DIGITAL MEDIA AND INNOVATION

This fully updated second edition explores the importance of innovation and innovative thinking for the long-term success of today's leading media, telecommunications, and information technology companies.

The book takes an in-depth look at how smart, creative companies have transformed today's digital economy by introducing unique and highly differentiated products and services. This edition provides a detailed overview of intelligent networks and analyzes disruptive business models and processes from companies involved in social media, artificial intelligence, the metaverse, smart cities, and robotics among other emerging areas. From Apple to Zoom, this book considers some of the key people, companies, and strategies that have transformed the communication industries. Exploring the power of good ideas, this book goes inside the creative edge and looks at what makes such companies successful over time.

Digital Media and Innovation is suited to advanced undergraduate and graduate courses in media management, media industries, communication technology, and business management and innovation, and provides up-to-date research for media and business professionals.

Richard A. Gershon is Professor Emeritus in the School of Communication at Western Michigan University, USA.

Media Management and Economics
Alan B. Albarran, Series Editor

DIGITAL MEDIA AND INNOVATION

Management and Design Strategies in Communication

Second Edition

Richard A. Gershon

Routledge
Taylor & Francis Group

NEW YORK AND LONDON

Designed cover image: Blackboard

Second edition published 2024
by Routledge
605 Third Avenue, New York, NY 10158

and by Routledge
4 Park Square, Milton Park, Abingdon, Oxon, OX14 4RN

Routledge is an imprint of the Taylor & Francis Group, an informa business

© 2024 Richard A. Gershon

First edition published by Sage 2017

Names: Gershon, Richard A., author.
Title: Digital media and innovation : management and design strategies
    in communication / Richard A. Gershon.
Description: Second edition. | New York, NY : Routledge, 2024. |
    Series: Media management and economics series | Includes
    bibliographical references and index.
Identifiers: LCCN 2023047484 (print) | LCCN 2023047485 (ebook) |
    ISBN 9781032278476 (hardback) | ISBN 9781032278469
    (paperback) | ISBN 9781003294375 (ebook)
Subjects: LCSH: Mass media—Management. | Organizational
    effectiveness.
Classification: LCC P96.M34 G47 2024 (print) | LCC P96.M34 (ebook) |
    DDC 302.23/068—dc23/eng/20231204
LC record available at https://lccn.loc.gov/2023047484
LC ebook record available at https://lccn.loc.gov/2023047485

ISBN: 978-1-032-27847-6 (hbk)
ISBN: 978-1-032-27846-9 (pbk)
ISBN: 978-1-003-29437-5 (ebk)

DOI: 10.4324/9781003294375

Typeset in Times New Roman
by Apex CoVantage, LLC

To my A. team:
Casey, Matthew, Brooke, and Oliver

CONTENTS

ABOUT THE AUTHOR

Richard A. Gershon, PhD (Ohio University), is Professor Emeritus at Western Michigan University where he specializes in media, telecommunications, and business strategy. Dr. Gershon has twice been selected for national teaching honors, including the Steven H. Coltrin Professor of the Year Award by the International Radio & Television Society (IRTS) and the Barry Sherman Award for Teaching Excellence by the Management and Economics division of the Association for Education in Journalism and Mass Communication (AEJMC). In 2007, he was the recipient of the Distinguished Teaching Award at Western Michigan University.

Dr. Gershon is an internationally recognized scholar having authored eight books and multiple journal articles and book chapters. His most recent works include *Media, Telecommunications and Business Strategy*, 3rd Ed. (Routledge, 2020). Dr. Gershon is a Fulbright scholar having held visiting appointments at the University of Navarra, Spain and Nihon University, Japan. He serves on the editorial board of three major journals, including *The International Journal on Media Management, Journal of Media Economics*, and *The Journal of Media Business Studies*.

Dr. Gershon is a founding member of the Information, Telecommunications Education and Research Association (ITERA) where he served as the organization's first president. ITERA is a consortium of 15 universities committed to the advancement of media and telecommunications education. Dr. Gershon served as President of the WMU Faculty Senate and twice chaired the Campus Planning and Finance Council. He was directly involved with a number of campus planning and design efforts, including Miller Plaza and the Heritage Hall remodeling initiative.

Dr. Gershon is one of a select number of professors who has been recognized by Western Michigan University's College of Arts and Sciences in three of its major award categories, including the Faculty Achievement Award in Teaching (2005), Research and Creative Activities (2015), and Professional and Community Service (2017).

Dr. Gershon welcomes you to visit him at his website, The Digital NavigatorEG: https://rgershon.com

PREFACE

I began my career as a High School instructor in northern Vermont where I taught English. At the interview, the principal asked me two questions: Can you teach a new course for us in Communication and can you coach the hockey team? I said yes to the first; I needed a job and no to the second; he had probably never seen me skate. Little did I know at the time that my teaching a course in Communication at Memorial High School in Burlington Vermont would set the trajectory for a career in media and telecommunications that now spans 40 years. Today, I am a Professor Emeritus at Western Michigan University where I served as the Director of the Telecommunications and Information Management program. I am old enough to remember having to use transparency overheads for the purpose of projecting an image. Today, I can call up a satellite in geosynchronous orbit from my laptop computer and project a video-streamed set of images in real-time on a 4K Ultra High Definition Television Screen. I have often said that what I learned about teaching, came as a result of my five years as a High School instructor. I wouldn't be the educator and writer that I am today were it not for the principal, Father Roland Rivard, who asked the question can you teach a new course for us in communication?

This book was several years in the making. It represents the direct outgrowth of a graduate course that I began teaching at Western Michigan University in 2009 titled *Strategic Planning, Communication and Innovation*. In this course, we look at the importance of strategic decision-making and innovation with a special emphasis given to the entrepreneurs, project teams, and companies responsible for some of today's most engaging media and telecommunications products and services. This course set the foundation for much of my current research in the field of media management and telecommunications. In 2011, I was fortunate to obtain a Fulbright scholarship that took me to the University of Navarra in Spain, where I was invited to be a visiting professor. While at Navarra, I taught a similar graduate course but used the time to refine the subject matter and sketched out the basic outline for the present text. In many ways, this book could just as easily be subtitled *The Navarra Lectures*.

About This Book

The first edition of *Digital Media and Innovation* was published by Sage in 2017. A lot has happened since the publication of the first edition. This book is about the power of good ideas. It's about those business enterprises that have harnessed the power of good ideas to become real difference makers in the field of media, telecommunications, and information technology. Advancements in technology, most notably, digital media arts, electronic commerce, and artificial intelligence are changing many of our basic assumptions regarding information, news, and entertainment. *Digital Media and Innovation* takes an in-depth look at how smart, creative companies (both past and present) have transformed today's digital economy by introducing unique and highly differentiated products and services. This fully updated second edition looks at such topics as social media, artificial intelligence, metaverse, smart cities, robotics, and many other emerging topical areas.

A Word About Legacy Companies

To some observers, companies such as Google, Amazon, HBO, Apple, and Facebook would seem like well-established companies (or legacy companies) rather than new, leading-edge business enterprises. In this book, I make the argument that what makes a business enterprise innovative is the degree to which they have had a transformative effect on their respective industry rather than how current they are as companies. Consider, for example, how a small start-up company called *Home Box Office* in 1972 challenged the conventional thinking of the time by introducing the concept of pay television. The principle of advertiser-supported "free" television was firmly engrained in the minds of the American public. What HBO did was change public perception about the nature of television entertainment. HBO offered a uniquely innovative service emphasizing recently released movies and other specialized entertainment that could not be found elsewhere on the general airwaves. Thus marked the beginning of a new business model called pay television. Fast forward 40 plus years later, and various online video streaming services such as Netflix, Amazon Prime, Disney Plus, Peacock, and Hulu owe their beginnings to HBO and the principle of premium television first advanced by that company.

Consider further a small Seattle, Washington-based start-up company called Amazon.com, which, in 1994, laid the groundwork for an altogether new business model called electronic commerce. The company founder Jeff Bezos began with the idea of selling books via the Internet given the large, worldwide demand for literature. The challenge at the time was that there did not exist a single, multipurpose catalogue that covered all contemporary books in the arts, sciences, and humanities. Such a book would require an encyclopedia-like size and would be far too expensive to mail. For Bezos, the solution was to create a mail-order catalog, albeit electronically, using the Internet and the power of intelligent networking. The Amazon website was perfectly suited for organizing and displaying an unlimited amount of information. Three decades later, Bezos presides over an electronic commerce (EC) company that has redefined online shopping for billions of people worldwide. But more importantly, Amazon helped to establish many of the EC business practices that now support our present-day digital economy.

Promising New Innovators

This current second edition also considers many new promising innovators that in a short period of time have left their mark in both business and technology. Starting in early 2021, the Covid-19 pandemic disrupted the world's economy by forcing the eventual shutdown of both large and small businesses alike as well as government and educational institutions. But the Covid-19 pandemic also set into motion a global tipping point that unleashed the full power of video-telephony and conference streaming technology for everyday use. The Covid-19 pandemic forced the relocation of working professionals from a dedicated place of business to a person's home, apartment, or remote setting. The home office would undergo a major redefinition in terms of setup and design. Few companies soared during the Covid-19 pandemic quite like videoconferencing specialist Zoom. The company proved to be a major technology innovator by helping to redefine the principle of video telephony. Nearly overnight, Zoom became the go-to conferencing service for business, education, government, and the general public.

The field of artificial intelligence is concerned with developing computer systems that are able to perform tasks that imitate human intelligence, such as visual perception, speech recognition, analytical problem study, and decision-making. It has taken center stage in discussions among business, educators, and government policymakers regarding the future of technology. The goal of AI is to develop new approaches to reasoning and problem-solving. The field of artificial intelligence breaks down into five areas. They include 1) intelligent network design, 2) expert systems, 3) natural language processing, 4) robotics, and 5) machine vision. All AI systems share in common the ability to reason, problem-solve, and take corrective action based on preprogramed assumptions and information inputs. One of the promising new innovators is a company called OpenAI and their work in creating a software product called Chatbot GPT.

have human-like conversations using a process known as natural language processing (NLP). It gives rise to a concept known as personal digital assistants.

Welcome to the Future

This book explores the importance of innovation and innovative thinking to the long-term success of today's leading media and telecommunications companies. From Apple to Zoom, this book considers some of the people, companies, and strategies that have transformed the communication industries. It goes inside the creative edge and looks at what makes such companies successful over time. In a book titled *Blue Ocean Strategy*, business authors Kim and Mauborgne make the argument that to create new market opportunities, innovative companies redefine the playing field by introducing an altogether new product, service, or idea. Instead of trying to outwit the competition in a zero-sum game of one-upmanship, blue ocean companies pursue the potential market space that has yet to be explored. The rules of competition are waiting to be set. Here, then, is our starting point for us to explore the world of digital media and innovation. Welcome to the future.

ACKNOWLEDGMENTS

My time spent teaching and doing research at the University of Navarra, Spain gave me the chance to affirm that this was a book worth writing. I am grateful to my colleagues and friends at the University of Navarra for their friendship, collegiality, and warm hospitality. A special thank-you goes to Dr. Mercedes Medina at the University of Navarra and the Fulbright foundation for providing the financial support that made my stay at the University of Navarra possible.

I am also grateful to several of my colleagues in the field of media and telecommunications who provided helpful comments and suggestions in the making of this second edition. They include Dr. Alan Albarran, Professor Emeritus, University of North Texas and Dr. Steven Wildman, Professor Emeritus, Michigan State University.

I want to thank several of my colleagues and friends at Western Michigan University, including Dr. Dennis Simpson, Dr. Mike Tarn, and Dr. Leigh Ford for their continued friendship and support. I am also grateful to the senior administration at Western, whom I consider to be both colleagues and friends. They have given me encouragement and support to engage the university in a number of special projects on campus. My thanks to Dr. Edward Montgomery, President; Dr. Tim Greene (former Provost and Vice President for Academic Affairs); and Ms. Jan VanDerKley, Vice President for Business and Finance. There are, of course, friends and family along the way who have provided continuous support and encouragement in a variety of ways. I want to take a moment to thank Peter Gershon, Jerry and Myral Robbins, Carol Levin, and the New Bern gang.

I am indebted to the editorial staff at Routledge for helping to make this project possible. In particular I want to thank Alexandra de Brauw (my editor) for her strong encouragement and belief in the value of this project. A special thank-you goes to Sean Daly, senior editorial assistant, who was critical to the project's success. I also want to take a moment to thank the Routledge production staff including Rajalakshmi Ramesh who serves as the team leader at Apex CoVantage, India and copy editor Preetha Vincent for their invaluable assistance in the development of this book.

Finally, the most important thank-you goes to my wife Casey for her continuous love and support. From camel rides on the Saharan desert of Morocco to Nordic walking along the North Carolina coastline, I so appreciate her grace, wisdom, and sense of humor. She is my North Star. And to my son Matthew, who has become a Master Chef; to our daughter-in-law Brooke—meditation instructor, and of course our grandson, Oliver, whose fascination with the video game Minecraft makes the adventure all the more fun . . .

Richard A. Gershon, PhD
Professor Emeritus, Western Michigan University

1

INNOVATION AND THE POWER OF A GOOD IDEA

> If I have seen further it is by standing on the shoulders of giants.
>
> Sir Isaac Newton

> There is one thing stronger than all the armies in the world, and that is an idea whose time has come.
>
> Victor Hugo

Introduction

The lessons of business history have taught us that there is no such thing as a static market. There are no guarantees of continued business success for companies regardless of their field of endeavor. In 1942, economist Joseph Schumpeter introduced the principle of *creative destruction* as a way to describe the disruptive process that accompanies the work of the entrepreneur and the consequences of innovation. In time, companies that once revolutionized and dominated select markets give way to rivals who are able to introduce improved product designs, offer substitute products and services, and/or lower manufacturing costs.[1] The resulting outcomes of creative destruction can be significant including the failure to preserve market leadership, the elimination of a once highly successful product line, or in the worst case scenario business failure itself.[2] The history of media and telecommunications is replete with examples of companies that were once high flyers (the best of the best) but who failed to plan for the future. Companies with iconic names like Eastman Kodak, Blockbuster Video, Blackberry wireless, Minolta camera, and RadioShack have been greatly reduced or are no more.

DOI: 10.4324/9781003294375-1

Today, the international business landscape has become ever more challenging. Global competition has engendered a new competitive spirit that cuts across countries and companies alike. No company, large or small, remains unaffected by the desire to increase profits and decrease costs. Such companies are faced with the same basic question; namely, what are the best methods for staying competitive over time? In a word, *innovation*. This book is about the power of good ideas. It's about those business enterprises that have harnessed the power of good ideas to become real difference makers in the field of media and telecommunications.

When we use the word innovation, there is a tendency to think of it in present-day terms. Companies like Apple and Google are considered innovative companies. Similarly, the term innovation is often linked to companies who are engaged in digital media and information technology. From the launch of the first PlayStation video game system by the project design team at Sony to the development of ChatGPT by a team of researchers at OpenAI, one of the goals of this book is to show the full measure of creativity and entrepreneurship both past and present. While there are numerous books on the subject of innovation (and specific corporate histories of well-known media companies), there are few books presently that are fully focused on the linkage between innovation and media and telecommunications. What has long fascinated me about the work of innovators, like Steve Jobs (Apple), Jeff Bezos (Amazon), and Akio Morita (Sony), to name only a few, is the chance to examine how such companies and individuals create groundbreaking products and services while addressing the challenges of staying innovative over time. This book provides a unique opportunity to look at the importance of innovation and innovative thinking in helping to advance the power of good ideas. Specifically, it will address four sets of questions. First, what does it mean to be an innovative media business enterprise? Second, what are the different types of media innovation, and who are some of the players that have proven to be real game changers in shaping the business of communication? Third, why do good companies fail to remain innovative over time? And fourth, how do the best companies foster a culture of innovation within their own organizational setting? This book will examine some of the people, companies, and strategies that have transformed the business of media and telecommunications.

What Is Innovation?

Renowned scholar Everett Rogers (1995) defines innovation as "an idea, practice or object that is perceived as new by an individual."[3] In principle, there are two kinds of innovation; namely sustaining technology and disruptive technology. A sustaining technology has to do with product improvement and performance. The goal is to improve on an existing technology or service by adding new and enhanced feature elements.[4] A computer manufacturer, for example, is routinely looking to improve on basic design elements like speed and throughput, processing power, and graphics display. For most companies, sustaining technology (or incremental improvement) is the most common form of innovation, often receiving more than 80% of the organization's total research and development budget.[5]

Sustaining technology is extremely important because it provides the steady and necessary improvements in product design that guard against rival product offerings. It also demonstrates a commitment to brand improvement. Such examples might include incremental improvements in Microsoft Office software or the steady progressions made in the Google search engine. The goal of sustaining innovation is to realize as much value as possible from an existing product or service without having to make a significant change in product design and/or a major retooling in production. By doing so, a company can preserve market share, extend brand awareness and maintain profitability for a long period of time.

In contrast, a disruptive (or breakthrough) technology represents an altogether different approach to an existing product design and process. It redefines the playing field by introducing to the marketplace a unique value proposition. By that, we mean a technology or service that proves to be an absolute game changer by fully disrupting the existing playing field (see Table 1.1). Consider, for example, the impact that music streaming technology has had on the music industry. The launch of the original Apple iPod in 2001 in combination with the introduction of the iTunes music service (using Mp3 file-sharing technology) created the first sustainable Internet music business model of its kind. The iPod product design and iTunes music service have steadily given way to our present-day music streaming services via one's smartphone as evidenced by such companies as Spotify, Apple Music, and Tidal to name only a few. The speed and efficiency of Internet-delivered music have fundamentally changed the cost structure of music recording and distribution on a worldwide basis.

TABLE 1.1 Media Innovation: Disruptive Effects and New Value Proposition

Amazon	Amazon.com	Created the world's first and highly successful business-to-consumer electronic commerce business model.
Apple	Apple iPhone	Created the world's first smartphone that combined mobile telephony and Internet as well as enhanced information and entertainment applications.
Home Box Office (HBO)	Paying for television	Created the first example of premium television programming. The HBO business model would later be adopted by other cable program services as well as future video streaming services including, Netflix, Amazon Prime, and Disney Plus.

(Continued)

TABLE 1.1 (Continued)

Netflix	Television and film entertainment rental	Created the first direct-to-home television/film entertainment rental service using DVD technology. This would later give way to Over-the-Top video streaming.
OpenAI	ChatGPT	ChatGPT is a natural language processing tool driven by AI technology that allows the user to have human-like conversations and information queries with the chatbot. The language model can answer questions and assist the user with tasks, such as composing emails, essays, and code.
Sony Inc. and Phillips	Compact disk	Transformed music recording and playback. The CD would help advance music and later the DVD television/film industry.
Surgical Theater	Virtual reality (VR) simulator	The company's VR software lets surgeons walk through and visualize complex surgeries in VR before ever touching the patient.
Walt Disney Company	Walt Disney World Theme Parks and Resorts	Created the world's best-known family friendly set of theme parks and resorts. The Disney name and brand would further expand in the field of television and film entertainment.

The Power of a Good Idea

There are any number of terms that we use in our day-to-day experience to describe the power of a good idea. Such words as *inspiration* and *inventiveness* are just a few of the terms to describe that moment in time when a good idea takes hold. The best innovators have natural curiosity about their environment. They are keen observers of human behavior and one's natural landscape. They are willing to juxtapose various idea combinations to see what happens. As author Steven Johnson points out, a good idea is really a network of possibilities. A good idea spawns infinite connections and opportunities.[6]

One of the important themes in this book is that the best innovators work in environments that allow them to be creative. From the original AT&T Bell Labs to the present-day Googleplex, there is a natural synergy that occurs when a project team combines talents and skills toward a common effort. A good idea has to be malleable; that is, it must be capable of adapting to various designs and configurations. As Ideo's Tom Kelley describes it, the best projects and design configurations are a collaborative effort; they never finish where they began. He describes it as the "magic of cross-pollination."[7]

The Serendipitous Discovery

Not all discoveries work out as planned. From Arthur Fry's Post-it notes to the development of the original telephone by Alexander Graham Bell, it sometimes happens that the inventor winds up creating something very different than what was originally intended. And some discoveries are the accidental offshoot from another idea. Take, for example, the Post-it note. A Post-it note is a small piece of colored paper with a strip of light adhesive on the back that allows it to be temporarily attached to papers, documents, books, and a variety of other things. In 1970, 3M chemist Spencer Silver was working to develop a strong glue. Instead, he wound up creating an adhesive that wasn't very sticky. Nothing came of it for four years. But it so happens that a 3M colleague by the name of Arthur Fry was a singer in a local church choir. Fry would sometimes find himself routinely losing his place in the church hymn book when the bookmarks he would use kept falling out. Why not try something different? Fry hit on a simple but elegant idea. He decided to coat a set of bookmarks with Spencer's glue. Now, for the first time, they stayed in place yet lifted off without damaging the pages. The Post-it note was born.[8] In time, the Post-it note would become one of 3M's most popular office products.

Probably, the most famous example of serendipitous discovery is the invention of the telephone itself. In setting out to create the harmonic telegraph, (multiple Morse code signals on a single wire), inventor Alexander Graham Bell wound up creating something far more compelling and futuristic than the original concept itself. Bell's extensive knowledge of sound (and sound waves) enabled him to consider the possibility of transmitting human speech electronically.[9] Both he and Elisha Gray are credited with having independently designed the first prototype devices that would later become the telephone. The telephone became the foundation for an entire worldwide system of communication that would take over 50 years to build and require telephone exchanges, (including operators, switches, and routers), long-distance lines, and assigned numbers. In time, the future AT&T would become the largest corporation in the world.

Research and Development

The words *research* and *development* is a 20th-century term that owes its beginning to the original industrial lab concept promoted by men like Thomas Edison, who built one of the first of its kind in Menlo Park, New Jersey (now called Edison in his honor). Menlo Park was home to one of America's first research and development labs that created such products as the phonograph and the incandescent light bulb as well as an estimated 400 patents. The laboratory's open floor plan allowed for easy communication between Edison and his associates. The layout created an informal environment that Edison felt would foster creativity. Edison had no rules for work and no time clock. But his team worked long hours and was highly successful in their endeavors.[10] In time, other high-tech companies would one day would follow suit and create their own version of the industrialized research and development lab. One such company was AT&T.

AT&T

The traditional research and development model assumes a more formal approach to research and product development. The goal is to enhance current product design as well as solve problems related to its implementation. Such research and development groups are assigned an annual budget with which to conduct research pertaining to product development as well as pure research (i.e., creating new knowledge) that may not have immediate benefit. The establishment of Bell Labs would prove to be an extremely fertile ground for the development of new and enhanced communication technology. Bell Research labs had more PhDs under the roof of its 21 branches than any single university could claim in the field of engineering and had turned out more than 19,000 patents since it began in 1925. As a research and development facility, Bell Labs could boast a number of firsts, including the first transistor, first laser, the first efficient communication satellite known as Telstar, early prototype designs in telephone and cellular telephone communications, and telephone switches and fiber optic communications.[11]

Bell Research Labs was unique for its time because it enabled its people to pursue pure research. One Bell Labs researcher described it as "managed anarchy." Pure research is an unpredictable path, with many hidden twists and curves. As so often happens, one discovery may not be useful for the moment but may eventually lead to another. Consider, for example, the work of Bell researcher Clinton Davisson who won the Nobel Prize for physics in 1927 for work that revealed the nature of subatomic particles. His work proved that electrons can behave like a wave. Decades later, his work would be critical to the understanding of how semiconductors and lasers work. Davisson, for his part, was simply trying to figure out how electrons behaved in a vacuum tube environment. Vacuum tube design was essential to AT&T's growing long-distance telephone network. It should be remembered that all communication signals suffer from a problem of attenuation; that is, the signal becomes weakened over distance.[12] A vacuum tube helps to restore and amplify weakened signals. But a vacuum tube has certain limitations.

Davisson's work attracted William Shockley, a young physicist from MIT to Bell Labs. Shockley headed up a group that included John Bardeen and Walter Brattain. They began doing preliminary research in the field of semiconductor design. This would require a deeper understanding of the switching and amplification of electrons. On December 12, 1943, Bell Research Lab physicists

Shockley, Bardeen, and Brattain demonstrated the transistor: the world's first semiconductor device that could do the work of a vacuum tube. The transistor would allow for the more efficient transfer, switching, and amplification of electrons. By replacing bulky and unreliable vacuum tubes with transistors, computers could now perform the same functions, using less power and space.[13]

The transistor set into motion a whole host of innovation that was to touch every aspect of future communication technology ranging from transistor radios to command and control telemetry for space flight. The development of the transistor would win Shockley, Bardeen. and Brattain a Nobel Prize for physics.[14] The transistor proved to be an important step that would lead to the development of the integrated circuit (i.e., multiple interconnected transistors on a single piece of silicon) popularly known as the computer chip.

Mavericks and the Power of a Good Idea

Very few entrepreneurs ever set out with the goal of becoming an entrepreneur. Rather, they are highly committed individuals who develop a deep-seated passion toward a problem or issue that they are working on. Some of the best innovation comes from the lone individual who I like to term the *maverick*. The maverick stands outside the box in terms of his/her thinking. Mavericks come in many forms. They may include those individuals who criticize deficiencies in current business processes and products. But likewise, mavericks can sometimes be the right person at the right time whose position and training offers a unique vantage point. There is a strong sense of curiosity and the ability to think up new ideas that have never been tried before. What if we did . . . They put an entirely different lens on a problem. Let's consider three such people.

Bill Gates, Microsoft—USA

Microsoft is a transnational computer and information company based in Redmond, Washington. The company was founded by Bill Gates and his childhood friend, Paul Allen. Microsoft is the world's largest software company. Both Gates and Allen attended Seattle-based Lakeside preparatory school. Both Gates and Allen were the proverbial computer geeks spending most of their spare time in the school's computer room. Paul Allen would later graduate and study computer science at the University of Washington while Gates attended Harvard but later dropped out.

In January 1975, Paul Allen read an article about the Altair 8800 microcomputer in *Popular Electronics* magazine. He showed the article to Bill Gates, who in turn called Micro Instrumentation and Telemetry Systems (MITS) makers of the Altair. Bill Gates offered both his and Paul Allen's services to write a version of the new BASIC programming language for the Altair. In signing the contract,

Allen and Gates left Boston, where Allen worked for Honeywell, and Gates was enrolled in Harvard and moved to Albuquerque, New Mexico where MITS was located. It took them eight weeks to successfully complete and demonstrate the new software package. MITS agreed to distribute and market the product under the name of Altair BASIC.

The success of the Altair project proved to be the important catalyst that motivated Gates and Allen to form their own software company called Microsoft on April 4, 1975. Bill Gates would serve as the company's new CEO. The company was later incorporated in the state of Washington in 1981. Microsoft soon established itself as one of America's first (and perhaps largest) producers of computer software; most notably, expanded versions of BASIC which had become the default standard on most available PCs to date. The real turning point for Microsoft came in 1981, when it signed a contract with IBM to write the operating system code for the company's soon-to-be launched IBM personal computer. Initially, Gates referred IBM to Digital Research (DRI), makers of the widely used CP/M operating system. The discussions were unsuccessful, and IBM came back to Microsoft, which agreed to develop a new operating system. Microsoft contracted with Tim Patterson of Seattle Computer Products, and together they combined to create MS-DOS for a one-time fee of $50,000. The most important part of the deal, however, was Gate's shrewd decision to retain the copyright on the PC operating system. That decision was prescient. Gates recognized that software development would drive the burgeoning computer industry. He believed that future PC manufacturers would need equivalent operating systems, and Microsoft was well positioned to be the principal supplier.

From Microsoft's founding in 1975 until 2006, Bill Gates served as the company's chief technology strategist. He helped expand the company's range of products, including the Windows operating system as well as the Microsoft Office suite of products. As the world's leading supplier of personal computing software, Microsoft developed a reputation for being aggressive and sometimes anticompetitive. Gates, himself, was generally recognized to be an inpatient and demanding boss. Gates met regularly with Microsoft's senior leadership team. Firsthand accounts of these meetings describe him as verbally combative, routinely challenging his managers for perceived flaws in their approach to business strategy or mistakes made in software development and execution.[15]

What is sometimes forgotten is the important role that Microsoft (and specifically Gates) has played in helping to advance personal computing. Microsoft set the de facto standards in business computing software. By shifting the value proposition in computing to software, Microsoft commoditized the manufacture of hardware equipment thus making personal computing accessible to the general public.[16] Microsoft, more than any company, took the mystery out of computing by transforming an industry that was once the purview of the guys in the white coats. Unlike Apple, Microsoft did not create a proprietary standard, thereby allowing all manufacturers to build computers using Microsoft software. Microsoft put a PC on everyone's desk. The company built a strong, reliable operating system and set of software products that enabled millions of users worldwide to engage in computing at a cost point that greatly advanced the field of personal computing.

Tim Berners-Lee, CERN—Great Britain

There is something to be said for the fact that good ideas often takes a while to germinate. Steven Johnson refers to it as the "slow hunch."[17] Consider, for example, the steady, evolutionary thought process that gave birth to the principle of hypertext linking. In 1980, Tim Berners-Lee began working on a software project called Enquire, which was an early version of hypertext linking and the World Wide Web concept. It was an idea that took several years to evolve. He would come back to it time and again during the next several years. In March 1989, Tim Berners-Lee, now a scientist at CERN, the European Organization for Nuclear Research, wrote a paper detailing the means by which members of the particle physics research community could easily research and share electronic documents.

At the start of the 1990s, the Internet was used primarily by the military, academic institutions, and business contractors. The basic system for communication was entirely text-based, relying on basic newsgroups and remote Telnet chat sessions to send messages between users. Tim Berners-Lee was challenged by the fact that searching for information meant having to log on to different computers with different protocol languages. As the popularity of the Internet increased, newcomers often found the arcane navigational commands a difficult task. Such would-be users had to master a complex set of computer commands and procedures before they could access the Internet. What was needed was an easy-to-use communication protocol that could link various program sites.

In March 1989, Tim Berners-Lee wrote a proposal to develop a large hypertext database with typed links. The initial proposal generated little interest. Later that same year, both he and colleague Robert Cailliau rewrote the proposal with the goal of developing a more improved navigational protocol for the Internet. The new protocol design was based on the principle of hypertext (or non-linear text), which is the foundation of multimedia computing.[18] Tim Berners-Lee's hypertext markup language (HTML) protocol would not require any specialized computer skills other than the ability to point and click on text or graphics. The hypertext protocol allows the user to navigate the Internet by moving from one document to another (or from one computer host to another).[19] The genius in Tim Berners-Lee's work lay in the fact that he found a way to link documents using a common protocol rather than having to access remote data bases as separate and distinct pieces of information. Tim Berners-Lee's contribution to the development of the Internet cannot be overestimated. The HTML protocol forms the basis for the World-Wide-Web concept. It should be noted that both he and CERN made the HTML source code available for free to the larger Internet community. For his contributions, Tim Berners-Lee was knighted by Her Majesty, Queen Elizabeth II in 2004.

Linus Torvalds, Finland

Finland's Linus Torvalds is a computer scientist who was the principal force behind the development of the Linux operating system. In 1991, while studying at the University of Helsinki, he purchased his first personal computer (PC). Torvalds was not satisfied with the computer's operating system (OS). His PC used MS-DOS, the disk operating system designed by Microsoft Corporation. Torvalds, for his part, preferred AT&T's UNIX-based operating system that was used on the university's computers.[20] He decided to create his own PC-based version of UNIX. Months of determined programming work yielded the beginnings of an operating system known as Linux. In 1991, he posted a message on the Internet to alert other PC users to his new system and made the software available for free downloading. As was a common practice among software developers at the time, Torvalds released the source code, which meant that anyone with knowledge of computer programming could modify Linux to suit their own purposes. Because of their access to the source code, many programmers helped Torvalds retool and refine the software, and by 1994, the Linux kernel (original code) version 1.0 was released.

Operating systems (OS) require a certain amount of technical acumen. The original Linux OS was not as easy to use when compared to the more popular operating systems such as Windows or Apple's Mac OS. However, Linux evolved into a remarkably reliable, efficient system that rarely crashed. In addition to Linux being free, its source code can be viewed and modified by anyone, unlike a proprietary operating system. This means that different language versions can be developed and deployed in markets that would be considered too small for traditional companies. By the late 1990s, the upstart Linux OS caught the attention of companies like Microsoft and Apple. What sets Linux apart from other operating systems is that it has become a major force in computing, powering everything from the New York Stock Exchange to mobile phones to supercomputers to consumer devices. As an open source system, Linux is developed collaboratively; that is, no one company is solely responsible for its continuation or ongoing support. Developers, from hundreds of different companies, contribute to every kernel release. Companies participating in the Linux economy share research and development costs with their partners and competitors.

The sharing in development costs among multiple individuals and companies has resulted in a free and efficient ecosystem that is unparalleled in software design. Less appreciated at the time, Torvalds set into motion the principle of *crowdsourcing*, which is the practice of obtaining information or input into a task or project by enlisting the services of a large number of volunteer contributors typically via the Internet. Today, walk into any public school, and you'll see millions of Linux machines. They're called Chromebooks. Chrome OS and Android are both based on the Linux kernel. Chromebooks are the fastest-growing segment of the traditional PC market. Much of that is driven by schools, where Chromebooks dominate now. It is an article of faith among educators that school-age kids (especially in developing regions of the world) need inexpensive, sturdy ways to log onto the Internet; specifically, Google Classroom and other programs like it. Linux provides a light, inexpensive approach to PC use in contrast to Windows and Macintosh personal computers. Linux has forever found a practical way to enable capable, low-cost machines for millions of users. Today, the Linux operating system is at the foundation of cloud, edge, embedded, and Internet of Things (IoT) technologies that enable the operations of billions of devices.

Three Strategic Approaches to Business Transformation

The most important discoveries are built on the fundamental principles set forth by others. Such companies and project teams benchmark and learn by example. At the same time, the innovator must be willing to let go of basic assumptions and consider a problem from an altogether different perspective. The project designer must be open to taking risks by approaching a problem in an entirely new way. That is what truly separates the innovator from the also-ran. In this book, we will consider three major types of innovation. They include 1) business model innovation, 2) product innovation, and 3) process innovation.

Business Model Innovation

Today, innovation is about much more than developing new products. It's also about building new markets to meet untapped customer needs. Business model innovation involves creating entirely new approaches for doing business. Authors Kim and Mauborgne make the argument that to create new growth opportunities, innovative companies must consider the unknown market space, untainted by competition. They advocate what they term a *Blue Ocean strategy* approach, whereby demand is created rather than fought over. Blue oceans denote all future industries not in existence today (i.e., the unknown market space). It describes the potential market space that has yet to be explored.[21] HBO, for example, created a demand for premium television entertainment. They changed a one-time consumer mindset that television should forever be free.

Likewise, Amazon.com demonstrated the potential of electronic commerce by developing a simple and efficient way to buy books and other goods using the

Internet and the power of intelligent networking. This gave rise to an altogether new business model known as e-commerce (EC). Both companies introduced a business model innovation that proved transformative. They redefined the competitive playing field by introducing an entirely new value proposition to the consumer.

Product Innovation

Product innovation refers to the complex process of bringing new products and services to market as well as improving (or enhancing) existing ones. Highly innovative companies display a clear and discernible progression in the products they make. They force themselves to create new and better products while challenging the competition to do the same. There is a natural progression in product design and development.[22] Being first to market can often provide a huge strategic advantage. If successful, a new product innovation will create lasting advantage while spawning a host of imitators. Consider, for example, the host of imitators that followed the launch of the original Apple iPhone and the principle of smartphone design in 2007.

Successful product innovation goes hand in hand with the creative process for developing unique and original ideas. The best companies foster a culture of innovation. They recognize that the source of good ideas can come from a wide variety of people and players both inside and outside the organization, including design engineers, project teams, business units, and individual customers.[23] One important consideration is whether the proposed idea fills an obvious gap or niche in the marketplace. Take, as an example, the success of the EC service known as Uber in providing ride-sharing transportation using the power of the Internet and customer feedback. The sharing economy has brought changes to many industries, but Uber has been one of the frontrunners in market disruption. Given its approach using online payments, GPS tracking, rating systems, and a wide network of drivers, Uber offers a greater degree of transparency and flexibility when compared to traditional taxi cab services.[24]

Business Process Innovation

Business process innovation involves creating systems and methods for improving organizational performance. Examples of business process innovation can be found in a variety of organizational settings and structures, including product development, manufacturing, inventory management, customer service, distribution, and delivery. If the organization wants to understand how to best hire employees or improve on manufacturing technique, it needs to fully evaluate its business process. The challenge is when organizations succumb to needless red tape or extra steps to accomplish specific goals and outcomes. Microsoft's Bill Gates has been known to say, "that a lousy process will consume ten times as many hours as the work itself requires." The benefit of business process innovation is that it creates internal efficiencies that translate into organizational cost savings, including a better use of time, people, and resources.[25]

A highly successful business process renders two important consequences. First, business process is transformative; that is, it creates internal and external efficiencies that provide added value to the company and organization. Second, a well-designed business process sets into motion a host of imitators who see the inherent value in applying the same business process to their own organization. As an example, Dell Technologies was an important innovator when it came to developing just-in-time manufacturing techniques as well as direct-to-home computer sales delivery. Similarly, Netflix harnessed the power of the Internet in providing consumers with the ability to directly order movies online thus creating an efficiency for the delivery of movies to the home. Netflix would later adapt the delivery process further by helping to advance the video streaming of movies to the home, thus eliminating the need for the physical delivery of DVDs. Both Dell and Netflix were game changers in the field of EC by demonstrating the power of intelligent networking in place of traditional "bricks and mortar" retail stores.

Three-Sided Innovation

It is not uncommon that some of the best companies discussed in this book are innovative in more than one area. As often happens, the demands of bringing a product to market may require the organization to develop a well-designed innovation process that combines a unique business model, a distinct product design or service, as well as a supply chain process. I call this three-sided innovation (see Table 1.2).

Digital Media and Innovation

Digital media represents the artistic convergence of various kinds of hardware and software design elements to create entirely new forms of communication expression. From e-commerce to the power of social media, digital media has transformed the way we live. We have entered the era of personalization where users personalize their music listening experience, and newspaper readers customize their news selection via their smartphone or computer tablet.[26] Also important to the discussion is the importance of mobile Internet access. Digital media has proven to be a major game changer when it comes to storytelling. Digital storytelling is fast and immediate (24/7) and can take a variety of forms including digital news, website display, social media, and a host of blogs and commentary. The once iconic family photo album has given way to multiple storage devices that include personal computers, smartphones, computer tablets, as well as social media sites that fully utilize cloud storage. All this points to the fact that the transition to digital photos and online video is no longer about a

TABLE 1.2 Three-Sided Innovation

Company	Business Model	Product/Service	Business Process
Amazon	Electronic commerce	General merchandise	Highly advanced AI supply chain management system and direct-to-home delivery
Spotify	Electronic commerce	Spotify Music (customized music)	Music streaming via the Internet
Dell Technologies	Electronic commerce	Laptop computers	Just-in-time manufacturing and direct-to-home delivery
HBO	Pay cable television and HBO MAX electronic commerce	Television/film entertainment	Satellite distribution and OTT video streaming
Netflix	Electronic commerce	Television/film entertainment	OTT video streaming

single product but rather a fundamental shift in thinking regarding storytelling, visual display, and the communication process. I call this *digital lifestyle*.

The Digital Economy

The *digital economy* is comprised of the billions of worldwide online business and financial transactions that occur daily. In today's digital economy, the Internet and EC serves as the central hub by which all economic activity occurs. The digital economy can take many forms ranging from online hotel and airline reservations to OTT video streaming services. International business has been transformed by the power of instantaneous communication. The combination of computer and telecommunications has collapsed the time and distance factors that once separated nations, people, and business organizations. We start with the premise that the intelligent network is not one network but a series of networks designed to enhance worldwide communication for business and individual users alike.[27] What gives the network its unique intelligence are the people and users of the system and the value-added contributions they bring to the system via critical gateway points (e.g., desktop and laptop computers, smartphones, and tablets).[28]

Artificial Intelligence

Artificial intelligence (AI) is concerned with developing computer systems that are able to perform tasks that imitate human intelligence, such as visual perception, speech recognition, analytical problem study, and decision-making. The goal of AI is to develop new approaches to reasoning and problem-solving and take corrective action based on preprogramed assumptions and information inputs.[29] The field of AI breaks down into five areas. They include 1) intelligent network design, 2) expert systems, 3) natural language processing, 4) robotics, and 5) machine vision. The intelligent network in combination with the power of AI provides the electronic pathways and information support systems that help define today's digital economy. Some of these signature features can be seen in Table 1.3 and is the subject of this book.

TABLE 1.3 The Digital Economy: Ten Signature Features

Artificial Intelligence	The development of information systems capable of performing tasks that normally require human intelligence and engagement, such as visual perception, speech recognition, decision-making, and reaction to moving objects. AI is often associated with such things as robotics, human–computer interface design, autonomous self-driving vehicles, and various types of computer software algorithms.
Cloud Computing	The expression *putting something on the cloud* refers to the idea of storing of information and data on a remote host site. Cloud computing provides both storage and the delivery of information services over a virtual platform using the networking capability of the Internet. The user is able to access such services on demand. Cloud computing comes in two general forms: public (i.e., social media—Facebook, YouTube, TikTok, etc.) versus private clouds (internal university or hospital network support services).
Electronic Commerce	Electronic commerce (EC) represents the ability to sell goods and services electronically via the Internet. The field of EC has come of age as evidenced by the success of such companies as Amazon, Apple, Netflix, Uber, and Bookings.com to name only a few. EC has created an altogether new business model that maximizes the potential for instantaneous communication to a worldwide customer base. There are three kinds of EC transactions: business-to-consumer (B2C), business-to-business (B2B), and consumer-to-consumer (C2C). In today's digital economy, the Internet and EC serves as the central hub by which all economic activity occurs.
Machine Learning	Machine learning is a subfield of AI which can be broadly defined as the ability of computer (or information) systems that are able to learn and adapt without following explicit instructions. Machine learning requires the use of algorithms and statistical models to analyze and draw inferences from patterns in data. Facial recognition used at airports is a good example of machine learning.

(Continued)

TABLE 1.3 (Continued)

Metaverse and Virtual Reality	Metaverse is a vision of what many in the media and computer industries believe is the future of the digital economy; specifically, a shared, immersive 3D space where users can engage in simulated experiences, involving business marketing, collaborative project design work, instructional training, gaming, and shopping. The Metaverse virtual world is facilitated by the use of virtual and augmented reality headsets. Virtual reality (VR) is the consummate form of Metaverse. VR involves constructing illusory realities out of data drawn from a variety of databases. It allows the user to enter into a three-dimensional space and interact with his/her surroundings. The simulated environment can be realistic (e.g., flight simulation, VR surgery etc.) or imagined (e.g., a trip to Mars). There is a shared common space involving action and reaction to one's movements.
OTT Video Streaming	Over-the-Top (OTT) represents the ability to video stream television programming via the Internet to both smart homes equipped with high-definition television sets and various kinds of mobile devices including smartphones, computer tablets, and laptop computers. The major game changer began with the start of Netflix, which demonstrated the possibility of streaming movies via a broadband connection directly to the end user's HDTV television set. OTT has redefined how television is delivered and given new meaning to the term *video-on-demand*.
Robotics	Robotics is a subfield of AI. The term *robot* refers to an artificial machine or agent that performs highly skilled tasks with a high degree of consistency. Robots are typically guided by highly sophisticated computer program software and electronic circuitry. Robots can take the place of humans in various types of manufacturing processes (i.e., car assembly) as well as performing tasks in dangerous environments (explosive ordnance disposal). Robots can resemble humans in appearance, behavior, and/or cognition. The branch of the field that deals with how people interact with robots is called *social robotics*.
Smart Homes	A smart home is a residential dwelling that uses highly advanced automatic systems for lighting, temperature control, information and entertainment services, window and door operations, security, and many other functions. A smart home relies heavily on Internet-connected devices and helps to enable digital lifestyle in its many forms. A smart home appears "smart" because a variety of sensors monitor the daily activities of house use. The *Internet of Things* (IoT) is a working concept that describes a smart, actively engaged network that monitors physical objects "things" and shares the said information between one or more devices and a system platform. It provides the basis for smart home design.

(Continued)

TABLE 1.3 (Continued)

Smartphone—Wireless Communication	Beginning with the introduction of the original Apple iPhone in 2007, today's generation of smartphone design combines the best elements of cellular telephony with mobile Internet access. What makes a smartphone "smart" are the many applications that can include but not limited to text messaging, email, music playback, photo storage, GPS, weather, as well as a host of other applications. Today's smartphone design has been described as "broadband on the go." At the heart of smartphone technology use is the principle of mobility, that is, the ability to communicate anytime, anywhere. Location should never be an obstacle.
Social Media	Social media represents a category of Internet-based activity where a virtual community of users share information through the use of individual profiles, contact information personal messages, blogs, commentary, and videos. Simply put, social media is about the power of networking and relationship building. Social media can range in size and scope from Facebook and Instagram (personal) to YouTube, TikTok, Snapchat (video), and LinkedIn (professional). Social media allows individuals to meet new people as well as strengthen existing relationships. The term *social media influencer* refers to a person on social media who has presumed credibility in a specific industry, trade, or art. These content creators are so-called *digital opinion leaders* who have access to a large audience and can share information and/or persuade others through their established presence and reach. The power of social media makes it possible to communicate in real time regardless of time, geographical borders, and physical space.

Discussion: Failure Is Not an Option

Change is never easy. Change is especially difficult when a new technology or start-up company is poised to displace a well-established business. Nowhere is this more evident than the impact that digital media and the Internet has had on traditional newspapers and magazines. Starting in 2004, the international newspaper and magazine industries felt the beginning tides of creative destruction and competitive decline. The United States then lost an estimated one quarter (or 2,100) of its newspapers. This included 70 dailies and more than 2,000 weeklies or nondailies. Similarly, hundreds of newspapers and magazines from around the world have shuttered their doors or moved to an all-digital format. The combination of news via the Internet along with computer tablets and other mobile devices has fundamentally challenged the long-term sustainability of print media. Today, the question for journalists, newspaper managers, and journalism educators are the same. What business are you really in?

In this book, we will see examples of companies that have overcome the challenges of business reinvention. We will meet a select number of media companies who have learned how to make innovation a sustainable repeatable process. Their lessons and experience are fully shared with the reader. We will also encounter companies that succumbed to the devastating effects of creative destruction and are today greatly reduced or are no more. In the life of all business enterprises, there comes a point when such companies are challenged by the moving tides of changing technology and market conditions. How they respond to such changes determines whether they will be successful or a business that failed to adapt. This juncture represents what former Intel CEO Andy Grove refers to as a *strategic inflection point*; a time when a triggering event in the competitive marketplace requires new solutions or faces the prospect of business extinction.[30] Put differently, as former NASA flight director, Gene Kranz once said to the members of his mission control team—responsible for the safe return of the disabled Apollo 13 spacecraft: "Failure is not an option!"

Notes

1 Joseph Schumpeter, *Capitalism, Socialism and Democracy* (New York: Harper & Row, 1942).
2 Richard Gershon, *Media, Telecommunications and Business Strategy*. 3rd ed. (New York: Routledge, 2020), 181.
3 Everett Rogers, *Diffusion of Innovation*. 4th ed. (New York: Free Press, 1995), 11.
4 Clayton Christensen, *The Innovator's Solution* (Boston, MA: Harvard Business School Press, 2003), 34.
5 Tony Davila, Marc Epstein and Robert Shelton, *Making Innovation Work* (Upper Saddle River, NJ: Wharton School Publishing, 2006).
6 Steven Johnson, *Where Good Ideas Come From: The Natural History of Innovation* (New York: Riverhead Books, 2010).
7 Tom Kelley, *The Ten Faces of Innovation* (New York: Doubleday, 2005), 68.
8 Nick Glass and Tim Hume, "The 'Hallelujah Moment' Behind the Invention of the Post-It Note," *CNN*, 2013, April 4, www.cnn.com/2013/04/04/tech/post-it-note-history/index.html
9 James Mackay, *Alexander Graham Bell* (New York: John Wiley & Sons, 1997), 91–130.
10 Randall Stross, *The Wizard of Menlo Park: How Thomas Alva Edison Invented the Modern World* (New York: Three Rivers Press, 2006), 39–58.
11 Jeremy Bernstein, *Three Degrees Above Zero: Bell Labs in the Information Age* (New York: Charles Scribner's & Sons, 1984), 77–107.
12 Jon Gertner, *The Idea Factory: Bell Labs and the Great Age of American Innovation* (New York: Penguin Press, 2012), 28–40.
13 Walter Isaacson, *The Innovators* (New York: Simon & Schuster, 2014), 131–170.
14 Bernstein, *Three Degrees Above Zero: Bell Labs in the Information Age*.
15 Ken Auletta, *World War 3.0: Microsoft and Its Enemies* (New York: Random House, 2001).
16 Pascal Gabry, "Yes, Microsoft Did Change the World More than Apple," *Business Insider*, 2011, September 8, www.businessinsider.com/yes-microsoft-did-change-the-world-more-than-apple-2011-9

17 Johnson, *Where Good Ideas Come From: The Natural History of Innovation.*

18 Tim Berners-Lee, *Weaving the Web* (New York: Harper Collins, 1999).

19 Gershon, *Media, Telecommunications and Business Strategy.* 3rd ed.

20 UNIX is a computer operating systems that developed in the 1970s at AT&T's Bell Research Labs. Designed originally for internal use within the Bell system, AT&T would later license Unix to outside parties (both academic and commercial) starting in the late 1970s.

21 W. Chan Kim and Renée Mauborgne, *Blue Ocean Strategy* (Boston, MA: Harvard Business School Press, 2005).

22 Gary Hamel, "The What, Why and How of Management Innovation," *Harvard Business Review,* 2006, February, 72–87.

23 Marty Cagan, *Inspired: How to Create Tech Products Customers Love.* 2nd ed. (Hoboken, NJ: John Wiley & Sons, 2018), 309–326.

24 Lana Pepick, "The Sharing Economy: Uber and Its Effect on Taxi Companies," *Acta Economica* 16,28 (2018): 123–136.

25 Susan Page, *The Power of Business Process Improvement.* 2nd ed. (New York: American Management Association, 2015).

26 Richard Gershon, "Digital Media Innovation and the Apple iPad: Three Perspectives on the Future of Computer Tablets and News Delivery," *Journal of Media Business Studies* 10,1 (2013): 41–61.

27 Don Tapscott, *The Digital Economy. Rethinking Promise and Peril in the Age of Networked Intelligence* (New York: McGraw-Hill, 2015), 11–50, See also: Eli Noam, *Interconnecting the Network of Networks* (Cambridge, MA: MIT Press, 2001).

28 Richard Gershon, "Intelligent Networks and International Business Communication: A Systems Theory Interpretation," *Media Markets Monographs.* No. 12 (Pamplona, Spain: Universidad de Navarra Press, 2011).

29 Stuart Russell and Peter Norvig, *Artificial Intelligence: A Modern Approach.* 4th ed. (New York: Prentice Hall), 1–5.

30 Alan Webber, "The Apple Effect," *The Christian Science Monitor,* 2011, September 19, 26–31.

2

BUSINESS MODEL INNOVATION

Introduction

Business model innovation involves creating entirely new approaches for doing business. Business model innovation is transformative; that is, it redefines the competitive playing field by introducing a unique value proposition to the consumer.[1] In the book *Blue Ocean Strategy*, business authors Kim and Mauborgne make the argument that to create new growth opportunities, innovative companies fundamentally change the business landscape by introducing an altogether new product, service, or idea. They use the metaphor of red and blue oceans to describe the market universe. *Red oceans* are all the industries in existence today (i.e., the known market space). Direct competition is the order of the day. The goal is to grab a bigger share of the existing red ocean market. Instead of trying to outwit the competition in a zero-sum game of one-upmanship, blue ocean companies pursue the soon-to-be discovered opportunities that await the entrepreneur. Competition is irrelevant because the rules of the game are waiting to be set.[2]

This chapter represents a unique opportunity to look at the importance of innovation and innovative thinking to the long-term success of today's leading media and telecommunications companies. Specifically, it will address two important questions. First, what does it mean to be an innovative media business enterprise? Second, how has business model innovation been used to transform the field of electronic commerce? The term *electronic commerce* (EC) represents the ability to sell goods and services electronically via the Internet. The blending of EC in combination with intelligent networking has created a vast global playing field where buyers and sellers from around the world are free to participate.[3] In this chapter,

DOI: 10.4324/9781003294375-2

we will consider three companies that exhibit the best features of business model innovation. They include Home Box Office Inc. (HBO), Amazon, and Google. These companies were selected because they introduced a unique business model that fundamentally changed the competitive business landscape following their respective product launch. In short, they were absolute game changers.

Why Is Innovation Important?

Innovation is important because it creates a competitive advantage for a company or organization. Successful innovation occurs when it meets one or more of the following conditions. First, the innovation is based on a novel principle that challenges management orthodoxy. When HBO introduced the principle of pay television in the 1970s, it was challenging the conventional wisdom of its day by promoting the belief that television was something worth paying for. Second, the innovation is systemic; that is, it involves a range of processes and methods. Amazon's commitment to direct-to-home sales delivery involves a whole host of supply chain management processes, including EC product display, an online ordering system, warehouse inventory management, customer service, shipping, and distribution. Third, the innovation is part of an ongoing commitment to develop new and enhanced products and services. There is a natural progression in product design and development.[4] See Table 2.1.

TABLE 2.1 Successful Innovation: Feature Elements

The innovation is based on a *novel principle* that challenges management orthodoxy.	**Home Box Office:** Developed the principle of premium television entertainment **Google:** Greatly advanced information gathering on the Internet through keyword search **Amazon.com:** Established the world's first and preeminent EC business model
The innovation is *systemic*; that is, it involves a range of processes and methods.	**Amazon.com:** EC product display and online ordering system, warehouse inventory management, shipping and distribution, direct-to-home sales delivery **Netflix:** Online video rental, global inventory management, original television/film development, OTT television/film video streaming.
The innovation is part of an ongoing commitment to develop new and enhanced products and services.	**Apple:** iPod, iTunes, iPhone, iPad $\rightarrow$ $\rightarrow$ $\rightarrow$ Apple Music Apple Watch Apple TV Streaming Media Vision Pro VR Headset

Source: R. Gershon, adapted from G. Hamel, (2006).

Business Model Innovation: Strategies and Approaches

While most organizations recognize the importance of innovation, there is a wide degree of latitude regarding the method and approach to innovation. For some business enterprises, innovation is the direct result of a *triggering event*, that is, a change in market conditions or internal performance that forces a change in business strategy.[5] The development of OTT video streaming services such as Disney Plus, HBO Max, and NBC Peacock (to name only a few) was a strategic response to the online video success achieved by Netflix and Amazon Prime. For other companies, innovation is deliberative and planned. It is built into the cultural fabric of a company's ongoing research and development efforts. Such companies display a clear and discernible progression in the products they make.[6] Careful planning leads the way. This can be seen in the method and approach adopted by Apple, starting with the original Macintosh computer and proceeding forward with the development of future Apple-based products and services. As entrepreneur and PayPal co-founder Peter Thiel writes,

> The greatest thing Jobs designed was his business. Apple imagined and executed definite multiyear plans to create new products and distribute them effectively . . . Jobs saw that you can change the world though careful planning, not by listening to focus groups, feedback or copying others' successes.[7]

Successful Business Model Innovation

Successful innovation is not a guarantee of success. Rather, it is an opportunity. As writer Steven Hoff notes, "inspiration is fine, but above all, innovation is really a management process."[8] There are no shortcuts when it comes to innovation. Putting the right structures, people, and processes in place should occur as a matter of course—not as an exception. Early in the project design process, a successful business model innovation should address five basic questions.

How Will the Firm Create Value?

This first question concerns the value proposition to the consumer. The term value refers to the unique or specialized benefits derived from the product or service offering. What value does the proposed product or service provide the consumer? Booking a flight and vacation on Booking.com is a very different value proposition than working with a travel agent. Purchasing a set of songs via

Spotify is an altogether different shopping experience than walking into a music store. From a planning standpoint, the firm starts with a clear understanding of the product or service mix. The level and type of innovation should match the company's larger overriding strategy. There should be a clear alignment of goals in terms of the proposed innovation strategy.[9]

For Whom Will the Firm Create Value?

This question focuses on the competitive environment in which the firm competes. Who is the target audience for the proposed product design or service? Such considerations as audience composition, geographic location, and user technology proficiency level can have a significant impact on strategy approach, resource requirements, and the nature of the product or service that is being developed for the consumer.[10] Netflix, for example, had to consider technology skill level as one important metric when designing its original Internet-based EC service. The same can be said for the international airline industry when it introduced self-check-ins at airports in the late 1990s. While the airlines have realized significant savings, they have also had to contend with passenger resistance to the technology as well as unique security threats introduced following the events of the World Trade Center attack on September 11, 2001. A successful product launch presupposes a clear understanding of how one's customers are realistically going to use the proposed product or service.

What Is the Firm's Internal Source of Advantage?

The term *core competency* describes something that an organization does well. The principle of core competency suggests that a highly successful company is one that possesses a specialized production process, brand recognition, or ownership of talent that enables it to achieve higher revenues and market dominance when compared to its competitors. Core competency can be measured in many ways, including brand identity (Disney, ESPN, Facebook); technological leadership (Apple, Google, Microsoft and Sony); superior business process logistics (Amazon, Netflix, and Ericsson); manufacturing and production capability (Samsung, LG, and Philips); and excellent customer service (Disney, Amazon and Spotify).

How Will the Firm Make Money?

The financial business model provides the inherent logic for earning profits. From Alexander Graham Bell to Mark Zuckerberg, it is not uncommon to find that some of media and telecommunication's best-known entrepreneurs are better inventors and software programmers than they are business people. The start-up of Google and Facebook are two such examples of companies that began with a good idea but didn't necessarily have a plan for how they would make money. Sometimes, the best ideas often require the business acumen of an outside person or capital investment firm to come up with a sustainable business plan that will enable such project start-ups to succeed in the long term.

The financial business model must take into consideration the strategy rationale for making money. The Spotify music service is based on a freemium model; that is, it makes money from subscriptions and advertisements. Spotify makes 91% of its revenue from subscriptions and the other 9% from advertisements. Of the revenue it generates, Spotify keeps 30% and splits the remaining amount between licensing, music deals, and payment to the artists. Alternatively, the ESPN cable sports network has two distinct revenue streams. First, ESPN makes money through a licensing fee arrangement, whereby it charges the cable operator (and other multichannel delivery systems) an estimated $9.00+ every month per subscriber for the right to receive the ESPN service. Second, ESPN makes money through the sale of national and international advertising.

How Does the Firm Plan to Position Itself in the Marketplace?

This question asks us to consider how the current or proposed business enterprise plans to position itself within its external competitive environment. Specifically, the business enterprise must determine how it plans to achieve a strategic advantage over all its would-be competitors.[11] This idea is closely related to the principle of core competency discussed earlier. Consider, for example, Korea-based Samsung corporation. Samsung has proven to be the organizational master in fast and efficient (almost military-like) production. Samsung has focused on becoming a superior manufacturer rather than original research and development. The company has learned how to manage and work through the highly volatile world of commoditized consumer electronics products. Speed and manufacturing dexterity are the keys to perishable commodities, from smartphones to digital television sets. As author S.J. Chang points out, unless a firm learns to introduce its products faster and sooner than its competitors, it quickly gets caught up in the hellish competition of commodities. Samsung Electronics has aggressively invested in product and process technology so that it can beat its competitors to market and capture price premiums before its offerings become commodities.[12]

Value Proposition

A value proposition involves creating a unique product offering or service enhancement that greatly improves the customer experience. Some notable examples of business model innovation in the field of media and telecommunications can be seen in Table 2.2. Each of the said companies developed a unique value proposition to the consumer. They were blue ocean companies in the best sense of the term. They would help set the standards for their respective area of business commerce.

TABLE 2.2 Select Examples of Media and Telecommunications Business Model Innovation

• Apple	Launched iTunes, the first sustainable MP3 music-downloading business of its kind. It later gave way to Apple's current music service.
• Alphabet (Google)	Helped advance Internet keyword search advertising and developed the principle of micromarketing.
• Amazon.com	Created the world's preeminent EC business model for goods and services online
• Bitcoin	Represents the first cryptocurrency; specifically, a virtual currency designed to act as money and a form of payment outside the control of a government nationality.
• eBay	Helped advance electronic auctioning on the Internet, creating the world's largest customer-to-customer online marketplace.
• HBO	Introduced the principle of pay television service. It became the forerunner for future pay television and OTT streaming services.
• Meta (Facebook)	Developed the world's preeminent social networking Internet site; helped advance online advertising.
• Netflix	Developed world's most successful online video rental service. It later gave way to its current OTT streaming service.
• PayPal	Introduced the first online EC payment systems of its kind, providing a significant alternative to checks and money orders. It became the forerunner for many of today's EC payment systems.

Being First-to-Market

Being first-to-market presents enormous opportunities for the organization that is able to establish a clear and recognized product or service before anyone else. All future competitors are faced with the task of having to compete with a well-established company possessing enormous brand recognition. This was certainly the case with companies like HBO and Amazon.com. Both companies became synonymous with their respective business model (i.e., HBO, pay television and Amazon, EC). At the same time, being first-to-market is not without its challenges. The start-up company is tasked with having to build consumer interest for a product or service that is entirely new and untested. Consider, for example, the challenges of being HBO in 1974 and having to convince a skeptical American public about the value of premium TV (i.e., paying for something that was otherwise free). Similarly, imagine the challenges faced by the Sony Corporation in 1990 when it tried to persuade America's television-viewing audience about the benefits of high-definition television ten years before the general public, television stations, and regulatory structures were in place to consider it realistically. Sometimes, the second- or third-place entrant has the opportunity to refine and improve on the product or service without having to undertake the initial upfront costs and product shortcomings. Before Google, there were search engines such as Yahoo and Infoseek. However, Google was able to customize its search engine to perform more effectively and efficiently. They now control over 90% of the world's Internet search market.

Boundary Spanning

In his book, *Where Good Ideas Come From: The Natural History of Innovation*, author Steven Johnson describes what he calls "the adjacent possible":

> We are often better served by connecting ideas than we are protecting them . . .
> Good ideas . . . want to connect, fuse, recombine. They want to reinvent
> themselves by crossing conceptual borders.[13]

The term *boundary spanning* means finding adjacent (or complimentary) areas that add value to one's current business or organizational enterprise. Boundary spanning leadership assumes the ability to establish direction, alignment, and commitment for an organization in terms of meeting a higher purpose or business goal.[14] A good example can be seen when Federal Express overnight delivery mail service acquired Kinko's printing, (located near many university campus environments), thereby creating a natural synergy among copying, packaging, and overnight mail delivery. Highly innovative companies are routinely engaged in boundary spanning by exploring the natural, ancillary meeting points of other business enterprises (see Table 2.3).

Home Box Office, Inc.

The real move to modern cable television began on November 8, 1972, when a new start-up company named Home Box Office began supplying movies to 365 subscribers on the Service Electric Cable TV system in Wilkes Barre, Pennsylvania. That night, Jerry Levin, then vice president for programming, introduced viewers to the debut of HBO. The feature programming for that inaugural night was a hockey game between New York and Vancouver and a film prophetically titled, *Sometimes a Great Notion*. HBO was the brainchild of cable entrepreneur

TABLE 2.3 Boundary Spanning—Select Examples

Company	Value Proposition	Business Model	Boundary Spanning
HBO	Premium television services	Pay-supported television	HBO Original Entertainment HBO International Television/film production OTT Streaming—HBO Max
Amazon	Online shopping and direct-to-home delivery of product goods	E-commerce	Amazon Kindle and digital books AWS cloud computing services Amazon Prime OTT streaming Amazon Prime—home delivery
Alphabet (Google)	Internet search	Keyword search advertising	YouTube Google Maps and Waze GPS Google internet search apps • Image • Earth • Calendar • Gmail • Analytics • Translate

Charles "Chuck" Dolan, who drew up the concept for a pay television service in the summer of 1971 while aboard the Queen Elizabeth II en route to France.

From the beginning, HBO developed two important innovations that helped to promote its rapid growth and development. First, HBO introduced the principle of premium television (i.e., business model innovation). Specifically, HBO achieved what no other television service provider had accomplished to date; namely getting people to pay for television. The principle of advertiser-supported "free" television was firmly engrained in the minds of the American public. What HBO did was change public perception about the nature of television entertainment. HBO offered a unique value proposition emphasizing recently released movies and other specialized entertainment that could not be found elsewhere on the general airwaves.[15] While HBO was not the first company to introduce a monthly per channel fee service, they were the first to make it work successfully. This marked the beginning of premium television entertainment. In September 1973, Time Inc. demonstrated its confidence in the young company by acquiring HBO as a wholly owned subsidiary. A year later, HBO quickly established itself as the largest pay cable program supplier in the United States. And by the start of the 1980s, HBO had become one of Time Inc.'s most successful business operations. From the beginning, HBO developed a number of strategies that helped promote its rapid growth including the use of a monthly per-channel fee and the use of microwave and later satellite communications for the transmission of programming rather than distribution by videotape.[16]

The HBO Business Model

HBO is first and foremost a subscription television service. Companies like Netflix, Amazon Prime, and Disney plus owe their beginnings to companies like HBO for having introduced the principle of pay television. Today, HBO's name recognition and past success make it one of the most profitable programming services in the world. The company is duly recognized for producing some of the industry's best television content including award-winning programs such as *Band of Brothers, The Sopranos, Sex in the City, Game of Thrones, Six Feet Under, The Wire,* and *John Adams* to name only a few. In addition to subscription income, another important revenue source is through the licensing of its program content to other networks and streaming services in return for a royalty or flat fee. HBO also makes money through the sale of licensed merchandise based upon the popularity of some of these said programs.

HBO and Boundary Spanning

Today, HBO has extended its geographical boundaries and reaches an estimated 73.8 million subscribers in more than 155 countries worldwide. Their extended reach has been greatly aided by the launch of its HBO Max OTT streaming service. For HBO, the company which originated the concept of pay television, the commitment to its HBO Max OTT streaming service represents a logical progression in strategy as it looks to the future. The HBO Max service has given the company the ability to be less dependent on traditional cable television, multichannel telephone service providers, and Direct Broadcast Satellite television. The new HBO Max streaming service can now traverse geographical borders globally.

As will be discussed throughout this book, many of today's television viewers have elected to "cut the cord" and not subscribe to a cable television or satellite service provider. They can, instead, access HBO Max as well as other OTT services directly. One important business change for the future is the acquisition of HBO's former parent company AT&T—Warner Media by Discovery Inc. for $30 billion. The new Warner Bros. Discovery will create one of the largest media companies in the world by combining the assets of Warner Brothers television and film studios, HBO, and the sports-heavy TNT and TBS networks with Discovery's vast library of nonfiction programming, which includes Oprah Winfrey's OWN, HGTV, the Food Network, and Animal Planet.[17] As the competitive environment for OTT streaming continues to grow, having an expanded base of original television programming becomes the all-important essential.

Amazon

Amazon Inc. is a US-based EC company headquartered in Seattle, Washington. Company founder, Jeff Bezos, incorporated the company in July 1994. The company is named after South America's Amazon river. Today, Amazon.com is the largest EC retailer in the world. In 1994, Bezos resigned his position as vice president at D.E. Shaw, a Wall Street firm, and moved to Seattle. He began to work on a business plan that served as the blueprint for what would become Amazon.com. The basic idea was to create a mail order catalog, albeit electronically, using the Internet and the power of intelligent networking. Bezos created a list of 20 products that could be marketed online. The list included books, CDs, computer hardware, computer software, and videos.[18]

Amazon.com started with online books given the large worldwide demand for literature, the low price points for books, as well as the large number of titles available in print. At the time, no significant mail-order book catalogs existed. The reason was simple. To build a substantial mail order catalog covering books in all areas of arts, sciences, and humanities would require an encyclopedia-like publication (if not bigger). And it would be too expensive to mail. The solution, of course, was the Internet which is ideally suited for organizing and displaying a limitless amount of information. It so happens that Bezos attended the American Booksellers' annual convention where he learned that books are among the most highly databased items in the world. At the time, most of the world's publishers had their works fully listed in CD-ROM format. Bezos reasoned that such information could be better organized and more efficiently put online. Within its first two months of operation, the company was selling and distributing books in all 50 states as well as 45 countries. While the largest of America's bookstore chains might carry 200,000 plus titles, an online bookstore could offer several times that, since it does not require physical storage space when compared to a traditional retailer. Said Bezos at the time,

Within the first few days, I knew this was going to be huge. It was obvious that we were onto something much bigger than we ever dared to hope.[19]

From the beginning, Bezos took a careful and long-term view of his business. He did not expect to make a profit for several years. His slow growth approach caused stockholders to complain about the company not achieving profitability fast enough to justify the level of investment. Amazon, for its part, survived the dot.com crash at the start of the 21st century and went on to achieve profitability by the end of 2001. Two years earlier, *Time* magazine named Bezos its Person of the Year, recognizing Amazon's success and contributions in helping to advance the principle of e-commerce.

> Bezos is a person who not only changed the way we do things but helped paved the way for the future . . . E-commerce has been around for four or five years . . . but 1999 was a time in which e-commerce and dotcom mania reached a peak and really affected all of us.[20]

Today, Jeff Bezos presides over an EC company that has redefined online shopping for billions of people worldwide. The value proposition for all would-be Amazon customers is exchange efficiency, which can be translated in one of three ways: selection, convenience, and low prices.[21] It is central to Amazon's business model and philosophy. Customers complete 28% of their purchases on Amazon in three minutes or less, and half of all purchases are finished in less than 15 minutes. Compare that to the typical shopping trip to a physical store—driving, parking, searching store aisles, waiting in the checkout line, finding one's car, and driving back to home.[22]

Amazon.com and Exchange Efficiency

The principle of *exchange efficiency* is an important concept found in management theory. It has to do with creating the optimum conditions through which a consumer can obtain a product or service. Traditional examples of exchange efficiency can be seen with speed lanes and self-checkout at a supermarket thereby allowing customers to move more quickly through the checkout line.[23] Similarly, the principle of exchange efficiency can be seen with ATM machines at banks as well as digital wallet services such as Apple Pay, PayPal, and Venmo. Today, EC has taken the principle of exchange efficiency to a whole new level in terms of retail trade and distribution. Companies such as Amazon (US), ASML Holdings (the Netherlands), Alibaba (China), and Rakuten (Japan), to name only a few, have developed highly sophisticated supply chain management systems with which to create this efficiency. A supply chain consists of all parties involved, directly or indirectly, in fulfilling a customer request. The supply chain consists of the online ordering systems as well as the manufacturer and suppliers, transporters, warehouses, retailers, and the customers themselves.

Amazon and Supply Chain Management

When an order is placed on Amazon, the EC site sets into motion a kind of software road map that will enable the said purchase order to be completed by the various players who make up the supply chain. From manufacturers and wholesalers to product shipping, everyone who comprises the supply chain has access to all of the pertinent information to complete the transaction, including the customer order information, credit rating (where appropriate), order history, production status, warehousing, and distribution. Supply chain in the Amazon sense is critically important when one considers that nearly 58% of all sales made on Amazon are the result of third-party sellers. To accomplish this, Amazon offers two EC options to sellers FBA (Fulfillment by Amazon) and FBM (Fulfillment by Merchant). With FBA, Amazon takes care of all logistics and customer support. Third-party sellers basically send bulk products to Amazon's fulfillment centers for the company to organize, pack, and ship. FBA is the appropriate choice for third-party sellers who don't possess the logistical support in place to handle small and lightweight products. The second EC approach is FBM, whereby third-party sellers are in charge of listing their products on Amazon and handling all of the storage and fulfillment aspects of the process on their own. Amazon has more than 175 fulfillment operating centers globally as well as 500 plus warehouses located near major metropolitan areas.[24]

To enhance product delivery, Amazon developed *Amazon Prime*. Part of any business-to-consumer EC model requires a mastery of cost-effective shipping and distribution. In 2005, Amazon initiated Amazon Prime; a two-day shipping service on all eligible purchases for a flat fee. For Amazon users, an annual subscription to Prime offers multiple benefits including free two-day shipping (free same-day delivery in select markets), access to Amazon Prime video streaming, Amazon Music, Audible (audio books), online photo storage as well as exclusive rewards and discounts on various goods and services.[25]

Amazon and Boundary Spanning

Amazon employs a multilevel EC business model strategy. In its formative years, Amazon focused on business-to-customer (B-to-C) e-commerce. The goal was to become more fully diversified in terms of product and service offerings. In time, they incorporated customer reviews and leveraged such information as a way to sell more products and services as well as improve the customer experience. Amazon is a highly innovative company and has adopted the principle of boundary spanning in three specific ways. Each area is a natural extension of what Amazon already does.

Amazon Marketplace

Amazon has also greatly expanded its third-party marketplace, where merchants all over the world can set up their own virtual stores on Amazon.com and sell their products alongside Amazon's—all the while leveraging Amazon's large customer base and credit-card-processing capability. Both retailers and individual sellers utilize the Amazon platform to sell goods. Large retailers like

Nordstrom and Target use Amazon.com to sell their products in addition to selling them via their own websites. In its communication with prospective sellers, Amazon articulates its goals as follows:

> We offer programs that enable sellers to grow their businesses, sell their products on our websites and their own branded websites, and fulfill orders through us. We are not the seller of record in these transactions. We earn fixed fees, a percentage of sales, per-unit activity fees, interest, or some combination thereof, for our seller programs.[26]

Amazon Web Services (AWS)

It is a collection of cloud computing services offered by Amazon via the Internet. In recent years, AWS has greatly expanded its cloud computing services by powering small and large businesses alike in over 190 countries around the world. The benefit for such enterprises is that they do not have to make large upfront investments in computing infrastructure. Amazon maintains data center locations in the United States, Europe, Brazil, Singapore, Japan, and Australia. Some of the better-known companies that use Amazon Web Services include BMW, Comcast, Walt Disney, Johnson & Johnson, NASA, Sony, and Netflix to name only a few.[27] It is interesting to note that some of these companies like Comcast, Disney, and Netflix are both customers and competitors.

Amazon Kindle and Digital Tablets

In November 2007, Amazon launched its Amazon Kindle e-book reader. Today, most analysts agree that Amazon probably sold its original Kindle hardware at breakeven or a small loss to subsidize media sales. With the original Kindle, Amazon pioneered the sale of digital books and as a result owns over 90% of their distribution. By July 2010, Amazon e-book sales for its Kindle reader outnumbered the sales of hardcover books for the first time ever. The Amazon Kindle is much more than an e-reader. It represents the foundation for an entire media ecosystem. Specifically, the Amazon Kindle is a series of e-readers designed and marketed by Amazon. Amazon Kindle devices enable users to browse, buy, download, and read e-books, newspapers, magazines, audio books (Audible), and other digital media products via a network connection to the Kindle Store. It is digital boundary spanning in its most essential form.

The display on the Amazon Kindle e-reader resembles a book page. The reader, however, can adjust the screen and size of the font to meet individual reading needs as well as underline passages and set bookmarks. The Kindle high-contrast screen allows the user to read even in bright sunshine with no glare. Also important to the discussion is the lightweight and carry feel of the

Kindle and similar digital tablet devices. The Amazon Kindle stores upwards of 1,400 books. Consider what this means for students attending universities as well as grade schools. Publishers are fully committed to the future of digital books because they know students appreciate the convenience of e-books, especially when it comes to large, heavy textbooks that can be burdensome to carry. Consider further the cost factor and what it means to download an entire academic years' worth of textbooks and readings onto one lightweight device. The cost of a digital textbook is significantly less expensive than a hardcopy edition. As the popularity of tablets increases, many schools are making the switch from textbooks to tablets, along with introducing one-to-one programs (one device per student use) into their districts.

Additional Amazon Subsidiaries

In addition to these three core areas, Amazon is parent company to a number of other business enterprises; most notably, Whole Foods (supermarket), Zappos (shoes and footwear), Kiva Systems (robotics), and Twitch Interactive (video live streaming). One area that is sometimes underrepresented is advertising. In 2020, Amazon claimed 10.3% of the U.S. digital ad space. With the influx of sellers and brands on Amazon, competition on Amazon is steep. But effective microtargeted advertising can help sellers and brands set themselves apart. Ad revenue is now one of Amazon's fastest-growing sectors.

Google

Google was founded by Larry Page and Sergey Brin while they were PhD students at Stanford University. Together, they formed a unique partnership based on intellectual curiosity and competitiveness. One of the toughest challenges facing the Internet at that time was the ability to organize and retrieve information from massive amounts of data. Together, Page and Brin began work on a search engine called *BackRub*, named for its unique ability to analyze the back-links pointing to a given website. Equally important was the development of PageRank; an algorithm that ranks websites in terms of search engine results. PageRank was designed to count the number and quality of links to a page and thus provide an estimate of how important the website is.[28] They received encouragement from David Filo, Yahoo co-founder and fellow Stanford alum. One of the company's earliest investors was Sun Microsystem's co-founder Andy Bechtolsheim, who wrote them a check for $100,000. The name *BackRub* was eventually changed to Googol (or Google); a term coined by Milton Sirotta in 1938, nephew of the American mathematician Edward Kasner. Google refers to the number 1 followed by 100 zeros. It implies organizing vast amounts of information on the Internet.

In September 1998, Google opened its door in Menlo Park California. The company would later move to its current home in Mountainview, California. It didn't take long before various business news and high-tech publications began to take notice of the new start-up company. In a matter of a few short years, Google would establish itself as the world's most widely used Internet search engine.

The Launch of Keyword Search Advertising

The launch of its keyword search advertising program in 2001 provided a unique business model that would transform Google into a major communications company. *Keyword search*, also known as contextual advertising, involves text-based ads and links that appear next to a search engine result. Keywords are words or phrases that are used to match a company or organization's ads with the terms people are searching for. The new advertising program was given the name AdWords (later changed to Google Ads.). An advertiser buys a keyword or phrase from the search engine site and pays only if consumers click-through to its site. An advertisement that generates a large number of hits can be considered successful in terms of promoting consumer interest.[29] The ads can appear in the results following search query as well as on non-search websites, mobile apps, and video.

As an example, if a user were to type *Hotel Le Bristol in Paris* into the Google search bar, the ads that might appear next to the search query are links to Booking.com, Expedia.com, as well as other hotel booking companies. These advertising links are listed on the display page as well as on the right-hand portion of the search results window. These ads are ranked for presentation based on a bidding process. Bidding is competitive with the bid range determined by the popularity of the search term. The higher the bid, the greater the likelihood that an advertiser's ad will appear on the first page of the Google search query. In principle, ads are supposed to reach only those people who actually want to see them thus providing benefit to both users and advertisers. More to the point, a keyword search allows an advertiser to target a message to an audience that is presumably already interested in it. Moreover, the advertiser can record the number of people who click though the advertisement. Google offers the advertiser different pricing options ranging from maximum cost-per-click where the advertiser sets a prescribed limit on the number of hits they are willing to pay for; to a cost-per-click option, where the advertiser pays for only those ads that are specifically queried by the user. Keyword search advertising set into motion the principle of micromarketing, that is, advertisements that are directed toward the individual user based on the user's query. It has proven to be a revolutionary Internet marketing strategy that is utilized today by a whole host of media and social media companies.[30]

Google Analytics

Google Analytics is a free website-tracking tool offered by Google to help a person or organization analyze their website traffic. For most persons and organizations, their website presence serves as the main entry point for all of their digital traffic. Google Analytics comes into play by measuring the effectiveness of their website's performance. This becomes especially important when the said organization is running a major marketing, sales, or recruitment campaign. With Google Analytics, the person or organization can track not only the number of users visiting a said website but select demographic features as well, including what marketing channels drive traffic to the host site, which sites users come from at different times of day, what landing page they arrived at, and how long the page took to load for them.[31] For many organizations, the increased use of smartphones and tablets has led to a larger need for tracking users across the Internet as well as the devices they use.

Google and Boundary Spanning

Google is unique among major media/tech companies given its willingness to explore ideas and working concepts outside its core areas of expertise. Writers A.G. Lafley and Mark Johnson refer to this as "seizing the white space." The term refers to the range of potential activities that are not part of the company's main business strategy.[32] Google's deep-seated commitment to experimental research can be seen in such areas as its autonomous self-driving vehicles. In 2009, Google started the self-driving car project with the goal of driving autonomously over ten uninterrupted 100-mile routes. In 2016, Waymo, an autonomous driving technology company, became a subsidiary of Alphabet, and Google's self-driving project became Waymo. Google launched its Waymo division to develop and market consumer-ready driverless vehicles around the globe.[33] The company, along with automobile giants like Tesla, Mercedes Benz, and GM, is betting that self-autonomous vehicles will revolutionize driver efficiency and safety in the future.

From its very start, one of Google's stated missions was to organize the world's information. This would require a very powerful set of intelligent networks to accomplish this goal. The power and networking capability of the Google search engine has proven highly adaptive and grown exponentially over time.[34] Google has indexed trillions of URL links since its beginning. This ever-increasing amount of data has created its own unique networking effect. In keeping with the principle of network evolution, there is an automatic self-learning quality that is built into the larger network design that has engendered the development of other Google software products and services (e.g., Gmail, Google Maps, Google Earth, Google Analytics, YouTube, Waze, etc.). The more people use the Google search engine, the more powerful the network becomes. Over time, the Google search engine network has become greater than the sum of its parts. Google's enormous information capabilities has enabled the company to boundary span in multiple directions. This is reflected in the company's 2015 decision to rename itself Alphabet to better reflect the many growth opportunities stemming from its various businesses. In a blog post, CEO Larry Page said:

> We liked the name Alphabet because it means a collection of letters that represent language, one of humanity's most important innovations, and is the core of how we index with Google search! We also like that it means alpha-bet (Alpha is investment return above benchmark), which we strive for![35]

Discussion

Business model innovation involves creating entirely new approaches for doing business. HBO, Amazon, and Google have each introduced a unique business model that has fundamentally changed the competitive business landscape following their respective product launches. Both HBO and Amazon.com were first-to-market and, thereby, established a market presence and brand recognition that would make them difficult to compete against in the future. HBO proved that there was a market for premium television services. From Blockbuster to Netflix, all of today's pay television services owe their beginnings to the original premium television concept developed by HBO.

Amazon.com took the early lead in EC development. Today, the company has become the world's preeminent EC company. Many of the company's SCM practices have become the standard for companies worldwide engaged in e-commerce. Amazon is also a major player in OTT video streaming with its Amazon Prime service. Finally, Amazon.com, through its Kindle media ecosystem, has taken the lead in defining the future of digital books, products, and services.

Google, for its part, has built the most widely used search engine in the world. In developing its keyword search advertising model, the company has greatly contributed to the principle of micromarketing, a marketing strategy widely adopted by numerous EC companies. Google continues to be a major innovator by introducing a whole host of software applications, most notably YouTube, Gmail, Maps, and Calendar that continue to expand the company's boundaries in multiple directions.

Successful business model innovation requires a commitment to a challenging management or design issue problem. It means blue ocean visioning and a letting go of traditional ways of thinking. Business model innovation is transformative; that is, it redefines the competitive playing field by introducing a unique value proposition to the consumer. The real test of business model innovation is the degree to which the model is later imitated by others. Each of the said companies discussed in this chapter proved to be an innovative game changer by introducing a business model as well as technology/service that has set the standard for others to follow.

Notes

1 Tanja Storsul and Arne Krumsvik, (Eds.) *Media Innovations: A Multidisciplinary Study of Change.* (Goteborg, Sweden, Nordicom, 2013). See also: Alexander Osterwalder and Yves Pigneur, *Business Model Generation* (Hoboken, NJ: John Wiley & Sons, 2010).
2 W. Chan Kim and Renée Mauborgne, *Blue Ocean Strategy* (Boston, MA: Harvard Business School Press, 2005).
3 Richard Gershon, *Media, Telecommunications and Business Strategy.* 3rd ed. (New York: Routledge, 2020).
4 Gary Hamel, "The What, Why and How of Management Innovation," *Harvard Business Review*, 2006, February, 72–87.
5 Heather McGowan and Chris Shipley, *The Adaptation Advantage* (Hoboken, NJ: John Wiley & Sons, 2020), 3–15.
6 Gershon, *Media, Telecommunications and Business Strategy.* 3rd ed.
7 Peter Thiel, *Zero to One* (New York: Crown Business, 2014), 79.
8 Robert Hoff, "Building an Idea Factory," *Business Week*, 2004, October 11, 194.
9 Raphael Amit and Christoph Zott, *Business Model Innovation Strategy* (Hoboken, NJ: John Wiley & Sons, 2021), 27–54.
10 C. Dal Zotto and H. van Kranenburg, "Introduction," in C. Dal Zotto and H. van Kranenburg (Eds.), *Management and Innovation in the Media Industry* (Cheltenham: Edward Elgar, 2009), ix–xxiv.
11 Lucy Küng, *Strategic Management in the Media.* 2nd ed. (London: Sage, 2017).
12 S. J. Chang, *Sony vs. Samsung: The Inside Story of the Electronics Giants' Battle for Global Supremacy* (Singapore: John Wiley & Sons, 2008).
13 Steven Johnson, *Where Good Ideas Come From: The Natural History of Innovation* (New York: Riverhead Books, 2010), 22.
14 Chris Ernst and Donna Chrobot-Mason, *Boundary Spanning Leadership* (New York: McGraw-Hill, 2011), 5–6.
15 Gershon, *Media, Telecommunications and Business Strategy*, 69–71.
16 Richard Gershon, "Pay Cable Television: A Regulatory History," *Communication and the Law* 12,2 (1990): 3–26.
17 J. Koblin, "Discovery's Merger with WarnerMedia Clears Antitrust Scrutiny," *New York Times*, 2022, February 9, www.nytimes.com/2022/02/09/business/discovery-warnermedia-merger-antitrust.html
18 Brad Stone, *Amazon Unbound: Jeff Bezos and the Invention of a Global Empire* (New York: Simon & Schuster, 2020).
19 Jeff Bezos, *Invent and Wander: Collected Writings of Jeff Bezos* (Boston, MA: Harvard Business Press, 2021).
20 J. C. Ramo, "Jeffrey Bezos: 1999 Person of the Year," *Time*, 1999, December 27, www.time.com/time/subscriber/article/0,33009,992927,00.html
21 Dave Chaffee, "Amazon.com Marketing Strategy 2022: E-commerce Retail Giant Business Case Study," *Smart Insights*, 2022, February 11, www.smartinsights.com/digital-marketing-strategy/online-business-revenue-models/amazon-case-study/
22 Amazon Inc., *2020 Annual Report* (Seattle, WA: Amazon Inc., 2021), 3, https://s2.q4cdn.com/299287126/files/doc_financials/2021/ar/Amazon-2020-Annual-Report.pdf
23 Gershon, *Media, Telecommunications and Business Strategy*, 192–193.
24 Moritz Bauer, "How Amazon Supply Chain Works," *Teikametrics*, 2021, February 23, www.teikametrics.com/blog/how-amazon-supply-chain-works/
25 Tim Chan, "Amazon Raises Price of Prime by $20, Promises Expansion' of Benefit," *Rolling Stone*, 2022, February 17, www.rollingstone.com/product-recommendations/lifestyle/amazon-prime-price-subscription-membership-1294862/

26 Chaffee, "Amazon.com Marketing Strategy 2022."
27 N. Suryawanshi, "The Biggest AWS Users," *Linked-In*, 2020, September 22, www.linkedin.com/pulse/biggest-aws-users-nikhil-suryawanshi/
28 Anna Crowley Redding, *Google It: A History of Google* (New York: Feiwel and Friends, 2018), 14–32.
29 Eric Schmidt and Jonathan Rosenberg, *How Google Works* (New York: Hachette, 2014).
30 Gershon, *Media, Telecommunications and Business Strategy*, 284–285.
31 "The beginner's guide to Google Analytics," *MOZ*, 2023, https://moz.com/beginners-guide-to-google-analytics
32 A.G. Lafley and Mark Johnson, *Seizing the White Space: Business Model Innovation* (Boston, MA: Harvard Business School, 2010).
33 Joe D'Allegro, "How Google's Self-Driving Car Will Change Everything," *Investopedia*, 2021, June 30, www.investopedia.com/articles/investing/052014/how-googles-selfdriving-car-will-change-everything.asp
34 Redding, *Google It: A History of Google*, 14–32.
35 Eugene Kim, "Larry Page Explains Why He Chose the Name 'Alphabet' for His New Big Company," *Business Insider*, 2015, August 10, www.businessinsider.com/why-googles-new-name-is-alphabet-2015-8#:~:text=Larry%20Page%2C%20who%20will%20now,we%20index%20with%20Google%20search

3

PRODUCT INNOVATION AND DESIGN

Introduction

Product innovation refers to the complex process of bringing new products and services to market as well improving (or enhancing) existing ones. It allows a business to develop and improve on its existing product line as well as preparing the groundwork for the future.[1] If successful, a new product innovation will create a first-of-its-kind market space. Highly innovative companies display a clear and discernible progression in the products they make. They force themselves to create newer and better products while challenging the competition to do the same.

This chapter looks at the importance of product innovation and design. Specifically, it will address the following question. What are some of the distinguishing features that characterize successful product design? This chapter will further consider some of the people, companies, and strategies that have transformed the business of media and telecommunications in the area of product innovation and design. Specifically, we will consider three important issues related to this topic. They include 1) ideation—the power of new ideas, 2) new product development, and 3) product design. Special attention is given to three media companies: Apple, Sony Inc., and the Walt Disney Company. These companies were selected because they introduced an altogether new product or service that fundamentally changed the competitive business landscape following their respective product launch (see Table 3.1).

Ideation: The Power of New Ideas

What is the value of one good idea or suggestion? Design thinking is a method and approach used by designers for the purpose of advancing new

DOI: 10.4324/9781003294375-3

TABLE 3.1 Media and Telecommunications Product Innovation

• Apple	Macintosh Computer and Apple iPhone	The introduction of the Macintosh computer made personalized computing much more accessible to the general public. The Mac featured a graphical user interface (GUI) design that allowed users to interact with computers through the use of graphical icons and computer mouse. The introduction of the Apple iPhone in 2007 represented the first all-in-one integrated cell phone that combines voice communication, Internet access, music, camera, and photo storage. The iPhone set the standard for future smartphone design.
• SONY	Walkman, Compact Disk (CD), and PlayStation Video Game System	The Sony Walkman became the first portable music playback device of its kind using audio cassettes and later CDs. The compact disk (CD) transformed music recording from analog-based vinyl records to digital recording on CD. The introduction of the PlayStation Video Game System in 1994 was among the first wave of consoles capable of delivering 3D visuals while gaining worldwide popularity. The PlayStation would redefine video game entertainment.
• Walt Disney Company	Animated films, theme parks and resorts	The founding of Walt Disney Studios (later renamed Walt Disney Feature Animation) gave rise to numerous award-winning children's animated films while developing many of the techniques and concepts that have become standard practices in the field of animation. In 2006, Disney acquired Pixar Studios thus advancing CGI-animated films. The introduction of Disneyland in 1955 and Walt Disney World in 1971 set the standard for family friendly theme park entertainment with a strong emphasis on quality design.

product development and/or developing creative solutions to practical problems. Ideation is the essential first step in the design thinking process. In principle, ideation has two main stages: 1) idea generation, where quantity and diversity of viewpoints matter, and 2) synthesis, in which ideas are discussed, refined, and narrowed down to a small set of viable options.[2] The source of good ideas can come from a wide variety of people and players both inside and outside the organization, including design engineers, project teams, business units, and individual customers. Walt Disney's Imagineering group, which is responsible for the design and development of Disney theme parks worldwide, makes the point that ideation is about generating ideas and staying open to any and all possibilities.

> The tiniest spark of an idea is no small thing. Even if born upon the tattered edge of a paper napkin, it may well grow up to be the size of something special . . . Each idea is approached with minds open to any intriguing possibility. Every aspect is questioned, admired, debated . . . until the first sketch can take a daring leap off the napkin into larger more defined drawings and paintings.[3]

Synthesis: Asking the Tough Questions

Part of the management challenge is learning how to work with a large assemblage of highly creative people. The task is to manage the dynamic tension between creativity and value capture. By value capture, we mean the ability to transform creative concepts into commercial realities.[4] The argument can be made that how an organization innovates determines what it will innovate. Stage two requires the ability to synthesize, that is, the ability to discuss and refine the best and most promising ideas into a working set of possibilities. This involves asking the tough questions. Synthesis is a winnowing down process. The following four questions are a type of rapid-fire test designed to help bridge the transition from concept stage into practical applications.

1. Does the Proposed Idea Fill an Obvious Gap or Niche in the Marketplace?

The most effective way for an entrepreneur to succeed in an otherwise established market is to identify an obvious gap or niche that is being underserved by the established leaders. Customers have real needs and want solutions to their problems. A clever idea is nothing more than a curiosity or experiment if nobody actually needs the resultant product. As Lorraine Marchand writes, a successful innovation must offer a solution to a real problem that needs to be solved.[5] Some of the best innovations often begin as a small project start-up. They start by capturing an underserved market. Think of it as playing along the edges. Once the innovator begins to dominate a niche market, he/she can gradually expand into complimentary and adjacent markets (i.e., boundary spanning).

2. Does the Idea Have a Shelf Life?

Are there pending, sweeping changes in technology that could render this idea moot? Companies not on guard for changes in technology can be swept away while competitors move ahead. Finland-based Nokia Corporation, for example, was once the world's leader in cell phone manufacturing. Yet even a company as big and successful as Nokia was not insulated from direct competition. For years, Nokia relied on the mass market production of its cell phones. Each generation of Nokia cell phone was incrementally better than the previous one. Starting in 2008, Nokia found itself outmaneuvered by the successful launch of the Apple iPhone. The launch of the Apple iPhone ushered in a mobile communications revolution. The iPhone proved to be a technological game changer in terms of smartphone design as well as mobile Internet connectivity. As a consequence, Nokia steadily lost market share and would never reclaim its mantle as the world's leading cell phone manufacturer.[6]

3. Is the Idea a True Stand-Alone Business, or Is It Simply a Promising Idea?

For the budding innovator or designer, it is sometimes hard to distinguish between a true business start-up and a promising idea in the early stages of development. Building and designing a business enterprise like Zoom required significant time, people, and investment. It was a technology and service well understood from the beginning. In contrast, so-called *minimum viable products* (MVPs) represent promising ideas but are often fragmented and incomplete during the early stages of development. Now, as sometimes happens, what starts out as an MVP can steadily transform into something much bigger with the right kind of investment of people and financial support. This was the case with such early start-ups such as Facebook, Uber, and Airbnb.[7] The next generation of MVPs can already be seen in the field of artificial intelligence.

4. How Much Funding Will Be Needed to Successfully Launch the Product or Service?

Innovators and project start-ups (both past and present) need financial backing. In the days of Guglielmo Marconi and the invention of the wireless telegraph, financial support came from his father as well as the British Post office. For Alexander Graham Bell, financial backing came from his future father-in-law, Gardner Green Hubbard. Depending on the size and scale of the operation, the funding requirements may be accomplished by the parent company. Alternatively, project start-ups will sometimes seek the assistance of venture capital firms. Kleiner, Perkins, Caufield & Byers, for example, provided the seed capital for such company start-ups as Amazon.com, Google, and Netflix to name only a few.

New Product Development

After the proposed idea has been fully screened and tested, the real work of product development begins. *New product development* (NPD) represents the process of transforming a working idea into a salable product or service. We begin with the idea of scalability; what kinds of people and talents will be required to get the product launched? NPD requires taking a highly disciplined and organized approach to strategy execution. The product manager (and team) must execute on the details. When new product development fails, it fails because of poor project execution.[8]

The Role of Project Teams and Product Manager

Strategy implementation has to do with project execution; specifically, getting it done, on time and on budget. In most organizations, strategy implementation begins with the development of an action plan. An action plan includes the essential steps needed to accomplish the said strategy. A successful action plan recognizes the value of designing a person's job around an outcome rather than a series of tasks. This is often best accomplished through project teams that are responsible for performing the whole process. The project team is a very specialized group because it has been formed for the specific goal of advancing a proposed strategy concept. The project team is typically headed by a product manager who is responsible for creating the system that will drive the project forward to completion. It is the responsibility of the product manager to make things happen. In practical terms, this means setting priorities, spending the many hours to keep the project on task, and having to say "no" on certain occasions when competing ideas and suggestions prove to be a distraction from the goals that have been established.[9] As writer Marty Cagan writes,

> It is my strong belief . . . that behind every great product there is someone—usually someone behind the scenes, working tirelessly—who led the product team to combine technology and design to solve real customer problems in a way that met the needs of the business.[10]

Product Design

Product design is the combined set of engineering and artistic activities that go into the creating of a product or service for the benefit of the end user. The design must balance a diverse set of requirements. It must possess the right aesthetics while being scalable enough to be manufactured and distributed in a cost-effective manner. The product designer should have a good eye for detail, including an appreciation for function, visual appearance, ease-of-use, and reliability. The designer works to ensure that all design specifications use materials and technology effectively and comply with all legal and regulatory requirements.

The Design Philosophy of Dieter Rams and Jonathan Ive

Dieter Rams (1932–) is a German industrial designer closely associated with the consumer products company Braun and the functionalist school of industrial design. Rams believes that technology routinely offers up new opportunities for innovative design. Good product design should go hand in hand with its functionality. It should be pleasing to the user while providing practical utility.[11] In Rams' view, a product should be understandable and easy to use. Good product design should display a kind of simple elegance. It should blend in with its surroundings.[12] Rams had a strong influence on the work of Apple's former chief designer Jonathan Ive, who similarly believes that design should be as important as the product's function. Ive was the principal designer behind the development of the Apple iPhone. Ive has received numerous accolades and honors for his design patents and was selected to be an Honorary Fellow of the Royal Academy of Engineering and Knight Commander of the Order of the British Empire. Ive is a strong believer in the importance of minimalism. This is reflected in a number of Apple products. From the Apple iPhone to the Apple iPad, Apple's products are not flamboyant or flashy but are instead clean and straightforward. For the user, the minimalist approach suggests a product that is inviting and easy to use. It also provides the right aesthetics while being fully functional. And lastly, there is room for interpretation and engagement, specifically, the ability to try and play things out.

The Problem With Complicated Design

An overly complicated product design becomes an immediate barrier to its use. As an example, the first set of personal computers (PCs) in the 1980s were typically accompanied with thick, highly detailed training manuals. The manuals, while well intentioned, proved very intimidating to the user who simply wanted to jump on to the computer and start using it. Implied in the manual's use was the underlying assumption that there was a correct way for using the computer. With time and experience, manufacturers of PCs began to recognize that the technical manual was having the opposite effect. Eventually, they began to scale back the pages and substituted an internal self-help guide that enabled users to have a better first-time experience with their computer.

Similarly, the videocassette recorder (VCR) in the 1980s was a difficult piece of equipment to use, especially when it came to prerecording programs for later viewing. The ability to time shift should have been a signature feature of the VCR. Instead, the manufacturers of VCRs at the time made the recording function needlessly complicated. Consequently, the recording function was rarely used by the vast majority of VCR users. The design problems associated with the VCR would offer up some important lessons for future manufacturers of digital video recording equipment. By comparison, today's generation of digital video recorder (DVR) and Over-the-Top (OTT) video streaming services combine a simple, organized menu structure with ease of use.

Product Integrity

Both Dieter Rams and Jonathan Ive believe that products should be made with integrity and built to last. There is no place for planned obsolescence. Such products should be honest and blend in with their surroundings. By this, they mean that a product does not attempt to manipulate the consumer with promises that cannot be kept. They are neither decorative objects nor works of art. The design should be both neutral and restrained. In sum, less is more because it concentrates on the essential aspects and is not burdened with nonessential features. Finally, good product design pays close attention to detail. This too is something that can be seen in the work of the Imagineers and the design work and construction found at Disney theme parks and resorts. Nothing is left to chance. Care and accuracy in the design process show respect for the user experience.[13]

Apple

Few companies are so closely identified with the strategy, vision, and aesthetic tastes of one person. Apple is one such company and is a direct reflection of its co-founder and CEO, Steve Jobs. Apple has a long-standing history of approaching product design by paying close attention to detail. This is reflected in both striving for perfection in product design and looking at entirely new ways to make products more user-friendly and useful. For Steve Jobs, one way to accomplish this was to have end-to-end software and hardware control for every product that Apple makes.[14] Taking an integrated approach was a central tenant to Apple's basic design philosophy from the company's very start.

Apple Computer was formed in April 1976 by 25-year-old Steve Wozniak and 21-year-old Steve Jobs. After selling a van for some extra start-up cash, the two set up shop in Jobs' family garage at 2066 Crist Drive in Los Altos, California, to start building computers. Steve Wozniak spent the summer of 1976 building the first prototype design for what would become the Apple I computer. Steve Jobs, for his part, took the lead in establishing the company's first customer; a small retail outlet called the Byte Shop located in Mountain View, California. Together, Jobs and Wozniak were able to build and sell 50 Apple I computers that summer.[15] The ideas and innovation techniques that emerged from the company's early start would set the foundation for building one of the world's most powerful and influential technology companies ever conceived.

Apple Computer

In 1977, Jobs and Wozniak began work on the Apple II with the help of a few tech-savvy friends and classmates. It was at this time that Steve Jobs first realized his true passion for the burgeoning computer industry. The successful launch of the Apple II made Apple a highly valued company in the field of personal computing. Soon thereafter, the company began work on the Apple III. The Apple III was meant to be Apple's bold entry into the field of business computing. The Apple III was the first Apple computer not designed by Steve Wozniak. Steve Jobs supervised the project and was very particular about some of the design features, including a specific demand that the computer not have a cooling fan because they were "too noisy and inelegant." The Apple III proved to be Apple's first commercial failure. Part of the problem was due to the fact that the Apple III was very expensive, retailing at a cost ranging between $4,340 and $7,800. Apple's next follow-up computer was the Lisa, named after Steve Job's daughter. The Lisa was targeted to business customers as well. The Lisa did not fare any better than the Apple III having sold only 10,000 units. The one important design element that became part of the Lisa project was Apple's involvement in graphical user interface (GUI) design. In the end, the Apple III and Lisa failures provided some important takeaway lessons that would be later applied to the development of the Macintosh computer.

Microsoft and Apple

Simultaneous to the release of the Apple III and Lisa computers, IBM had been developing a PC of its own whose target market was the business community. IBM, of course, was synonymous with business computing. IBM was the undisputed leader in large mainframe computers. In 1981, IBM introduced its own PC at a cost of $1,565. More importantly, the IBM PC could do more in the way of business software applications. IBM's operating system and beginning software products were being developed by a then unknown company called Microsoft. In time, Microsoft would set the de facto standard in business computing software. By shifting the value proposition in computing to software, Microsoft commoditized the manufacture of hardware equipment, thus making personal computing accessible to the general public. Unlike Apple, Microsoft did not create a proprietary standard, thereby allowing all manufacturers the capability to build computers using Microsoft software. While Microsoft software was not as elegant as the Macintosh, it built a strong, reliable operating system and set of software products that enabled millions of users worldwide to engage in computing at a cost point that greatly accelerated the field of personal computing.

Throughout their respective histories, Apple and Microsoft have had a kind of symbiotic relationship. They have been both competitors and innovation partners. Specifically, Microsoft developed a number of key software products that are featured on Mac computers, including Microsoft Word and Excel; two of the most widely used programs in professional software. It should also be remembered that Microsoft rescued Apple in August 1997 with a $150 million in cash to ensure Apple's survival. This came at a time when Apple was seriously at risk of failing. Steve Jobs had just recently returned to the now struggling company. Dreams of revolutionizing the music and telephone industries with the Apple iPod and iPhone were still several years away.[16]

Macintosh

The Macintosh project was begun in 1979 by Jeff Raskin, an Apple employee who envisioned an easy-to-use, low-cost computer for the average consumer. He wanted to name the computer after his favorite type of apple, but the spelling was changed to *Macintosh* for legal reasons. Raskin was given the responsibility to hire a number of new engineers and designers to the team. In time, the Mac team would bring together some of the most talented individuals ever to work on the same design team. Steve Jobs left the Lisa project team and focused his full attention on the Macintosh project. In 1981, Raskin left the team due to professional differences (and personality conflict) with Steve Jobs.

Graphical User Interface

The Mac featured a *graphical user interface* (GUI), that is, a type of interface that allows users to interact with computers through graphical icons, as opposed to typing in text-based commands. The GUI concept was developed by Xerox PARC laboratories. Xerox Corporation's Palo Alto Research Center (Xerox PARC) was established in 1970 for the purpose of performing research and development work in the area of business machine equipment and computing. The Mac project team was somewhat familiar with the work being done at Xerox PARC. Steve Jobs arranged for a meeting and negotiated rights to the technology in exchange for Apple stock. Steve Jobs and his team were able to immediately seize on the possibility of what GUI could mean to the future of personal computing.[17] It has been suggested that the Apple raid on Xerox PARC represents one of the great technology thefts of all time. Steve Jobs, for his part, takes a different view stating that what transpired was less of a heist by Apple and more of a fumble by Xerox. "They were copier-heads who had no clue about what the computer could do . . . Xerox could have owned the entire computer industry."[18] Writer Walter Isaacson makes the point that Steve Jobs and his team of engineers were able to take the basic design concept and greatly improve upon it in ways that Xerox could not have envisioned. The use of visual icons in combination with a computer mouse was a real breakthrough in the organizing of computer files and the manipulation of software applications.

On January 24, 1984, at the Flint Center on De Anza College's campus in Cupertino, California, Apple formally announced the Macintosh at its shareholder meeting, in front of an audience so packed that large numbers of people who owned Apple stock couldn't get in at all. The introduction of the Macintosh computer would set the foundation for personal computing for an entire industry. In the beginning, the Macintosh was a commercial failure. But, in time, the Mac would become more than a stand-alone computer. It would become a computing platform spawning a whole host of computer, laptop, and notebook derivatives. The Macintosh, like all Apple products, emphasized the importance of combining both hardware and software elements into a seamless integrated design. Today, the Mac is the only personal computer with a 40 year history. Most other leading computer companies of the time, Atari, Commodore, Compaq, Kaypro, and RadioShack no longer exist. Even IBM left the field of PC manufacturing in 2004. The true look and feel of personal computers today can be attributed to the early design features found in the original Macintosh computer.

The Apple iPhone

The Apple iPhone is a line of cellular "smartphone" devices designed and marketed by Apple. The iPhone is designed as a multimedia platform that can support a whole host of applications, including voice communication, mobile Internet access, music playback and storage, as well as a camera and photo storage. Apple CEO Steve Jobs introduced the iPhone at the Macworld convention at the Moscone Center in San Francisco California on January 9, 2007. In his presentation, Steve Jobs described the iPhone as a three-in-one device that included music, phone, and a mobile Internet connection.

> Every once in a while a revolutionary product comes along that changes everything . . . Today we're introducing three revolutionary products of this class. The first one is a widescreen iPod with touch controls. The second is a revolutionary mobile phone. And the third is a breakthrough Internet communications device. Are you getting it? These are not three separate devices, this is one device, and we are calling it iPhone.[19]

Technical Design Features

The iPhone is built using GUI and a multi-touch screen capability. It utilizes both Wi-Fi and cellular 4G and 5G connectivity. The iPhone runs on Apple's iOS mobile operating system. The launch of the Apple iPhone redefined mobile wireless communication by changing public perception of what a cell phone should be able to do. In developing the iPhone, Apple created an entire digital media ecosystem by combining 1) voice communication, 2) mobile Internet access,

3) text messaging and email, 4) music playback and storage, 5) camera, video, and photo storage, as well as helping to advance thousands of apps, such as weather, news, calendar, and GPS by way of example. What was not fully appreciated at the time of the iPhone's launch was how much of a technology game changer it would prove to be.

The iPhone Design Philosophy

Apple's design philosophy is a direct reflection of its co-founder Steve Jobs. Aesthetics in design should be as important as the product's function. From the iPhone touch screen to the Apple stores (where they are retailed), there is a commitment to simplicity in design. Apple's abiding philosophy is that such devices should be simple to the touch, display clean lines, and exercise a less-is-more quality. Author Walter Isaacson makes the point that at most companies, engineering tends to drive design. The engineers set forth their specifications, and the design team comes up with cases and displays that will accommodate them.[20] At Apple, it's often just the opposite. Design drives the engineering. For chief designer Jonathan Ive, the most important aspect to the iPhone experience is the display screen. The iPhone's ergonomic design and high-resolution graphics should be simple and attractive. All applications should defer to the screen.[21] In time, other companies would introduce their own version of smartphone design including Samsung, LG (Korea); Huawei, Xiaomi, Lenovo (China); Google (USA); Nokia (Finland); and Alcatel (France). The Apple iPhone (and smartphones in general) have become an essential part of today's digital lifestyle.

Sony Corporation

Sony Corporation is a leading transnational media corporation in the production and sale of consumer electronics, music, film entertainment, and video game technology. Throughout its more than 60-year history, the Sony name has been synonymous with great product design and innovation. During that time, Sony has introduced a number of firsts in the development of new communication products. Words like *Walkman, Compact Disk*, and *PlayStation* have become part of the global lexicon of terms to describe consumer electronics.[22] Early on in his tenure, Sony president and co-founder Akio Morita developed the kind of business skills that allowed him to successfully enter into foreign markets. Morita did not initially have a global strategy in mind. Instead, he tended to focus on those markets that he believed were important and where Sony's products would be readily accepted. The United States represented a first step in realizing that objective. In time, Sony would establish a foreign office in both the United States and Europe to handle the sales and service of its products.[23]

The Sony Walkman

The creation of Sony's highly popular Walkman portable music player was highly serendipitous in its origins. From 1966 onwards, Sony and other Japanese manufacturers began the mass production of cassette tapes and recorders in response to a growing demand. At first, cassette tape recorders could not match the sound quality of reel-to-reel recorders and were mainly used as study aids and for general purpose recording. By the late 1970s, audio quality had steadily improved, and the stereo tape cassette machine had become a standard fixture in many homes and automobiles.

It so happened that Masaru Ibuka (who was then honorary Chairman of Sony) was planning a trip to the United States. Despite its heaviness as a machine, Ibuka would often take a TC-D5 reel-to-reel tape machine when he traveled. This time, however, he asked Norio Ohga for a simple, stereo playback version. Ohga contacted Kozo Ohsone, general manager of the tape recorder business division. Ohsone had his staff alter a Pressman stereo cassette by removing the recording function and had them convert it into a portable stereo playback device. When Ibuka returned from his US trip he was quite pleased with the unit, even if it had large headphones and no recording capability.[24]

Ibuka soon went to Morita (then chairman) and said, "Try this. Don't you think a stereo cassette player that you can listen to while walking around is a good idea?"[25] Morita took it home and tried it out over the weekend. He immediately saw the possibilities. In February 1979, Morita called a meeting together that included a number of the company's electrical and mechanical design engineers. He instructed the group that this product would enable someone to listen to music anytime, anywhere. It was understood that the target market was to be students and young people and that it should be introduced just prior to summer vacation of that year. In developing a new portable music device, Morita would have to overcome two resistance barriers. The first was the notion that cassette tapes could provide good sound quality and second that people would be willing to wear headsets; albeit, well-designed headsets in public. As author John Nathan, writes:

> The Walkman project was founded on Morita's certainty and determination; there was no conventional development process, and no market testing. From the outset, Morita insisted that the product must be affordable to teenagers.[26]

Akio Morita was the quintessential marketer. He understood how to translate new and interesting technologies into usable products. After rejecting several names, the publicity department came up with the name "Walkman." The product name was partially inspired by the movie *Superman* and Sony's existing *Pressman* portable tape cassette machine.[27] The Walkman created an altogether new market for portable music systems and unleashed an important change in consumer lifestyle. From public parks to public transportation, portable music and the wearing of headsets gave us a new way to appreciate music.

The Compact Disk

In 1975, Sony Corporation entered into a partnership with the Netherlands-based Philips Corporation to begin work on the digital recording of information onto laser discs. Sony President Norio Ohga, a former student of music, was enamored with the possibilities of digital recording. He designated a small group of Sony engineers to give the laser disc top priority. From 1979 to 1982, both teams of engineers worked together to refine the compact disk (CD) player. Demonstrations of the CD were made worldwide in preparation for the planned launch of the CD in October 1982.

Norio Ohga was convinced that the CD would eventually replace vinyl records given the technology's superior sound quality. At the same time, Ohga recognized that the development of the CD would meet with fierce resistance from many in the recording industry who felt threatened by CD technology. To them, the CD format was an unproven technology made by hardware people who knew nothing about the software side of the business. Worse still, the conversion to a CD format would require enormous sums of money while possibly destabilizing the entire music industry. In one product demonstration in Athens, Greece, a group of executives stood up and shouted back in unison, "The truth is in the groove."[28] On August 31, 1982, an announcement was made in Tokyo that four companies—Sony, Philips, CBS, and Polygram—would work together to introduce the first CD system. In time, the Sony/Philips CD became the de facto standard throughout the industry. By 1986, the production of music CDs had topped 45 million titles annually, overtaking records to become the principal recording format. In time, CD technology would ultimately redefine the field of recording technology and spawn a whole host of new inventions, including the portable CD music player, the CD-based video game console (i.e., PlayStation and XBox Video game systems), digital video disc (DVD), and Blu-Ray DVD systems.[29]

PlayStation

The Sony PlayStation was the brainchild of an engineer named Ken Kutaragi, who was fascinated with designing an entertainment device that could combine the power of a computer workstation with high-resolution graphics. For two years, Kutaragi operated without a sponsor until his friend, Teruo "Terry" Tokunaka, a senior executive at Sony, interceded on his behalf. Tokunaka took Kutaragi to see Sony CEO Norio Ohga to discuss his idea. Ohga was sufficiently impressed that he authorized Kutaragi to begin building a working prototype of his video game console. Not everyone at Sony was enamored with the idea of video game technology. In the beginning, the senior leadership at Sony did not view themselves in the business of video game technology, which was seen as a children's toy. Worse still, companies like Nintendo and Sega were the established leaders in video game technology and software. Nevertheless, Sony's executive planning committee approved $50 million in start-up costs to allow Kutaragi and his design team to develop the basic computer chip necessary for a future video game console.

One of Sony's major challenges was to convince the major video game software developers to create innovative games to support the new platform system. Sony's future success in video game technology would depend on high-quality software games. In November 1993, Sony Computer Entertainment (SCE) was created for the purpose of marketing and licensing video game consoles and titles. One of the most critical elements to the new Sony video game platform was the use of CD technology instead of the existing 16-bit cartridge. It was recognized that the CD possessed greater storage capacity than a video game cartridge and was much cheaper to produce. Sony was able to play to its own strengths since both they and Phillips Corporation were the coinventors of the CD. On December 3, 1994, the Sony PlayStation was launched in Japan with eight game titles. Sony sold some 300,000 units in the first month alone, more than three times what company strategists had expected. The PlayStation was launched a year later in the United States and achieved immediate success. By 1998, PlayStation had sold 33 million units worldwide and had become the international leader in video game consoles.

In 2000, Sony's PlayStation 2 was launched and became the bestselling console ever built. Since then, there have been multiple iterations of PlayStation consoles designed and sold worldwide as well as different mobile versions. Sony has likewise developed the PlayStation "gaming" network, which allows users from around the world to play online. The development of PlayStation ultimately changed the landscape of the medium forever, becoming the foundation for gaming as we know it today. In time, the Sony PlayStation would become more than a video game system. It would develop into an all-inclusive broadband delivery system to the home, capable of allowing users to play games, watch television, and listen to music. The year 2020 saw the launch of the Sony PlayStation 5 (PS-5), which has developed a strong international following including growing markets in South America, Africa, India, China, Eastern Europe, and Russia.[30] It's worth noting that PlayStation 5 gamers are much older when compared to the original PlayStation 1 which suggests strong brand loyalty among its many users. In addition, 41% of PS-5 owners are women, when compared to 18% on the original PlayStation 1 system.

The new PS-5 is a powerful and well-designed console that offers a compelling next-generation gaming experience. Its library of exclusive games continues to be a showcase for the PS-5's DualSense controller that is designed to immerse the player more fully in the game by simulating sensory touch experiences in the user's hand. This, of course, is the creative first step in virtual reality gaming. One product review described it this way:

> You can feel the crunch of sand as you walk across a beach, the cracking of glass as you smash through a panel, the pitter-patter of raindrops on an umbrella, or the elastic tension as you pull on a loose cable. Even more impressive: often, you can feel these sensations coming from different parts of the controller.[31]

The DualSense controller has spatial 3D audio tech which means creating sound in 360 degrees around the user. And lastly, the DualSense controller uses super-fast solid state drives (SSD), which involve flash-based memory to store data and thus has no moving parts. This enables a faster, smoother gaming experience and loading time for the game itself.

Video Game Design

While companies like Sony, Microsoft, and Nintendo have built the best-known and most highly recognized video game platforms, there is also the software side to consider. A video game is an electronic game whose purpose is entertainment by engaging in a competitive challenge or overcoming a set of tests and trials. Today's modern-day video games typically involve the use of a controller, keyboard, or joystick. The first video games were prototyped in the 1960s, but by the 1970s there was a whole industry created around video games. Such game designs have evolved significantly from the early days of computer games and the first versions of Nintendo and Atari. The video game industry is immensely large. By 2025, analysts predict the industry will generate more than $260 billion in revenue. Video game industry sales performed especially well early in the Covid-19 pandemic as business shutdowns and social-distancing measures limited people's entertainment options. Because consumers can play video games in the home, they became a popular form of entertainment.

The creation and development of a video game involves a few basic design principles. First, there needs to be some kind of goal or outcome that people can work toward. The more concrete and defined these are, the easier it is for people to participate. Second, there need to be some defined constraints on what players can or cannot do when achieving those objectives. The constraints should be relevant, related to each other, and be part of a coherent whole. Third, and most importantly, there needs to be some type of success criteria; that is, a point at which the player knows that the game's objectives have been met. This can take a variety of forms such as winning at a sports game or overcoming or defeating an enemy (i.e., space aliens or war-time adversary).[32] An important design principle is "flow," which means giving the player the ability to perform actions that match or exceed the requirements of the game.[33]

What makes a video game fun and entertaining is that it transports the player into new realities and satisfies the need for achievement and recognition. The best video games are highly immersive with captivating visual and audio displays featuring heroes, superheroes, sports teams, mythical creatures, aliens, and a host of bad guys and women. What's more, the well-constructed video game gives the player the ability to temporarily live in these unique and other worldly type settings.[34] Graphics and audio are extremely important in the design of any video game. Simply put, it's what the player sees and hears. The combination of setting and environment, the characters, lighting, and sound all contribute to the look and feel of the game. Video game design is an example of media convergence in its most essential form.

Video games offer a type of simulation for the person who might not otherwise get to experience what it's like to be a professional football player, a combat soldier in a hostile environment, or a superhero fighting alien monsters. Simulation teaches several important skills for the player, including improved problem-solving skills, the ability to adapt to a fast-paced changing situation (i.e., hand-to-eye coordination), and faster and more accurate decision-making. To that end, one important change to the industry is the development of eSports. The term *eSports* (electronic sports) describes the world of competitive video gaming that features team-oriented multiplayer online competitions, to single player first person shooters, to virtual reconstructions of physical sports. Competitors from different leagues or teams face off in the same games that are popular with at-home gamers including *Fortnite*, *League of Legends*, *Counter-Strike*, *Call of Duty* and *Madden NFL*, to name only a few. These competitive gamers are watched and followed by millions of viewers worldwide who attend live events and/or watch online. These types of tournaments can attract viewing crowds that can often rival many traditional sports competitions.[35] One such example includes *The League of Legends World Championship*, which is the world championship tournament hosted by Riot Games. Teams compete for the champion title, the 70-pound Summoner's Cup, and a multimillion-dollar prize award.

Online Gaming

Another important change is the greatly expanded interest in online gaming; specifically, the ability to access and play games via the Internet with both friends and other virtual competitors. Starting in 2002, both Sony and Microsoft committed themselves to the start of creating online gaming networks. In the beginning, Microsoft pushed the benefits of online gaming more so than Sony and developed the more successful Xbox Live pay service. The launch of the PlayStation 3 in 2006 set the foundation for the all new PlayStation Network (PSN), which included downloadable content from the PlayStation Store. For most users, playing games online is about connecting with friends. The value of an online gaming service is the opportunity to socially engage with other players while having the opportunity to play different kinds of games.

The Walt Disney Company

The name *Disney* has become synonymous with family entertainment. The result has been an ongoing relationship with the public that spans more than 90 years. The Walt Disney Company is the largest transnational media corporation in the world in terms of capital assets and revenue. Since the company's original 1996 acquisition of Capital Cities/ABC (including ESPN), the Walt Disney Company has steadily evolved into various media and entertainment brands.

Film Animation

At the end of World War I, Walter Elias Disney returned home to the United States after having served as an ambulance driver for the American troops overseas. Prior to his enlistment, Disney trained as a commercial artist having studied at the Kansas City Art Institute. Disney's plan, upon his return, was to pursue a career as a commercial artist. In 1919, Disney formed his own animated cartoon company in partnership with artist, Ub Iwerks. Despite several attempts, the four-year partnership proved unsuccessful. The company went bankrupt, and Disney left to join his brother, Roy, in Hollywood. Together, they formed the Disney Brothers Cartoon Studio in 1923. Walt Disney would be responsible for the creative side while brother, Roy, would devote himself to the business end.[36]

Soon thereafter, word came from New York that a film distributor by the name of Margaret J. Winkler was interested in buying the rights to a series of Disney's live-action cartoon reels, later to be called *Alice Comedies*. Winkler offered $1,500 per reel. Disney agreed and soon became Ms. Winkler's production partner. In 1927, Disney began developing a series of short animated films called *Oswald the Lucky Rabbit*. The series was an instant hit with the general public. However, the name, *Oswald the Lucky Rabbit* was copyrighted in Winkler's name. As a result, Disney did not receive the recognition or commercial benefits of his creative time.[37] That decision proved momentarily costly. He would not make that same mistake twice. Thereafter, Disney made it a point never to relinquish the copyright and creative control to one of his character inventions.[38]

Disney would eventually conceive of an altogether different type of animated character. This time it was a charming and high-energy mouse named Mortimer—later shortened to *Mickey*. Disney drew up several sketches and, together with his brother Roy, invested their own money in the production of two Mickey Mouse films. The third Mickey Mouse film represented a major step forward with the introduction of sound. The film *Steamboat Willie* was a technological achievement and went on to become an all-time classic. Soon thereafter, Mickey Mouse became a cultural sensation and the name Walt Disney was firmly established.

The founding of Walt Disney Studios (later renamed Walt Disney Feature Animation) would give rise to numerous award-winning children's animated films. The company developed many of the techniques and concepts that would later become standard practices in the field of animation. Starting in the 1980s, Walt Disney Studios was responsible for producing an ongoing series of animated film hits, including *The Little Mermaid, Beauty and the Beast, Aladdin, The Lion King, The Hunchback of Notre Dame, Pocahontas*, and *Tarzan* to name only a few. Several of these films, most notably, *Beauty and the Beast* and *The Lion King* would eventually be turned into stage productions as well as regular films.

The Walt Disney Company Today

The Walt Disney company is currently organized into six major divisions (see Table 3.2).

TABLE 3.2 The Walt Disney Company

Walt Disney Theme Parks and Resorts	Disneyland
	Walt Disney World
	Disneyland Paris
	Tokyo Disney Resort
	Hong Kong Disneyland
	Shanghai Disney
	Disney Cruise Lines
	Disney Store
	Disney Vacation Club
	Walt Disney Imagineering
Studio Content	Walt Disney Studios
	Wald Disney Animation
	Pixar Animation
	Marvel Studios
	Lucas Film Ltd.
	20th Century Studios (formerly 20th Century Fox)
	Searchlight Productions
	Disney Theatrical Group

(Continued)

TABLE 3.2 (Continued)

Disney Media & Entertainment Distribution	Disney Plus
	ESPN Plus
	Hulu
	Disney Music Group
	Hotstar
General Entertainment	ABC Television Entertainment
	ABC Television News
	20th Television (formerly 20th Century Fox)
	FX
	National Geographic
	Free Form
	Disney Branded Television
ESPN and Sports Content	ESPN
	ABC Sports Entertainment
International Content and Operations	Developing Local and Regional Entertainment
	International Streaming and Licensing
	Advertising Sales

When Robert Iger was selected to become President and CEO of Disney in 2005, he set into motion three major strategic initiatives.

Expand the Company's Program and Branded Content

The first key strategy was the need to improve and expand the company's television and film content. This was evidenced by the $7.4 billion purchase of Pixar entertainment in 2006 which greatly enhanced and made the Walt Disney Company the world's leading producer of television and film animation. Later, Disney, under Iger's direction, acquired Marvel Entertainment (2009), Lucasfilm—*Star Wars* (2012), and 21st Century Fox (2019). Taken together, these various acquisitions have greatly added to the company's branded television/film entertainment as well as creating cross-marketing opportunities for the many Disney theme parks and commercial merchandise.[39]

In addition, Disney greatly expanded the ESPN brand into becoming the world's leading cable television program service. ESPN has become synonymous with sports entertainment. The ESPN brand has ushered in a sports revolution in terms of media entertainment. ESPN is considered one of the most valuable media properties of its kind. With this name and brand recognition, today's ESPN exercises a level of authority and control in all areas of professional and collegiate sports. This is especially true when it comes to collegiate sports where it exercises considerable influence in helping to determine college and football schedules, including specific sports match ups, days, and times of the week. The ESPN business and programming model has proven so successful that it has been imitated by television sports entities around the world.[40]

The Development of the Disney + OTT Streaming Service

A second important strategy was the need to embrace changing technology; specifically, Disney's commitment to the future of OTT video streaming. In 2019, Disney launched its Disney + OTT streaming service. This included television and film entertainment based on Disney films and animation, Pixar Animation, Marvel Studios, Star Wars, and National Geographic. Given the breadth and depth of program choices, there is something for kids, teenagers, and adults alike. The company attained ten million subscribers in its first 24 hours of operation and a hundred million global subscribers by March 2021. The Disney Plus streaming service also benefited from Disney's investment (and later controlling interest) in the Hulu streaming service, which provided a parallel platform for showcasing Disney Plus. It is worth noting that the success of Disney Plus as well as other leading OTT services was due in part to the Covid-19 pandemic which resulted in a major increase in worldwide subscribership.

Theme Parks and Resorts

The third key strategy was to expand internationally in the area of theme parks and resorts. The Disney Theme Parks and Resorts division is responsible for the operation of the company's six worldwide theme parks and corresponding venues. The two primary theme parks are Disneyland and Walt Disney World. Disneyland was founded in 1955 and is located on 500 acres in Anaheim California. It features the original Magic Kingdom as well as numerous rides and attractions. Disney also owns and operates Walt Disney World located in Lake Buena Vista, Florida. It was founded in 1971. This resort features four major theme parks: *the Magic Kingdom, Epcot, Hollywood Studios*, and *Animal Kingdom*. Walt Disney Attractions is also an equity investor in Disneyland Paris (formerly Euro Disney) located in the suburbs of Paris, France as well as Hong Kong Disneyland located on Lantau Island, 30 minutes from downtown Hong Kong. The company also has a licensing agreement with the Oriental Land company that operates Tokyo Disneyland located in Tokyo, Japan. In November 2009, Disney received approval from the central government of China to build a Disney theme park in Shanghai's Pudong district. China, of course, is considered one of the most sought-after markets in the world. The launch of Disney Shanghai in China in 2016 is 11 times the size of Disneyland at a cost of $6 billion. Also included in the theme parks and resorts division is the Disney Vacation Club and Disney Cruises. The Walt Disney Company is a strong adherent to the principle of vertical integration. The company takes full advantage of its name by cross-promoting its products and services among the company's various films, theme parks, stores, and cruise ships. Several of Disney's more notable animated film characters are regular featured attractions throughout.

Walt Disney Imagineering

Walt Disney Imagineering (WDI) is the creative design and development team of the Walt Disney Company, responsible for the creation and construction of Disney theme parks, resorts and major staged events worldwide. The Imagineering group was founded in 1952 to oversee the construction of Disneyland in California. The term *imagineering* was popularized in the 1940s by the Alcoa corporation to describe the blending of imagination and engineering. It was later and adopted by Walt Disney a decade later to describe the unique artistic and engineering skills that characterized the company's creative design team. Most of the Imagineering design team are based in the company's headquarters in Glendale, California. Often, members of the Imagineering group are sent on various locations around the world to work on specialized projects. In its beginning years, Imagineering was best known for the development of Audio-Animatronics, a form of robotics featured in many Disney theme park attractions including *Pirates of the Caribbean, the Haunted Mansion,* and the Hall of Presidents to name only a few. Throughout its history, the Imagineering group has been granted numerous patents in areas such as ride systems, special effects, interactive technology, live entertainment, and advanced audio systems. More than anything, it is the Imagineering group that shapes the building design, landscape, and color that are featured throughout the various Disney worldwide theme parks and resorts.[41]

Discussion

Product innovation refers to the process of bringing new products and services to market as well as the refinement (improvement) to existing ones. Product innovation is important because it creates a long-term competitive advantage for a company or organization. The principle of ideation represents the creative process for generating, developing, and communicating new ideas with the goal of helping to advance new product development. Successful product design balances function, value, and appearance for the benefit of the end user.

Mobility is a signature feature of the digital economy. The launch of the Apple iPhone demonstrated the first, fully integrated smartphone. The use of GUI multi-touch screen capability would set the standard for all future mobile devices including both smartphones and computer tablets. Also important to the discussion would be the development of thousands of future apps that would give breadth and depth to smartphone capability. The development of the Google

Android operating system in 2008 would help facilitate new and enhanced smartphone designs by various international smartphone manufacturers, thereby making it a worldwide product.

The development of the Sony/Philips compact disk in 1982 redefined the field of music delivery by introducing an altogether new way of recording and playing music. The CD played on the inherent strengths of digital technology by eliminating scratches and surface noise while being able to produce a cleaner sound than was true for analog-based vinyl records. As a one-time student of music, Sony President Norio Ohga firmly supported the product's development despite a well-established music industry that was resistant to change. The CD would eventually replace vinyl records as the new standard in recording technology. As noted earlier, successful innovation leads to a progression in new product offshoots. The CD would set into motion the future development of CD-based video game systems as well as DVD and Blu Ray DVD video recording and playback.

The introduction of Disneyland in 1955 and Walt Disney World in 1971 helped to create an altogether new type of family friendly theme park experience. This, in combination with Disney animated films, has helped establish an entertainment brand that is known worldwide. Words like *magic* and *fantasy* have become part of the glossary of terms to describe a Disney vacation experience. The Disney experience is driven by a strong attention to detail. Both the theme parks and the Disney-owned hotels, resorts, and cruises feature highly detailed design, landscaping, and period architecture. One of the more interesting facts about Disney World is the 70% return rate of first-time Disney visitors. A 70% return rate says a lot about customer satisfaction and loyalty. Walt Disney World is the mostly highly visited tourist destination in the world after the cities of London and Paris.

Product innovation and design have the power to redefine an industry. Apple, Sony, and the Walt Disney company were blue ocean companies in the best sense of the term. They helped set the direction for an entire industry by introducing an altogether new type of product design. What each of these companies share in common is a strong attention to detail. Each product was more than a product. They became a fully engaging experience for the user.

Notes

1 Karl Ulrich and Steven Eppinger, *Product Design and Development*. 7th ed. (New York: McGraw-Hill, 2019).
2 Andrew Pressman, *Design Thinking: A Guide to Creative Problem Solving* (New York: Routledge, 2019), 13–42.
3 The Imagineers, *Walt Disney Imagineering* (New York: Disney Enterprises Inc., 1996), 21.
4 Philippe Davidson, *Democratizing Innovation in Organizations* (Berlin, Germany: De Gruyter, 2022), 67–74.

5 Lorraine Marchand, *The Innovation Mindset* (New York: Columbia University Press, 2022), 20–36.
6 Richard Gershon, *Media, Telecommunications and Business Strategy*. 3rd ed. (New York: Routledge, 2020), 253.
7 Michael Georgiou, "7 MVP App Examples that Became Huge Successes," *Innovation Insider*, 2020, October 22, https://imaginovation.net/blog/mvp-app-examples-successful-businesses-takeaways/
8 Antonio Nieto-Rodriguez, *Harvard Business Review Project Management Handbook* (Boston, MA: Harvard Business Review Press, 2021).
9 Scott Berkun, *Making Things Happen: Mastering Project Management* (Sebastopol, CA: O'Reilly, 2008), 260–267.
10 Marty Cagan, *Inspired: How to Create Tech Products Customers Love*. 2nd ed. (Hoboken, NJ: John Wiley & Sons, 2017), 6.
11 Sophie Lovell, *Dieter Rams: As Little Design as Possible* (London: Phaidon, 2012).
12 *Dieter Rams, 10 Principles of Good Design, Heurio*, www.heurio.co/dieter-rams-10-principles-of-good-design
13 Lovell, *Dieter Rams: As Little Design as Possible*.
14 Adam Lashinsky, "The Decade of Steve," in *The Legacy of Steve Jobs 1955–2011* (New York: Fortune Books, 2011).
15 Walter Isaacson, *Steve Jobs* (New York: Simon & Schuster, 2011), 56–68.
16 John Bell, "Apple Rescued by Microsoft," *Wired*, 1997, August 6, www.wired.com/2009/08/dayintech_0806/
17 Adam Lashinsky, *Inside Apple* (New York: Business Plus, 2012).
18 Isaacson, *Steve Jobs*, 98.
19 Steve Jobs, *Keynote Address, Macworld Convention* (San Francisco, CA, 2007, June 9), www.engadget.com/2007/01/09/live-from-macworld-2007-steve-jobs-keynote/
20 Isaacson, *Steve Jobs*.
21 Lashinsky, *Inside Apple*.
22 Richard Gershon, "The Sony Corporation: Market Leadership, Innovation Failure and the Challenges of Business Reinvention," in Fu Lai Yu and Ho-Don Yan (Eds.), *Handbook in East Asia Entrepreneurship* (London: Routledge, 2014), 225–239.
23 Richard Gershon, "The Transnational Media Corporation and the Economics of Global Competition," in Yahya R. Kamalipour (Ed.), *Global Communication*. 3rd ed. (New York: Rowman and Littlefield, 2020), 37–54.
24 Sony Corporation, *Genryu*. 2nd ed. (Tokyo, Japan: Sony Inc.).
25 Sony Corporation, *Genryu*. 2nd ed., 207.
26 John Nathan, *Sony: The Private Life* (New York: Houghton-Mifflin, 1999), 152.
27 Richard Gershon and Tsutomu Kanayama, "The Sony Corporation: A Case Study in Transnational Media Management," *The International Journal on Media Management* 4,2 (2002): 44–56.
28 Nathan, *Sony: The Private Life*, 143.
29 Gershon and Kanayama, "The Sony Corporation: A Case Study in Transnational Media Management."
30 C. Dring, "PlayStation Targets Over 50% of the Games Console Market with PS5," *Gamesindustry.biz*, 2021, May 21, www.gamesindustry.biz/articles/2021-05-27-playstation-targets-over-50-percent-of-the-games-console-market
31 Andrew Webster, "How the PS5's Dualsense Controller Makes Games Like Fortnite and NBA 2K21 Better," *The Verge*, 2020, November 12, www.theverge.com/21562206/ps5-dualsense-controller-review-games-features-vibrations
32 "Seven Principles of Game Design," *The Design Gym*, 2022, September 2, www.thedesigngym.com/seven-principles-of-game-design-and-five-innovation-games-that-work/

33 Anthony Palomba, "Gaming Industry," in M. Mahoney and T. Tang (Eds.), *The Handbook of Media Management and Business* (New York: Rowman & Littlefield, 2020), 285–305.

34 Aphra Kerr, "Game Production Logics at Work: Convergence and Divergence," in M. Deuze and M. Prenger (Eds.), *Making Media: Production, Practices, and Professions* (Amsterdam, Netherlands: Amsterdam University Press, 2019), 413–425.

35 A.J. Willingham, "What Is eSports? A Look at an Explosive Billion Dollar Industry," *CNN*, 2018, August 27, www.cnn.com/2018/08/27/us/esports-what-is-video-game-professional-league-madden-trnd

36 Neal Gabler, *Walt Disney: The Triumph of the American Imagination* (New York: Vintage Books, 2006).

37 Ron Grover, *The Disney Touch* (Homewood, IL: Irwin, 1991).

38 Louise Krasniewicz, *Walt Disney: A Biography* (Santa Barbara, CA: Greenwood, 2010).

39 Robert Iger, *The Ride of a Lifetime* (New York: Random House, 2019), 127–188.

40 Gershon, *Media, Telecommunications and Business Strategy*. 3rd ed., 77–80.

41 The Imagineers, *Walt Disney Imagineering*.

4
BUSINESS PROCESS INNOVATION

Introduction

Today, innovation is about much more than developing new products. It is about reinventing business processes and building entirely new markets to meet untapped customer needs. A business process implies a strong emphasis on how work gets done within an organization. Business process innovation can take many forms and touch on a number of different organizational parts, including product manufacturing, inventory management, research and development, customer service, marketing, and distribution. From Henry Ford's original design for an assembly line in automobile manufacturing to Amazon.com EC order fulfillment, the focus is on increased productivity and reduced costs. What made Ford's assembly line unique for the times was the conveyor system and the mass production of motor vehicles. Henry Ford famously remarked that the use of the moving assembly line allowed for the work to be taken to workers rather than the worker moving to and around the vehicle.[1] Fast forward to the present day, and EC fulfilment of orders by Amazon, better known as FBA, represents an altogether different type of business process of receiving, processing, and delivering EC customer orders. FBS starts with a customer placement order, inventory management (tracking and locating customer item), automated warehousing, selecting and packing products, and shipping and handling returns.[2]

A well-constructed business process renders two important consequences. First, it is transformative; that is, a successful business process creates internal and external efficiencies that provide added value to the organization. Second, it sets into motion a host of imitators who see the inherent value in applying the same business process to their own organizations.[3] The goal for both Ford

DOI: 10.4324/9781003294375-4

then and Amazon today is to ensure accurate and timely delivery of products to customers while minimizing errors and costs. Their business design process has been emulated by companies worldwide.

This chapter will look at the importance of business process innovation. Special attention will be given to Dell Technologies, eBay, HBO, Netflix, Spotify, SAP, and the Walt Disney Company (specifically, the Walt Disney World theme park). Each of these companies were selected because they represent a different kind of business process (see Table 4.1). They have proven to be industry leaders rendering a host of imitators in terms of the design of their business process.

TABLE 4.1 Seven Media and Technology Companies: The Transformative Impact of Business Process Innovation

Dell Technologies	Dell Technologies is a US-based manufacturer of computers and related equipment. The original Dell Computers developed a highly successful business process in the area of PC manufacturing, utilizing just-in-time manufacturing techniques, global inventory management as well as direct-to-home sales capability.
eBay	eBay is one of the oldest and best recognized online auctioning websites. eBay's success can be attributed to its unique business plan; specifically, allowing individuals or businesses to list new or used items for auction for a fee. To accomplish this, eBay had to develop a business process that would enable sellers to create listings for their items which include the item description, photos, payment, and shipping options.
Home Box Office (HBO)	HBO is one of the world's leading pay television and film services. It was the first of its kind to establish the current pay television model in the United States. Starting in 1975, HBO helped advance the principle of satellite and cable networking by using satellite communication to advance long-haul television distribution.
Netflix	Netflix is a subscription-based television streaming service. In its beginning years, Netflix became the world's largest EC online DVD rental service offering subscribers flat-rate rental| by mail. Starting in 2007, the company started transitioning to its current online video streaming service.
SAP	SAP is a German multinational software that develops enterprise software to manage business operations and customer relations. The company is the world's leading enterprise resource planning software vendor. SAP Data Intelligence is a cloud service that combines AI and machine learning to better integrate the IT and data science departments of an organization.

(*Continued*)

TABLE 4.1 (Continued)

Spotify	Spotify is a Sweden-based digital music, podcast, and video service that gives the user access to over 40 million songs and other content from creators all over the world. The user for his/her part creates playlists on their smartphone. Basic functions such as playing music are free, but the user can also choose to upgrade to Spotify Premium.
Walt Disney Company	Walt Disney is a brand name that has become synonymous with family entertainment. At its multiple theme parks, Disney has championed the belief that customer service is a business process as evidenced by how it manages large numbers of people at its theme parks with special attention given to guest flow and line waiting as its attractions as well as transportation.

Business Process Innovation

Business process innovation involves creating entirely new systems and methods for improving organizational performance. Throughout the latter half of the 20th century and early 21st century, there has evolved a number of theoretical traditions that are central to any discussion involving business process innovation, including Total Quality Management, Six Sigma, Business Process Reengineering, and Lean Process Management. What each of the theoretical traditions shares in common is an exacting focus on finding new ways to improve quality and organizational performance.

Business Process and Organizational Performance

Business process innovation focuses on creating new and adaptive systems for improving organizational performance. Researchers Davenport and Short define a business process as "a set of logically related tasks performed to achieve a defined business outcome."[4] In their view, an effective business process cuts across organizational boundaries in support of both internal and external customers. For manufacturing companies, business process innovation can include such things as integrating new production methods to help advance product quality, engaging in just-in-time manufacturing techniques, or developing an enterprise resource management network that provides both the manufacturer and the customer with timely, up-to-date information. For cable television programmers, business process innovation is about finding the best technology and software combination to provide high-quality digital television programming and high-speed Internet delivery to the end consumer. Technology alone is rarely the key to unlocking economic value. A business enterprise creates real value when it combines technology with new ways of doing business.

Lean Process Management

Business process innovation involves creating systems and methods for improving organizational performance. One technique for identifying a business process within an organization is based on a set of principles known as lean process management. The goal is to offer the customer a level of value that exceeds the cost of the activities, thereby resulting in improved organizational performance. Lean process management looks at ways to improve organizational performance by focusing on business processes. All business enterprises consist of both primary and secondary processes. They are the series of steps that must be carried out to create value for customers. The goal is to maximize customer value while minimizing waste. A lean organization understands customer value.[5] There are four goals of lean process improvement.

Improve Quality

Quality is the ability of one's product or service to meet or exceed your customer requirements. Everyone within the organization from senior management to the worker on the floor has a responsibility to improve product and service quality. Continuous improvement means that the organization benefits from a shared sense of responsibility to regularly improve products and business processes.

Eliminate Waste

Waste is the activities that take up time, resources, and space but do not add value to a product or service. There are multiple contributing factors that contribute to waste, including product defects, waiting for parts from suppliers, overproduction (i.e., producing too much of something), transportation failures or breakdowns, and the underutilization of people.

Reduce Lead Time

Lead time is the total time it takes to complete a series of tasks within a process. Accurate forecasting goes a long way in determining the time it will take to produce and distribute a product to the end customer.

Reduce Total Cost

Total costs are the direct and indirect costs associated with the production of a product or service. For example, how much money does the organization spend in terms of its sales staff (i.e., customer expense account, food, lodging, etc.).[6]

Lean process management utilizes the principle of value stream mapping as a way to identify and chart the flow of information processes across an organization's entire supply chain from supplier to the end user. A *value stream* is all the actions, both added and taken away, that are required to bring a product to market. Lean systems are customer driven. Products and services should be created and delivered in the right amounts to the right location at the right cost.

Supply Chain Management

Supply chain management (SCM) is a complex business model that takes into consideration the entire set of linking steps necessary to produce and deliver a product to the end consumer. A *supply chain* consists of all parties involved, directly or indirectly, in fulfilling a customer request. The supply chain includes not only the manufacturer and suppliers but also product ordering, manufacturing, inventory management, warehousing, transportation, retailers, and customer service. SCM has two distinct and equally important parts: 1) the philosophy and 2) the methodology. SCM philosophy is grounded in the belief that everyone involved in the supply chain is both a supplier and a customer and requires access to timely, up-to-date information. The goal is to optimize exchange efficiency and meet the needs for both suppliers and customers. SCM methodology has to do with the specifics of strategy implementation. Information is key. At issue, is the ability to share timely information across the entire supply chain system. A well-designed SCM system gives automated intelligence to an extended network of suppliers, manufacturers, distributors, as well as a host of other trading partners.[7] A supply chain is connected by transportation and storage activities and coordinated through planning and networked information activities.

Enterprise Resource Planning

A supply chain is connected by transportation and storage activities and coordinated through planning and networked information activities. Central to any discussion of SCM and intelligent networking is the principle of enterprise resource planning (ERP), which attempts to integrate all departments and functions across an entire company onto a single computer system using a common database and a shared set of reporting tools. Researchers Deredden and Bergdolt define ERP as "information systems that integrate processes in an organization using a common database and shared reporting tools."[14]

There is a tendency among large (sometimes older) organizations to compartmentalize information. In the past, it was not uncommon to find several divisions within an organization having their own separate databases and often duplicating select work tasks. This was especially true for such organizations as General Motors, Eastman Kodak, and the U.S. based National Security Agency, to name only a few. The duplication of effort was both costly and inefficient. Today, the emphasis is on the sharing of information resources across divisional lines, thus promoting greater efficiency in product planning, manufacturing, marketing, and distribution. A well-constructed ERP system allows various players within an organization to be a part of a larger network of shared information in real time. ERP attempts to integrate all departments and functions across an entire company onto a single computer system using a common database and a shared set of reporting tools.[15] The goal of an ERP system is to replace stand-alone programs such as accounting, manufacturing, human resources, warehousing, and transportation and replace them with a single, unified software program.[16] This is lean process management in its most essential form.

Cloud Computing

Many of today's business and technology enterprises have moved away from stand-alone computing facilities and have elected instead to use various kinds of cloud-based services to host an organization's business and operational data. The expression "putting something on the cloud" refers to the idea of storing information and data on a remote host site. Cloud computing provides both storage and the delivery of information services over a virtual platform using the networking capability of the Internet. Cloud computing users are able to access such information and services on demand. In general, the public is most familiar with public cloud services such as Facebook, Google (Gmail and Calendar), YouTube, Instagram, and TikTok. The third-party vendor is responsible for managing the entire service. The end user has little control over where the data is stored, software design and formatting applications and how the data is protected and secured.

Private cloud services or community clouds operate within the structured boundaries of an organization. Private clouds are managed internally by an organization and are therefore responsible for organizing and securing all information. As a result, the organization will typically make a major financial commitment in software and hardware capability as well as utilizing in-house expertise to manage information flow and data protection throughout the entire organization. Examples might include the international banking and airline industries. In general, there are three types of cloud computing service models including 1) infrastructure as a service, 2) platform as a service, and 3) software as a service.

Infrastructure as a Service (IaaS)

This represents the most basic kind of cloud support model. IaaS refers to those kinds of facilities that provide business users with extra storage space on a remote server. The basic premise is that cloud service providers manage an organization's complete data information needs remotely and host all information via a series of virtual links. The principal advantage is cost savings by not having to manage and host one's own database system of documents and records.

Platform as a Service (PaaS)

This category of cloud computing services provides a highly refined computing platform and set of subsystems. In this model, the user creates a set of software tools using programs and/or library from the provider. The user also controls the software deployment and configuration settings. The cloud service provider helps to advance the network, servers, storage, and other services. Examples of PaaS might include a community-based Geographic Information System.

Software as a Service (SaaS)

This service model is used for purposes of software deployment. The cloud service provider licenses various kinds of software applications on demand to customers as needed. The end-user does not manage or control infrastructure planning as it pertains to the network, servers, operating systems, storage, or software applications. Instead, SaaS provides a cost-effective alternative from having to purchase software support outright as well as simplifying maintenance and support. In a sense, the organization is leasing the software as compared to having to purchase it outright. All updates are automatically fitted into the software as a service. SaaS has proven to be a useful approach for start-up companies with limited resources that don't want to make the large upfront investment in software costs.

Data Security

With the growth of cloud computing comes the associated challenges of information security. Both businesses and individual users who have their information stored on a third party's server are subject to security and compliance standards of operation to ensure the protection of their information. Preserving security on the cloud is one of major concerns by users who chose to store their data remotely. The overriding concern is the control of data; specifically, how data is entered into a system, where it resides, how it is managed and processed, and who can access it. One of the important consequent issues is data loss or misuse. A single point of failure or intrusion could prove catastrophic for business and individual users. To offset this possibility, cloud computing services provide built-in security as well as redundancy (i.e., back-up systems) to ensure client safety of their data.

Dell Technologies

Dell Technologies (formerly Dell Inc.) was established by Michael Dell in 1984 and has grown to become one of the world's preeminent manufacturers of desktop and laptop computers. What is interesting about the Dell story is not so much the hardware itself but rather the innovative business processes that the company put into place from a manufacturing and delivery standpoint. Dell builds computers to customer order and specification using just-in-time manufacturing techniques. The company has built its reputation on direct-to-home sales delivery combined with strong customer support. Dell's business model is simple in concept but very difficult to execute in practice. It is premised on a highly sophisticated SCM system.

Michael Dell started out as a pre-med student at the University of Texas. Dell soon became fascinated by computers and created a small niche in the assembly and sale of PCs and PC components out of his dormitory room. Dell bought excess supplies at cost from IBM dealers, which allowed him to resell the components at 10% to 15% below the regular retail price. He then began to assemble and sell PC clones by purchasing retailers' surplus stock at cost and then upgrading the units with video cards, hard disks, and memory. Dell then sold the newly assembled IBM clones at 40% below the cost of an IBM PC.[8] By April 1984, with sales reaching $80,000 a month, Dell dropped out of university and formed a company called PCs Limited. The ability to sell directly to the end user at a discounted price proved to be a winning formula, and by the end of 1986, sales had reached $33 million. PCs Limited was renamed Dell Computers in 1987, and the company soon opened its first set of international offices.

From 1990 to 1993, Dell experimented with traditional retail distribution in hopes of faster growth but soon realized that bricks-and-mortar stores were less profitable and refocused his efforts on direct sales. By 1996, Internet sales had taken off, and the company realized that computer-savvy shoppers preferred the convenience of custom ordering what they wanted directly from Dell and having it delivered to their door. During this time, Dell had become master innovators involving several important business processes. The first process was customization using a just-in-time manufacturing capability. Dell built computers to customer order and specification, thereby eliminating excess inventory and the need for storage.

Just-in-Time Manufacturing

Most large-scale companies have access to excellent hardware and software capabilities that enable them to operate in an international business environment. The distinguishing factor often centers on speed and turnaround time. Just-in-time manufacturing (JITM) is a production model that allows a company to meet customer orders by producing goods and services on demand. The purpose of JITM is to avoid waste associated with overproduction and excess inventory. JITM is designed to meet a customer order in the least amount of time. To accomplish this, JITM relies on the use of SCM and ERP systems for the purpose of tracking customer orders. They are designed to interface with Universal

Product Codes (i.e., bar codes) or Radio Frequency Identification (RFID) tags, which enables Dell to track the status of a product throughout the entire manufacturing and delivery cycle. This can include reacting to customer needs (i.e., answering customer inquiries about production status, delivery dates etc.). In sum, a well-designed JITM capability is designed to integrate both internal and external processes of the organization.

Global Inventory Management

Telecommunications has collapsed the time and distance factors that once separated nations, people, and business organizations. Communication is instantaneous. Faster product cycles and the ability to train and produce worldwide production teams have transnationalized the manufacturing process. It is the ability to apply time-based competitive strategies at the international level that enables companies like Dell to manage inventories across borders.[20] We call this global inventory management.

Today, Dell Inc. is one of the largest PC manufacturers in the world. The company has an international workforce of more than 133,000 employees in 374 locations in 77 countries around the world. The company has major business facilities located in the United States and India as well as manufacturing facilities in Ireland, Brazil, China, India, Malaysia, and the United States.[9] Dell's selection of geographic locations and production facilities has largely been driven by it foreign direct investment strategy, including the perceived profitability of the market and growth potential. Dell's international market presence and JITM capability requires a global network of suppliers and contract manufacturers to support each production facility. Instead of producing all of the necessary components themselves, Dell contracts with other manufacturers to produce subassembly parts, such as circuit boards, monitors, and so forth. Dell, for its part, maintains control over the final assembly portion, paying particular attention to customized feature elements.[21] Dell's global inventory management system requires an efficient method of communication to meet customer demands and ensure a ready supply of parts on hand to support various kinds of configuration requests. Over time, Dell has built a complex, global inventory management system that tracks information among suppliers, distributors, and other key component players involved in product manufacturing and support.

The final piece to Dell's SCM is direct-to-home delivery. Dell was among the first computer manufacturers to create online ordering. Once the personal or laptop computer was assembled, it was then a matter of engaging in direct delivery to the home or end user. This provided the obvious benefit of not having to create physical retail store outlets thus avoiding major infrastructure costs in terms of building facilities and staffing. It was a business process approach that other computer manufacturers would later adopt.

Dell Technologies Today

Throughout most of its history, Dell has primarily been a PC manufacturer. Michael Dell explained that there is a tendency to think incrementally about the future at most companies. But he believes that Dell needs to engage in boundary spanning by reimagining itself for the future. Hence the name change to Dell Technologies. Starting with the acquisition of EMC in 2015, Dell's product line has greatly expanded to include servers, peripherals such as monitors and projectors, smartphones, televisions, computer software, and security products. Equally important, Dell Technologies has steadily moved toward becoming more of a solutions-based full-service provider for its information technology customers.[10]

eBay

Like so many of the companies started during the dot com bubble, eBay is the ultimate success story of a company that went from a person's personal hobby into one of the largest global online marketplaces of its kind. The original site was developed in 1995 by computer programmer, Pierre Omidyar and was called Auction Web. The name was later changed to eBay in September 1997.[11] In keeping with one of its early slogans; "Whatever it is, you can get it on eBay," the company has experienced tremendous growth since its original founding. What differentiates eBay from other EC sites is its value factor as an auctioning site as well as the ease and efficiency of being able to list and sell both large and small items alike. eBay, not surprisingly, has sometimes been described as the world's largest garage sale. What makes eBay innovative from a business process standpoint is the ability to use the power of the Internet to both streamline and globalize traditional person-to-person EC. The marketplace is the world as are its users. In the past, personalized trading was accomplished through dedicated brokers, traditional auction houses, specialized trade and collectible shows, garage sales, and flea markets. In its formative years, eBay purchased PayPal as an efficient payment method for its users. The company also purchased Stub Hub, an online ticketing service. Both companies have been subsequently sold off; PayPal in 2015 and Stub Hub in February, 2020.

The eBay Business Model

As an auctioning site, buyers and sellers are brought together via an EC platform where sellers are able to list items for sale while buyers are able to bid on items of interest. The real power of eBay as an EC site is in the estimated 1.7 billion daily listings including more than 135 million worldwide users and 2 billion plus transactions per day.[12] The computer intelligence to sustain these many listings and auctions in real time is what makes eBay's business process highly unique. The items for sale are arranged in topical categories. The buyer simply types in the item of interest in the eBay search menu and is directly linked to the said item category. eBay estimates that more than three out of every ten US mobile users use the eBay app, which makes it the third most popular mobile shopping app behind Amazon and Walmart. Browsing and bidding on auctions are free of charge, but sellers are charged two kinds of fees:

- When an item is listed on eBay, a nonrefundable insertion listing fee is charged depending on the seller's opening bid on the item.
- A secondary fee may be charged for additional listing options to promote the item.
- A final value fee (commission) is charged at the end of the seller's auction. This fee generally ranges from 1.25% to 5% of the final sale price.[13]

eBay notifies the buyer and seller via email at the end of the auction if a bid exceeds the seller's minimum price, and the seller and buyer finish the transaction independently of eBay. The binding contract of the auction is only between the winning bidder and the seller. Part of eBay's appeal is the opportunity to find rare, collectible items and other unique products. If, for example, the person is a collector of rare, vintage license plates, he/she has simply to type those words into the eBay search menu and is immediately linked to a set of listings. It is the responsibility of the seller to provide a brief description of the listed item, (possible background history), set an opening price, and describe the said item's condition. During the auction setup, eBay provides shipping-method choices to sellers: ordinary mail, express mail, and/or courier service. The seller may choose to offer only one shipping method to buyers, or the seller may offer buyers a choice of options. The shipping cost is often factored into the listing cost. Part of the eBay experience is being part of a competitive auction; the ability to bid and sometimes pay less than what the item is worth. In addition to the company's original auction style sales platform, eBay has evolved and expanded to include an instant "Buy It Now" shopping option. This is more in keeping with traditional EC sites like Etsy and Walmart.

eBay uses AI and machine learning technologies to match buyers with the right sellers. eBay uses AI for improved search and discovery which often involves understanding context by showing a full spectrum of relevant topics.[14] The search term "smart homes," for example, yields a brief listing of related topics such as smart home compatibility (Alexa, Siri, Google Assistant, etc.), smart home electronics, home surveillance, and so forth. AI is also used to advance a process known as Image Search, which allows buyers to use images as part of their search query. The right photo can make it easier for the user to find exactly what he/she is looking for. AI is also used for translation of product listings and descriptions between worldwide sellers and buyers. Machine translation reduces the language barriers that encourage sellers to sell internationally and for buyers to do the same.[15] While eBay may try and compete with the likes of Amazon and

Walmart, its key strength lies in its ability to list and sell unique, specialty products. This, in turn, has helped eBay solidify its position as the go-to marketplace for both smaller and midlevel sellers and international artisans and entrepreneurs.

eBay distinguishes between what it calls its casual shoppers and its so-called power buyers who make purchases of nearly $1,000 multiple times a year. The power buyers are the users who go online regularly to shop. At the same time, eBay has proven to be the preferred EC platform for the hard-to-find and less expensive items. This was especially true during the Covid-19 pandemic when people who lost their jobs wanted a reliable site for everyday products like auto parts accessories, house furnishings, home and garden equipment, and so forth. E-commerce sites like eBay provide unlimited shelf space that makes such niche selections possible. The computer intelligence necessary to track an estimated two billion transactions daily and in real time is an important part of what makes eBay's business process highly unique and valued.

Home Box Office

As was mentioned earlier, it so happens that some of today's best-known media and technology companies are innovative in more than one area. In addition to demonstrating the future of premium television, HBO also demonstrated the feasibility of using satellite communication for long-haul television distribution (i.e., process innovation). A communication satellite is essentially a microwave relay in the sky, operating at 22,300 miles above the earth's equator. It receives microwave signals in a given frequency and retransmits them at a different frequency. Satellites provide an efficient means of reaching isolated places on the earth and are considerably less expensive than terrestrial communication links for select applications. What distinguishes communication satellites from other forms of wireless communication are their high orbital position and movement. The term *geosynchronous orbit* refers to a satellite that operates at 22,300 miles above the earth's equator. The satellite rotates at the speed of the earth. Hence, the satellite appears to be stationary in its orbital position.

When considering any distance greater than a few hundred miles, the cost of broadcasting via satellite is significantly less expensive than landline transmission. This is because only one relay station is involved, namely the satellite. The satellite's footprint (or area of coverage) permits many earth stations to simultaneously receive the same signal. Therefore, any earth station that falls within the footprint of a satellite-fed signal and that is locked on to the appropriate transponder is capable of receiving the same signal. Stated differently, an economy of scale is realized because it costs no more to transmit television to one earth station than it does 5,000 so long as they fall within the same footprint.[16] See Figure 4.1. This is the underlying economic/technical assumption that made HBO's use of satellite communication a highly innovative business process.

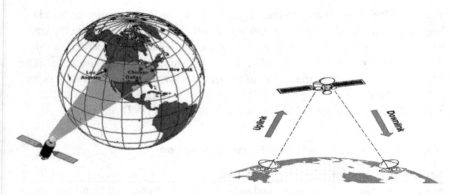

FIGURE 4.1   Satellite Communication Distribution

Source: Illustration: Chan, Chin Bong.

As a consequence, HBO was able to create an efficient distribution network for the delivery of its programming to cable operators. Second, the development of the satellite/cable interface would usher in a whole new era of cable program-mers that were equally capable of leasing satellite time and delivering their programs directly to cable operating systems, including WTBS, 1976; ESPN, 1979; CNN, 1980; and MTV, 1981. Thus was born the principle of satellite/ cable networking, that is, television programming designed exclusively for cable operating systems and later direct broadcast satellite systems. The satellite/cable network design would transform the business process of long-haul television distribution.[17]

Netflix

Netflix is an online, subscription-based television and film service. Netflix was founded by Reed Hastings, Marc Randolph, and a team of engineers in 1997. Netflix was conceived at a time when the home video industry was largely domi-nated by two major home video retail chains, Blockbuster Video and Hollywood Video, as well as a number of smaller retail outlets. Customers rented movies, primarily on VHS cassettes, from a retail location for a specified time period and paid a $3 to $4 fee for each movie rented. Companies like Blockbuster fully rec-ognized that renting a movie is largely an impulse decision. Having access to the latest movies was a high priority for most would-be renters. Market research at the time showed that new releases represented more than 70% of total rentals.[18]

The business that emerged from Hastings and Randolph was a rental company that in its first 15 years used a combination of the Internet and the U.S. Postal Service (USPS) to deliver DVDs to subscribers directly. Netflix was founded during the emergent days of EC, when companies like Amazon.com and Dell Computers were starting to gain prominence. The challenge for Hastings and co-founder Marc Randolph was whether to try and duplicate the traditional bricks-and-mortar approach used by companies such as Blockbuster. Most video rental store outlets at the time were still using VHS cassette tapes. The alternative was to utilize the power of the Internet for placing video rental orders and providing online customer service. Early on, Netflix focused their efforts on early technology adopters who had recently purchased DVD players.[19]

The Netflix Business Model and Process Innovation

Netflix, in its beginning years, offered its customers a great value proposition, namely unlimited DVDs for a fixed monthly price. In practical terms, the average consumer might receive only two to five DVDs in a week's time given the particular service plan as well as the subscriber's personal viewing habits. The general perception was that Netflix offered greater value to the consumer when compared to traditional video rental stores, which charged by the individual DVD rental unit. Netflix offered consumers greater convenience in the form of "no late fees." The subscriber was free to hold on to a specific video as long he or she wants.

Early on, Netflix proved to be a master of business process innovation and developed a number of strategies that enabled the company to be successful. First, Netflix developed a highly sophisticated SCM system that enabled the company to offer subscribers good selection as well as a fast turnaround time. As part of that effort, Netflix made the decision to partner with the USPS to deliver DVDs to its online subscriber base. DVDs are small and light, enabling inexpensive delivery, including the highly recognizable red envelope, which has become synonymous with the Netflix brand. Second, Netflix harnessed the power of the Internet to create a virtual store. The company then maintained a set of regional centers, which served as hub sites for DVD collection, packaging, and redistribution.[20]

Third, a big part of Netflix's success was the direct result of personalized marketing, which involved knowing more about the particular interests and viewing habits of one's customers. Netflix fully utilized a proprietary software recommendation system. The software recommendation system would make suggestions of other films that the consumer might like based on past selections and a brief evaluation that the subscriber was asked to fill out. The proprietary software recommendation system had the added benefit of stimulating demand for lesser-known movies thus taking the pressure off recently released feature films, where demand sometimes outstrips availability. This was in keeping with Chris Anderson's "long tail" principle where the power of intelligent networking enables companies like Netflix and Amazon to sell a small number of hard-to-find items to a large number of customers.[21]

Netflix and OTT Video Streaming Services

Starting in 2007, Netflix began the first stages of video streaming by offering its customers a Watch Instantly feature, which enabled subscribers (at additional cost) to stream near-DVD quality movies and recorded television shows instantly to subscribers equipped with a computer and high-speed Internet connectivity. During the course of the next decade, Netflix would steadily transition away from DVDs to what we now term *Over-the-Top* (OTT) video streaming services. OTT users pay for a high-speed Internet connection directly without having to subscribe to a multichannel cable or telephone-based television service. The user subscribes directly to Netflix, Amazon Prime, Disney+, or an equivalent OTT service. OTT subscribers are then able to access their preferred service on a variety of devices that can include television, computer, or smartphone.

Netflix uses Amazon's AWS for its primary computing and storage needs, including program storage databases, video transcoding, analytics, and billing. As part of that effort, Netflix has designed what it calls its *Open Connect* program by locating 17,000 plus servers in 158 countries to ensure continuous, reliable service. The challenge is to offset the potential for delivery speed slow-downs (latency), disjointed buffering, and breakdowns in quality of service. The goal, therefore, is to put a server as close to the end user as possible.[22] Netflix also uses Open Connect Appliance boxes at select ISPs designed to improve their customers' user experience by localizing Netflix traffic. The Open Connect Appliance box stores copies of Netflix television/film content, thereby creating a dedicated set of channels for Netflix traffic, separate and apart from general Internet traffic. The Open Connect Appliance box is refreshed daily.[23] The Netflix Open Connect delivery system is considered the most reliable streaming service of its kind among the major OTT program services.

Strategic Challenges

The main strategic challenge for Netflix is product inventory. In its formative years, the company had wide-ranging contracts with all of the major US and select international studios for the rights to use their movie inventory as part of the Netflix program service. That began to change as various television and film studios started to recognize the potential earnings and technical efficiency of streaming their own television and film programs. The decrease in program inventory (and discontinued contracts) has forced Netflix to develop more original programming and various made-for-television series.[24] The same challenge, of course, faces other OTT service providers as well, including Amazon, Disney, Hulu, HBO, YouTube, and so forth. In practical terms, Netflix has become more of a television/film channel rather than the aggregate, wide-ranging programming service of the past. Tomorrow's Netflix will have to compete for the same viewers as does any of the current OTT service providers. This is evidenced by the fact that in April 2022, Netflix announced the loss of 200,000 subscribers the first time since 2011.[25] Netflix is still considered the industry leader and is well-positioned for the future. But the competitive playing for OTT viewers will become increasingly more challenging in the years to come.

SAP

SAP is one of the world's leading producers of enterprise resource management software in support of an organization's business processes. SAP's integrated applications connect all parts of a business on to a fully digital platform suite with the goal of developing solutions that facilitate effective data processing and information flow across the entirety of the organization. Founded in 1972, the company was initially called System Analysis Program Development later abbreviated to SAP. Since then, it has grown from a small, five-person partnership into a transnational enterprise headquartered in Walldorf, Germany, with more than 105,000 employees worldwide. With the introduction of its original SAP R/2 and SAP R/3 software, SAP established itself as one of the world's leading ERP software developers.

The present generation SAP S/4HANA software has fully advanced the goals of ERP to the next level by using the power of in-memory computing to process vast amounts of data and to support advanced technologies such as AI and machine learning. At issue, in all supply chain management systems is the question of optimization; specifically, the ability to make adjustments to ensure "optimization" in the supply chain operation. Such peak performance capability is based on select key performance indicators that include the control of operating expenses pertaining to manufacturing, transportation, inventory management, and so forth. SAP's use of quantum mechanics is capable of performing parallel real-time optimization calculations at high-speed, with precision on a scale with classical computing.

SAP Data Intelligence is a cloud service that combines AI and machine learning by helping to assist in data analytics; specifically, the process of analyzing raw data (from various location points) to draw out meaningful, actionable insights, which can then be used for strategic planning, technical forecasting, and financial planning. By adding AI to ERP software, the organization can also automate repetitive and manual tasks, such as data entry, invoice processing, inventory management, and workflow schedules. Today, SAP is ranked number one in Europe and is used by more than 100,000 companies in over 130 countries around the world.[26]

Spotify

Spotify is a Swedish music streaming and media service founded in Sweden by Daniel Ek and Martin Lorentzon in April 2006. It is the world's largest music streaming service provider, with over 422 million active users. Spotify offers both music and audio podcasts as a service to its users based on a monthly subscription. The Spotify subscriber can search for music based on artist, album, or genre and can create/edit a variety of music playlists on one's smartphone or computer tablet.[27] What makes Spotify and other music services appealing is access to a virtual library of music and artists than can then be compiled and edited into various kinds of music playlists based upon the unique listening interests of the subscriber. Personalization is a signature feature of digital lifestyle.

Spotify also offers a more scaled-down freemium version of its service to its listeners. As a freemium service, basic features are free with advertisements and limited control in terms of song selection and presentation. Spotify makes 91% of its revenue from subscriptions and the other 9% from advertisements. Spotify is currently available in 180+ countries. As one of the first music services of its kind, Spotify earned the status of becoming a reference brand, that is, it became the best-known music streaming service internationally.

Spotify, like most Internet music services, audio streams music to the user's smartphone or computer. Spotify uses a combination of its own major servers as well as peer-to-peer (P2P) shared networks to stream audio to the end user. When the user selects a song, Spotify's computers directly begin sending the data to the person's smartphone or computer. As part of the premium service, Spotify stores (caches) the requested songs directly onto the person's phone or computer hard drive, which means that the user's device plays the song instead of Spotify. Most songs stream at about 160 kbps (kilobits per second), although many songs available to Premium users stream at a higher-quality delivery rate of 320 kbps. Once songs have been fully downloaded to the said phone or computer device, the user is able to customize various types of music playlists.

Spotify Helped Redefine Music Listening

Spotify helped redefine the way people listen to music and how artists distribute their music. Spotify has also helped to reduce music piracy by offering a legal and convenient alternative. During the early 21st century, peer-to-peer file-sharing platforms like Napster and LimeWire, cost the U.S. music industry billions of dollars in lost sales. The Recording Industry Association of America (RIAA) estimates that music revenue dropped from an all-time high of $14.6 billion in 1999 to $6.7 billion in 2014 and 2015. The introduction of the Apple iTunes music streaming service in 2003 (later Apple Music) as well as Spotify (2006) helped change all that. Music streaming saved the music recording business, and companies like Spotify and Apple helped create stability and growth for the music industry today.

The Power of Music Playlists Today

The ability to create music playlists has transformed the listening experience for millions of music listeners worldwide. Initially designed as organizational tools for radio DJs, music playlists have become far more significant and important than what was originally intended. With the growth of digital streaming services such as Spotify and Apple Music, the music industry has undergone a fundamental shift from album oriented production to a focus on creating a wide variety of music genres and themes. These collections have helped advance music discovery and marketing, thereby, giving a ready-made platform for the musician as well as enabling the listener to "try out" artists and music that was previously too costly or experimental in the past. For the individual listener, music playlists means the ability to customize a thematic playlist of songs on his/her smartphone according to the user's unique tastes and interests. The future role of music playlists will continue to evolve in keeping with ever changing technology and services, including smart home design (Smart TVs,) streaming music parties, special events planning, social media and virtual reality simulation. Their influence in helping to facilitate the type of music that is played as well as shaping the audience listener experience will likely continue into the foreseeable future thus creating unique opportunities for both artists and listeners alike.

Walt Disney's Parks and Resorts

Successful product design often requires a well-considered business and logistics process. The design and operation of both Disneyland and Disney World presuppose a deep appreciation for the fact that customer service is a process. The Walt Disney Company employs one of the most sophisticated employee training programs in the world. To ensure that employees at all levels are guided by a common sense of purpose, founder Walt Disney established a formal training program that has come to be known as Disney University Training. It begins with an appreciation for the fact that appearance is everything. Disney employees are referred to as cast members. Training includes everything from the way in which Disney employees interact with the public to the clothes they wear. In creating the right appearance, cast members are taught to be polite. They are taught to understand that park attendees are to be treated as guests.[28] The issue of employee training becomes all the more important when one considers Disney's multiple worldwide facilities.

In creating the original Disneyland, Disney knew that delivering an enjoyable experience was dependent on developing a set of processes that ensured a successful visit each and every time. From professional staff in costume to clean restrooms, there is a strong attention to detail. Nowhere is this more evident than in managing people, lines, and transportation at the company's various parks.

Guest Flow

Managing the thousands of daily visitors to Disney World (and other theme parks) requires a deep understanding of logistics and transport. There is a distinct science in managing large numbers of people when they have to wait in line for an upcoming ride or attraction. As a starter, guests staying at one of the many Disney hotels, lodging, and camping properties learn the different modes of transportation that are available to them depending on the specific theme park. This includes bus, monorail, boat, and automobile. Those guests staying at any of the Disney properties are allowed to arrive one hour early. They are given a smart bracelet that serves as an admissions pass as well as a direct charge card for food, merchandise, and services purchased at any of the theme parks, hotels, or entertainment venues. The combined bill is sent and tallied at the respective Disney property where the guest is staying.

Standing in line and wait time are the biggest customer complaints that visitors have when attending Disney World. Some lines during peak hours of the day can be as long as 90 minutes. Part of the guest flow challenge is finding ways to entertain (sometimes distract) guests while they wait in line.[25] Planners refer to it as the psychology of the queue. The sight of a long line can be discouraging. To offset that, planners create lines that make it difficult for people to see the full extent of the line. Most of the longer lines feature videos, interactive games, and animatronic characters to entertain park attendees. Beneath Cinderella Castle at Disney World is an operational command center that oversees logistics, including problems associated with long line waits. Disney's operations staff monitor large screens that depict various attractions using different colors to represent wait-time gradations.[29] Sometimes, the solution is technical (i.e., order more conveyance vehicles at select rides and attractions). Other times, the decision is made to have Disney characters and other entertainers fill in where lines are extra-long. One of the more important ways to speed up the waiting process is to offer guests the right to purchase what are known as Disney Genie and Lightning Lane passes which enable attendees to enter a separate, lightning lane entrance for faster admission to a popular attraction or ride. The Disney Genie and Lightning Lane passes work as part of an app, called *My Disney Experience* on one's smartphone. To use a lightning lane entrance, the attendee must select in advance one of the designated time windows made available before entering the said attraction or ride. Guests are also encouraged to make reservations or preorder fast food in advance at one of the many Disney World restaurants, cafes, and canteens. This too works as a mobile app on one's smartphone. Preordering has the advantage of not having to stand in line for a food order, thereby enabling the guest to go straight to a designated Pick-Up Counter or Waiting Area for their food selection. All food purchases can be charged to the guest's smart bracelet or credit card.

Transportation Management: Entering and Exiting the Park

Disney combines creativity with practical function when it comes to moving people to and from the various theme parks. As noted earlier, Walt Disney World uses a variety of transportation modes including buses, watercraft vehicles, a monorail system, and automobiles. The creativity part comes in the form of watercraft (ferries and boats) and a monorail system that provide unique ways to access park attractions. The Disney bus system provides the most direct transportation from hotels to all of the major park locations. Disney utilizes trams to take guests from the park entrances to the exterior visitor parking lots. At the end of the day, for those guests using cars, they should not leave the park only to find that they have difficulty locating their vehicle. Consider it the postscript to the Disney experience. Each parking lot area has its own identifier. In addition, tram drivers keep a simple list of what rows they work each morning, which is distributed to team members at the end of the day. This allows guests to simply mark the time they arrived, and the late afternoon and evening drivers will know what location each guest parked in. Transportation and the management of large numbers of people are very important when it comes to planning major sporting events in terms of time, efficiency, and security. It is not surprising that the Disney Institute provides regular training for prospective planners of large-scale, international sporting events including the Olympics and World Cup soccer.

Discussion

Sometimes, the beauty of a great innovation lies in the process. Business process innovation is about creating added value for both the organization and its customers. Innovation, without value creation, is simply a technology-driven effort that may provide incremental improvements to the organization but does not address the larger question of how to make the customer experience better. Value creation can translate in many different ways and formats. Dell's direct-to-home retail sales strategy was greatly aided by its just-in-time manufacturing capability and global inventory management system. eBay has used the power of the Internet to both streamline and globalize person-to-person EC thus making it the world's largest auctioning site. HBO helped advance the principle of satellite and cable networking by using satellite communication to advance long-haul television distribution to cable operators and by extension the end consumer. Netflix has harnessed the power of the Internet to create the world's best-known EC video streaming enterprise. SAP is the world's leading ERP software vendor and has made organizations more efficient in their data use. Spotify is the world's leading music streaming service by having developed a highly successful music archive and efficient system of delivery to the end user. The Walt Disney company's knowledge of guest flow and transportation management greatly aids the visitor experience at Disney World. Disney recognizes that customer relations is a process. Event planners when hosting major events like the world cup and Olympics often consult with Disney about guest flow traffic issues.

What each of these companies shares in common is the development of a unique and specialized business process. Process innovators are obsessive problem-solvers. There is a constant focus on finding new ways to improve quality and optimize performance. Each of the said companies proved to be major innovators by creating internal business efficiencies while improving customer experience. They established process improvement models that proved transformative, thereby setting into place a method and approach used by others.

Notes

1 Ford Inc, "The Moving Assembly Line and the Five-Dollar Workday," 2023, https://corporate.ford.com/articles/history/moving-assembly-line.html#:~:text=What%20made%20this%20assembly%20line,built%20step%2Dby%2Dstep

2 Brad Stone, *Amazon Unbound: Jeff Bezos and the Invention of a Global Empire* (New York: Simon & Schuster, 2020), 165–171.

3 Richard A. Gershon, "Business Process Innovation and the Intelligent Network," in Z. Vukanovic and P. Faustino (Eds.), *Managing Media Economy, Media Content, and Technology in the Age of Digital Convergence* (Lisbon, Portugal: Media XXI/Formal Press, 2011), 59–85.

4 T. Davenport and J. Short, "The New Industrial Engineering: Information Technology and Business Process Redesign," *Sloan Management Review*, 1990, Summer, 11–27.

5 Peter King, *Lean for the Process Industries* (New York: Routledge, 2019), 3–8, 19–21.

6 Monroe Engineering, "The Four Goals of Lean Manufacturing," 2016, May 17, https://monroeengineering.com/blog/the-4-goals-of-lean-manufacturing/#:~:text

7 Sunil Chopral, *Supply Chain Management*. 7th ed. (New York: Pearson, 2018), 117–149.

8 Michael Dell, *Play Nice But Win: A CEO's Journey from Founder to Leader* (New York: Portfolio/Penguin, 2021).

9 Statista, "Dell Technologies Number of Employees Worldwide from 1996 to 2023M," 2023, www.statista.com/statistics/264917/number-of-employees-at-dell-since-1996/

10 Tim Bajarin, "Looking Back, Looking Forward: Dell's Transformational Decade," *Forbes*, 2019, December 9, www.forbes.com/sites/timbajarin/2019/12/09/looking-back-looking-forward-dells-transformational-decade/?sh=1e3032056062

11 Brian O'Connell, "History of eBay: Facts and Timeline," *The Street*, 2021, July 16, www.thestreet.com/markets/history-of-ebay; See also, Corinne Watson, "The eBay Marketplace: Opportunities for Ecommerce Shops," *Big Commerce*, 2023, www.bigcommerce.com/blog/ebay-marketplace-statistics/

12 "10 eBay Statistics You Need to Know in 2021," *Oberlo*, 2021, June 20, www.oberlo.com/blog/ebay-statistics

13 "Selling Fees," *eBay Technical Briefing*, 2023, www.ebay.com/help/selling/fees-credits-invoices/selling-fees?id=4822

14 Bernard Mar, "The Amazing Ways eBay Is Using Artificial Intelligence," 2019, April 26, www.forbes.com/sites/bernardmarr/2019/04/26/the-amazing-ways-ebay-is-using-artificial-intelligence-to-boost-business-success/?sh=137925602c2e

15 Sanjeev Katariya, "eBay's Platform Is Powered by AI and Fueled by Customer Input," *eBay Technical Briefing*, 2019, March 13, https://tech.ebayinc.com/engineering/ebays-platform-is-powered-by-ai-and-fueled-by-customer-input/

16 Richard A. Gershon, *Media, Telecommunications and Business Strategy*. 3rd ed. (New York: Routledge, 2020), 165–172.

17 Patrick Parsons, "The Evolution of the Cable-Satellite Distribution System," *Journal of Broadcasting & Electronic Media* 47,1 (2003): 1–17.

18 Gershon, *Media, Telecommunications and Business Strategy*. 3rd ed., 100–102.

19 Marc Randolph, *That Will Never Work* (New York: Little Brown and Company, 2019).

20 Gershon, *Media, Telecommunications and Business Strategy*. 3rd ed., 100–102.

21 Chris Anderson, *The Long Tail: Why the Future of Business Is Selling Less of More* (New York: Hyperion, 2006).

22 "What Is OTT?" *Endavo*, 2023, www.endavomedia.com/what-is-ott/#netflix

23 Catie Kleck, "A Look Under the Hood of the Most Successful Streaming Service," *The Verge*, 2021, November 17, www.theverge.com/22787426/netflix-cdn-open-connect

24 James Miller, *Tinderbox: HBO's Ruthless Pursuit of New Frontiers* (New York: Henry Holt and Company, 2021).

25 Peter Kafka, "Why Netflix Is Suddenly Losing Subscribers," *Vox*, 2022, April 19, www.vox.com/recode/23032705/netflix-subscriber-loss-streaming-wars

26 Thompson Data, "Companies that Use SAP," 2023, www.thomsondata.com/customer-base/sap.php#:~:text=

27 A. Iglehart, "How Well Does Spotify Know You?" *Digital Initiative*, 2020, April 17, https://digital.hbs.edu/platform-digit/submission/how-well-does-spotify-know-you/

28 Theodore Kinni, *Be Our Guest: Perfecting the Art of Customer Service* (Burbank, CA: Disney Enterprises Inc., 2011).

29 Brooks Barnes, "Disney Tackles Major Theme Park Problem: Lines," *New York Times*, 2010, December 28, www.nytimes.com/2010/12/28/business/media/28disney.html?_r=0

5

THE DIGITAL ECONOMY I

Information Search, Exchange, and Interactivity

The Digital Economy

Today, the Internet has become steadily woven into all aspects of work and leisure. It has grown in size and complexity due to the many contributions of its users, including powerful search engines, unique website design, aggregation of content, electronic commerce, and social media to name only a few. The *digital economy* comprises the billions of worldwide online business and financial transactions that occur daily. In today's digital economy, the Internet and EC serve as the central hub by which all economic activity occurs. The digital economy can take many forms ranging from EC to OTT video streaming services. This, in turn, enables such economic activity to be global in scope as well as making the delivery of goods and services both fast and immediate. The digital economy is fast paced and available round the clock. The digital economy has transformed the way businesses operate.[1] It has increased the productivity of businesses by enabling them to automate their operations and processes. In both this chapter and Chapter 6, we introduce The Digital Economy Business Model as a way to explain seven network design principles. They include 1) information search, 2) exchange, 3) interactivity, 4) personalization, 5) mobility, 6) virtual communication, and 7) convergence (see Figure 5.1). These seven network design principles provide the structural basis for today's digital economy.

Digital Media

Digital media represents the artistic convergence of various kinds of hardware and software design elements to create entirely new forms of communication expression. Digital media has transformed the way to communicate and access

DOI: 10.4324/9781003294375-5

Internet – Artificial Intelligence – Metaverse

Network Design: Signature Features

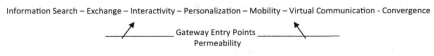

Information Search – Exchange – Interactivity – Personalization – Mobility – Virtual Communication - Convergence

Gateway Entry Points
Permeability

Internet Connection Devices

Desktop Computers – Laptop Computers – Smartphones – Computer Tablets – Game Consoles
– Smart Watches – Smart TV's

FIGURE 5.1 The Digital Economy Business Model

Source: Richard A. Gershon, 2023.

information.[2] It has proven to be a major game changer when it comes to visual presentation. *Digital storytelling* is the art of using enhanced media and information tools to tell a story. From online newspapers to a highly engaging website display, digital storytelling assumes a wide range of electronic media narratives that include text, still, and moving imagery and enhanced sound effects, as well as being interactive and nonlinear. Such stories no longer conform to the conventions of traditional storytelling.[3] The personal diary has given way to regular public demonstrations of one's ideas and opinions using the power of social media. Nowhere is this more evident than in social media sites like Facebook, YouTube, TikTok, and Instagram. The once iconic photograph album has become more decidedly multipurpose in approach with digital photos now available on one's smartphone, computer tablet, and/or social media account.

Digital Lifestyle

The digital economy has also changed the way consumers obtain information about prospective goods and services by giving them more power to comparative shop. Booking a vacation and hotel stay on Bookings.com or TripAdvisor is a very different value proposition than working with a travel agent. Streaming a set of songs to one's smartphone via Spotify or Apple Music is an altogether different shopping experience than walking into a music store. And shopping online for kitchenware at Amazon or Taobao (China) is an altogether different purchasing experience than going to a department store. These types of e-commerce activities are part and parcel of what I call *digital lifestyle*. In a digital economy, businesses and organizations will more typically accept credit cards, debit cards, mobile payments, digital wallets, and varying degrees of cryptocurrency exchange. Digital payments require a higher degree of authentication which makes financial transactions more secure. In the 21st century, digital lifestyle requires a special appreciation for speed, mobility, and convenience.

Principles of Digital Communication

Historically, older forms of communication and information technology, including radio and television broadcasting, vinyl records, and VHS tapes are considered analog forms of communication. An *analog signal* (or analogy) is a representation of something else. It is a continuous signal that can be physically measured. One of the major problems associated with analog systems of communication is their susceptibility to unwanted noise. Consider, for example, that a traditional telephone performs the function of translating one's voice into an electrical signal and transmitting it via a long-distance network of switches, routers, and amplifiers. Each time the signal is re-amplified, there is the potential to introduce unwanted noise into the transmission. The same problem occurs with audio recording formats as well. When using an analog tape recorder, the signal is taken straight from the microphone and laid onto tape. If one wants to make a tape of a tape, each successive generation suffers a degradation in quality. Whereas, in an all-digital link, the signal is an exact replication of the original, thus eliminating any unwanted noise factors. The cut-and-paste function on a computer provides a simple illustration. If one types the word *innovation* and copies it, the quality and accuracy of the paste function is the same whether it's the first repeat or the one-hundredth. The same principle is equally true for audio recording and the reason why a digital audio stream or CD copy is as good as the original.

Binary Logic and Coding Schemes

All forms of digital communication are based on the principle of binary logic which presumes that a signaling system is essentially in one of two states: open or closed. Binary logic uses the numbers 1 and 0 arranged in different sequences to exchange information. The numbers 1 and 0 are called bits from the word *binary digit*, which is the lowest possible unit of information that can be transferred or handled[4] (see Figure 5.2). A digital signal is made up of pulses of discrete duration, that is, a stream of bits that are either on or off.

Pulse Code Modulation

Traditional analog technologies and devices are incompatible with digital signaling and communication. Consequently, the situation requires a conversion process, whereby the analog signal is converted into a digital format. Consider, for example, the task of converting a Gordon Lightfoot music album recorded in the 1970s into an audio music stream or compact disk. Pulse code modulation

FIGURE 5.2 Digital Data Signal

(PCM) is a conversion process whereby the analog signal is sampled and converted into binary format, that is, a sequence of 1s and 0s.[5] The conversion process requires two steps: 1) sampling and 2) quantizing (companding) (see Figure 5.3).

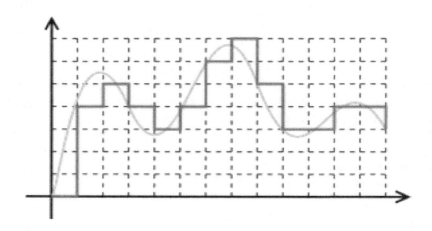

FIGURE 5.3 Pulse code modulation

The first step in the conversion process involves sampling the analog signal at regular time intervals. The goal is to accurately reflect the original signal. The higher the level of sampling per second, the more accurate the reflection of the original signal. Sampling rate refers to the number of times the analog signal is sampled per second.[6] The sampling rate must be at least twice the highest frequency component of the analog source to faithfully reproduce the signal when it is converted into digital form. The second step in the process involves quantizing the sampled pulse, that is, forcing it to occupy a discrete set of 1 and 0 values.[7] The information is now fully digitized. Once the information has been converted to digital format, distribution and storage costs have been significantly lowered. There is an inherent economies of scale. Creating an audio music stream or compact disk is much less expensive to produce when compared to vinyl records.

More Efficient Use of Bandwidth

The electromagnetic spectrum is a fixed and limited resource. Yet all wireless services, including television, smartphones, and satellites (to name only a few), depend on available spectrum. The critical challenge for broadcasters, cable television operators, and Internet service providers is how to optimize and make more efficient use of the electromagnetic spectrum. The term *bandwidth* refers to channel width or information-carrying capacity. As an example, FM Radio requires 200 KHz of bandwidth to provide an acceptable signal to a potential radio listener. In contrast, a typical TV signal requires 4 MHz of bandwidth. By the time one adds in sound, (vestigial sideband) and a little buffer space, a TV signal requires 6 MHz of bandwidth. The implementation of high-definition television requires about two times as much information-carrying capacity than was originally needed with analog TV. The solution, therefore, is to create a system that compresses existing bandwidth space allocations more efficiently.

Digital Video Compression

Digital video compression (DVC) refers to digitizing and compressing video pictures so that they may be processed, stored, and distributed with greater flexibility and ease. DVC refers to the technical ability to reduce the size of video signals so that it can be more efficiently transmitted and stored. Digital TV relies on a compression and encoding scheme known as MPEG-4 (Motion Picture Experts Group 4) to fit its high-resolution images into a lesser amount of bandwidth space. MPEG-4 reduces the amount of data to about 20% of the original amount. MPEG-4 is the industry standard for Internet video streaming as well as satellite television broadcasts.

DVC operates on the premise that some of the data present before compression is not essential for achieving good picture quality. Video compression operates off a grid system using square-shaped groups of neighboring pixels (often called macroblocks). These pixel groups are compared from one frame to the next, and the video codec sends only the differences within those blocks.[8] The term *lossy* is used to describe those situations where there is a high degree of redundant information within the video display. DVC works well in those situations where there is limited or no motion. The court surface, during a televised basketball game, for example, can be repeated with very little transmitted data. DVC is fully utilized by such diverse technologies as 1) cable television, 2) direct broadcast satellite (DBS) television, 3) video streaming and 4) video games.

Information Search (Network Design Principle 1)

Search Engine Design

Searching for information represents the most basic reason why someone uses the Internet, namely to gather information about topics and issues that are important to the user. A search engine is a software tool that helps the user perform keyword searches and locate specific information available on the Internet. The search engine in combination with hypertext linking provides a structured road map and makes the Internet more accessible to navigate. Search engines come in varying gradations of design and performance starting with general information search engines like Google, Bing, Baidu, Yahoo, and Yandex. Different countries of the world have an equivalent version of Google such as *Google India* or *Google Brazil* that accommodates differing search queries by language and more specialized information and news focus. Alternatively, some countries of the world have their own search engine equivalents such as Baidu in China and Yandex in Russia. Baidu is available worldwide but only in Chinese.

Less understood by the general public, however, is the importance of specialized search engine websites like WebMD (health care), Tripadvisor (travel), and Kelley Blue Book (automobile comparison shopping) that offer the user a more specialized focus. These kinds of search engines are responsible for organizing information resources that are distinct to a particular discipline or area of specialization. Typically, a specialized search engine works by sending out a spider to fetch as many documents as possible within a defined set of research parameters and databases. A *spider* is a software program operated by a search engine that surfs the web and records/saves to its hard drive all relevant words on each site and as well as links to other sites. This is followed by a software program called an indexer, which reads these documents and creates an index based on the words contained in each document.[9] The search engine uses a proprietary algorithm to create a set of listings that correspond to the user's query. WebMD, for example, advertises itself as the number one search engine site for obtaining information about health issues. The WebMD website, available at www.webmd.com/, provides useful medical news and information about a variety of health issues as well as information related to finding doctors, hospitals, and specialized treatment centers. Such specialized websites as WebMD, Tripadvisor (www.tripadvisor.com/), and Kelley Blue Book (www.kbb.com/) are very attractive to advertisers who are looking to direct their marketing focus toward the type of audience who are likely to query topics found on these types of specialized search engines.

Planning and Design Considerations

The basic reason for creating a search engine is simple. By becoming a major gatekeeper of people's online experience, Internet search companies hope to build a set of loyal users who will rely on them not only for trusted information but to buy goods and services as well. Many of today's better-known search engines are considered multilevel Internet companies. They have positioned themselves as a full service information site with links to a variety of information, entertainment, and value-added services. For a company like Google, Internet search is the jumping off point to a whole host of value-added services such as YouTube, Google Maps, Google Translate, Google Scholar, and so on. Similarly, Yahoo has created its own full service ecosystem, as well, including news, weather, finance, food, and Flickr photo sharing.

Two important features found in all search engine sites are the aggregation of content and personalization. The primary responsibility of a search engine is to collate data from a variety of information sources around the world. This is accomplished through international alliances and distribution partnerships. The search engine is responsible for the organization and arranging of information content thus making it possible for keyword- and context-based search information. A successfully designed search engine should provide added value to the user including relevant information, presentations, commentary, video, as well as related links to other sites. Search engine software helps facilitate registered users to receive personalized information in the form of specialized content (daily news briefings, weather and stock reports, newly released articles and commentaries, etc.). The same search engine can also make it easier for the user to comparison shop between different product and service providers. In sum, the key to building a successful search engine is to make it both a helpful and highly relevant part of the user's Internet experience.

Website Design

A well-designed website serves as the digital address for any business, organization, or person looking to provide information and engage prospective customers and clients. In today's digital economy, all major and minor business enterprises, government agencies, nonprofit organizations, educational institutions, and individual educators, commentators, and entrepreneurs maintain a website. The design and setup of a website has become an essential information, marketing, and sales tool. An effective website display provides the user with:

1. Contact information
2. Description and listing of products and service offerings
3. EC and point-of-sales links
4. Directory and description of key persons, professional staff, and sales contacts
5. Current news information and press releases
6. Investor relations, including a copy of the company's annual report
7. Information items, including reports, conference slide presentations, relevant URL links

The importance of creating the right kind of website design cannot be understated. Google, for example, has developed a search engine tool called SEO (search engine optimization) whereby it helps prospective web designers develop the best ways to be found and listed on Google. In practical terms, SEO means the process of improving the website's visibility when people search for information related to the user's work or business.

Wikipedia

Wikipedia was started by Jimmy Wales and Larry Sanger in January 2001 and serves as an online encyclopedia written and maintained by a community of volunteers through open collaboration and a wiki-based editing system. A wiki is a piece of server software that allows users to freely create and edit web page content using a simplified mark-up language. A wiki provides the basis for user-generated content since it allows the contributor to add information to a source page as well as enabling a person to engage in an open editing process. Wikis are often used to create collaborative websites and to promote a sense of collective ownership of website information and material. Wikipedia's contributed articles are written by an estimated 300,000 active volunteers around the world working in 270 languages. Nearly all of its articles can be edited by anyone with access to the Wikipedia website. Wikipedia is operated by the Wikimedia Foundation, a San Francisco-based nonprofit that takes care of the servers, fundraising, legal challenges, and many initiatives that advance the project.[10]

The Wikipedia website, available at www.wikipedia.org/, has taken the place of the once important encyclopedia. Wikipedia's easy access makes it the number one starting point when the user wants to conduct a preliminary search or answer starting questions like "who is and what is" about a topic. One of its guiding principles is the importance of neutrality, that is, the writing should be objective in tone and avoid social and political advocacy. As an open source process, readers can correct what they perceive to be errors and possible biases through contributor discussions. Critics of Wikipedia will sometimes target the website's biases and inaccuracies and its policy of favoring consensus over credentials in its editorial process. It should be noted that the Encyclopedia Britannica, arguably once the best of its kind, ended its last print edition in 2010. In its place, the company created its own online version called Britannica (see www.britannica.com/).

Table 5.1 provides a listing of the 12 most widely visited international websites based on monthly traffic. These websites represent a combination of search engines, e-commerce, and social media sites. They have also become the go-to apps for users and their smartphone.

Exchange (Network Design Principle 2)

The principle of *exchange* refers to something that is sent (distributed) and received. It can also mean a reciprocal agreement between two parties. A variation on this idea is the term *exchange efficiency* which has to do with creating the optimum conditions through which a consumer can obtain a product or service. The principle of exchange efficiency is central to the setup and organization of any electronic commerce (EC) system. Specifically, it refers to the transfer of goods and services between a manufacturer/distributor and the consumer.

Electronic Commerce

Electronic commerce (EC) represents the ability to sell goods and services electronically via the Internet. The field of EC has come of age as evidenced by the success of such companies as Amazon, Apple, Spotify, Netflix, Uber, and Bookings.com to name only a few. EC has created an altogether new business model that maximizes the potential for instantaneous communication to a worldwide customer base. There are three kinds of EC transactions: business-to-consumer (B2C), business-to-business (B2B), and consumer-to-consumer (C2C). The combination of EC combined with the power of intelligent networking has created a vast global playing field where international buyers and sellers are free to participate.[11]

TABLE 5.1 The 12 Most Widely Visited Global Internet Websites

Google	Google is the world's preeminent Internet search engine.	USA	
YouTube	The site is the best-known video-sharing website. Most of the content featured is user generated, which includes video clips, music videos, amateur content, etc. YouTube also has a TV/film streaming service.	USA	
Facebook	Facebook, owned by Meta, is the world's preeminent social media networking site. Facebook reaches an estimated 2.9 billion users worldwide.	USA	
Baidu	Baidu is the leading Chinese language search engine.	China	
Instagram	Social media website owned by Meta, parent company to Facebook.	USA	
Wikipedia	Wikipedia is the world's largest online encyclopedia. Wikipedia's contributed articles are written by volunteers from around the world.	USA	
Amazon	Amazon is the world's largest EC site.	USA	
Qq.com	Qq.com is China's largest and most-used Internet service portal owned by Tencent, Inc. Today, Qq.com tries to provide its users with one stop shopping in terms of information search and EC.	China	
Yahoo	Search engine, news and media	USA	
Taobao	Taobao Marketplace is the preeminent EC site for Chinese consumers. Shoppers choose from a wide range of products and services on Taobao Marketplace.	China	
xVideos	Adult	Czech. Republic	
Yandex	Yandex is a search engine and internet-related news, technology for Russian language users.	Russia	

Business-to-Consumer

Business-to-consumer EC involves selling products and services directly to consumers via the Internet. B2C comes in two general formats, traditional retail sales (e.g., Target, Walmart, and L.L. Bean) and those companies whose primary business model depends on the Internet as the basis for retail trade (e.g., Amazon, Zappos, Dell Technologies, Spotify Music, etc.). The EC merchant, in turn, is willing and able to provide prospective customers with 24/7 technical support capability as well as the ability to track the status of a physical package delivery via the Internet (e.g., Federal Express, UPS etc.)

Business-to-Business

Business-to-business EC involves online communication between businesses for the purpose of selling products and services as well as providing information exchange and technical support. B2B dramatically changes the structure of the traditional business supply chain which normally consists of raw material suppliers, a manufacturer, distributor, and retailer. Any one of these parties can now transact with any other via an Intranet exchange, that is, private internal network communication. Information flows in all directions between various members of the supply chain via their ERM system. Moreover, any one of these parties can also transact with the customer directly. The so-called middlemen (i.e., distributors and retailers) become less important to the direct delivery of goods and services.

Consumer-to-Consumer

Consumer-to-consumer (C2C) EC involves the exchange of goods, services, and information directly between consumers. EC websites like eBay, Etsy, Craigslist, Uber, and Airbnb provide opportunities for consumers to display and sell personal goods and services. C2C also includes the exchange of information through Internet forums that appeal to special interest groups. Through these forums, buyers do more than consume product information. They help generate useful information, which in turn can influence and facilitate purchasing decisions. Consumer ratings become especially important for sharing economy services like eBay, Airbnb, Uber, and Vacation Rental by Owner. This becomes an important factor in establishing credibility for the seller while giving the customer greater confidence in his/her purchasing decision.

Exchange and Financial Markets

The principle of exchange efficiency can be seen in the design of various kinds of financial networks. The world's financial markets have been revolutionized by the application of computer and telecommunications to the banking and investment process. The international transfer of electronic funds is premised on strong, interdependent relationships between banks, the investment community, business, and individual participants. Electronic funds transfer (EFT) operates as information (or the promise of actual funds) and not as physical currency. The real impact of EFT on organizations and the public is greater convenience and cost savings by not having to physically handle money during routine transactions. There are prescribed rules governing both the foreign exchange and the financial credit markets. EFT has permeated the world of business and personal finance in seven major ways (see Table 5.2).

TABLE 5.2 Seven Types of Electronic Financial Exchange

1. **Electronic Funds Transfer**—the national and international transfer of money between banks and other financial institutions.
2. **Direct Deposit**—the transfer of money directly into the bank account of an organization's employees.
3. **ATMs**—the public use of terminals and automated teller machines which enables the user to deposit and withdraw funds via electronic access.
4. **Credit and Debit Cards**—the public use of credit and debit cards as the basis of payment, between users and retailers that can include, restaurants, gas stations, supermarkets, department stores, and so on.
5. **Electronic Commerce**—the purchase of goods and services via the Internet which enables the transfer of funds from one's bank or online payment system.
6. **Digital Wallets**—contain a digitized version of one's credit and debit cards that are stored as apps on the person's smartphone device.
7. **Cryptocurrency**—is a digital currency designed to work as a medium of financial exchange. Cryptocurrencies are typically decentralized networks based on blockchain technology which requires the use of an agreed-upon virtual ledger system and cryptography methods for data security.

Credit Card Transactions and the Principle of Exchange Efficiency

A credit card transaction provides a good example of exchange efficiency and the power of intelligent networking. Let's assume for a moment that a person elects to pay for dinner using a credit card. The credit card transaction sets up a three-way interdependent relationship between the person buying dinner, the restaurant, and the credit card company. At the restaurant, the cashier swipes the credit card through a reader at the point of sale. The credit card terminal dials a stored telephone number via computer to the credit card company (CCC). The CCC maintains an internal database that authenticates the person and guarantees to the merchant that the said person has a sufficient line of credit to cover the cost of purchase. Specifically, the CCC authenticates the person by examining the magnetic stripe (or magstripe) or computer chip on the face of the card indicating a valid card number, expiration date, and credit card limit. Afterwards, the credit card transaction requires the physical administration and processing of the credit card claim, including direct payment to the merchant and issuing a billing statement to the credit card holder. The person, in turn, must make a full (or partial) payment to the CCC, and that information must be processed accordingly. In sum, no part of a credit card transaction can take place without the interdependent relationship of the three main system parts.

Digital Wallets

A digital wallet (or electronic wallet) is a financial transaction application that runs on mobile devices. It securely stores the user's credit card and debit card information and passwords. These applications allow the user to pay for goods and services while shopping, thereby taking away the need to carry physical credit cards or checkbooks. The smartphone takes the place of said credit cards to pay for purchases. The digital wallet is also used for other types of financial exchanges as well, including plane tickets, sports and music tickets, hotel reservations, and membership cards. Some of the better known examples of digital wallets include Venmo, Apple Pay, and Google Pay.

Today's mobile devices are designed to read QR (or Quick Response) codes which are bar codes consisting of black squares and dots. When scanned, the unique pattern on the barcode translates into stored, readable information (see Figure 5.4). QR codes vary in design and function. When dining out, for example, a QR code listed on a table card can direct the user to the evening's menu located at the restaurant's homepage. This, in fact, was done quite regularly during the Covid-19 pandemic for purposes of safety and security. Similarly, a person collecting tickets at a concert might give the attendee a small sheet of paper containing a QR code that provides a link to that evening's featured program. Another use of a QR code might be a technology salesperson who places a QR code on the back of their business card to direct the person to their LinkedIn profile and contact information. The QR can be used for direct sales as well. When the user holds their phone over a QR point of sale to make a purchase, the digital wallet becomes fully engaged to conduct the transaction.[12]

Cryptocurrency

Cryptocurrency is a digital currency designed to work as a medium of financial exchange. Cryptocurrencies are typically decentralized networks based on blockchain technology which requires the use of a virtual ledger system and cryptography methods for data security. Unlike the U.S. Dollar or Euro, there is no central authority that manages and maintains the value of a cryptocurrency. Instead, these tasks are broadly distributed among a cryptocurrency's users via the Internet.

FIGURE 5.4   Quick Response (QR) Code

While cryptocurrency can be used to buy regular goods and services, most investors approach cryptocurrencies as they would other assets, like stocks or precious metals. Bitcoin is recognized as the first cryptocurrency, first outlined in principle by Satoshi Nakamoto in a 2008 paper titled "Bitcoin: A Peer-to-Peer Electronic Cash System."[13] Nakamoto described the project as "an electronic payment system based on cryptographic proof instead of trust." Today, there are multiple types of cryptocurrencies available for purchase and sale, including Ethereum, Tether, U.S. Dollar Coin, and Binance USD to name only a few.

There have been many attempts in the past to create digital money, but they have always failed. What gives a currency value? The main issue is trust; first that the currency has legitimate value and second that the people and organizations developing the currency are trustworthy. As an example, the issue of trust (and what can go wrong) occurred in November 2022, when cryptocurrency FTX specializing in derivatives and leveraged products filed for bankruptcy protection in the United States. At issue was the fact that FTX CEO Bankman-Fried was arrested in the Bahamas and charged with wire fraud, securities fraud, and money laundering. Bankman-Fried is alleged to have taken about $10 billion in FTX customers' funds for his trading firm Alameda Research. As FTX collapsed, it set into motion a massive cascading run on the FTX cryptocurrency exchange among its customers who suddenly looked to withdraw their money. At least $1 billion in customer funds is reportedly missing.[14] Bankman-Fried was subsequently found guilty of fraud for his role in the collapse of the now bankrupt FTX cryptocurrency exchange. It took a jury just over four hours to convict him in what is now considered one of the biggest financial frauds in history.

The value of any recognized currency (the U.S. dollar, the Euro, the Japanese Yen, the British pound) comes from the governments that created them as well as international recognition of their legitimacy. The trust factor also comes into play when a nation's people believe that their government will do everything they can to protect and ensure the currency's value over time.

Blockchain

One way to ensure the integrity of cryptocurrency system is through a blockchain system of accounting. A blockchain is essentially a digital ledger of transactions that is duplicated and distributed across the entire network of computer systems located on the system. Each block in the chain contains a set number of transactions, and every time a new transaction occurs on the blockchain, a record of that transaction is added to every participant's ledger. Within the blockchain system, everyone who is part of the network has their own copy of this ledger, thereby ensuring a transparent and unified transaction record. The decentralized database (or ledger) managed by crypto's multiple participants is known as distributed ledger technology (DLT). As each new transaction is logged, everyone's blockchain copy is simultaneously updated with new information, keeping all records identical and accurate.[15] In principle, digital currencies like Bitcoin, Ethereum, and Tether cannot be faked or double spent. The people who own such money can trust that it has real value.

Moving digital currency into an actual bank account is similar to converting currencies at an airport when first arriving in a new country. The digital currency holder is essentially selling their digital currency and "buying" the equal value in dollars, euros, or other major international currencies. In a regular foreign currency exchange, the exchange rate is determined by the government or the country's central bank. Whereas, with digital currency, the exchange rate is determined by rising demand and the perceived value of the currency. Supply and demand is a big factor in determining the trade value of a digital currency. For example, if more people are trying to buy more Binance Coin than is available for sale, the price will go up as is true in reverse. Because digital currency is not mediated by governments and central banks, the exchange of digital currency to regular currency happens privately through third-party exchange brokers. These crypto exchange brokers will buy, sell, and store digital currency for prospective clients. For the person looking to sell their digital currency holdings, the crypto exchange will simply sell/exchange digital currency for cash at a given rate. There are a variety of factors that can influence a user's decision as to which crypto exchange to choose from, including ease of use, trading fees, security measures, and the number of coins available for trading. Table 5.3 provides a brief listing of some of the better-known international crypto exchanges.

Bitcoin

Bitcoin is the world's first successful decentralized cryptocurrency and payment system, launched in 2009 by creator and founder Satoshi Nakamoto. Bitcoin, as

TABLE 5.3 Notable Examples of Cryptocurrency Exchanges

1. Bitcoin
2. Coinbase
3. Binance
4. Ethereum
5. Kraken
6. FTX (declared bankruptcy)
7. Tether
8. Gemini
9. Cripto.com
10. XRP
11. Dogecoin
12. Solana
13. USD Coin

with all cryptocurrencies, is secured and verified using cryptography, an applied process of encoding and decoding data. All Bitcoin transactions are stored on computers located and distributed throughout the world using blockchain ledger technology. Bitcoin has no single, centralized location or controlling authority. Instead, Bitcoin is designed so that users can exchange (sell or trade) Bitcoins with one another directly through a peer-to-peer network, whereby all users have equal power and are connected directly to each other without a central server or intermediary company. This allows Bitcoin payments and corresponding data to be sent, shared, and stored between parties.

Due to the public nature of the blockchain, all network participants can track and monitor bitcoin transactions in real time. Blockchain technology is what allows cryptocurrency transactions to be verified, exchanged and stored in a consistent and agreed-upon way. Whenever new transactions are confirmed and added to the ledger, the network updates every user's copy of the ledger to reflect the latest changes. This infrastructure reduces the possibility of an online payment issue known as double-spending. Double-spending occurs when a user tries to spend the same cryptocurrency twice. Just as banks regularly update the balances of their users, everyone who has a copy of the Bitcoin ledger is responsible for confirming and updating the balances of all bitcoin holders.

Since Bitcoin is not controlled or issued by a central bank, there is a fixed supply of bitcoins currently in circulation. In principle, the total supply of bitcoin is supposed to have a cap of 21 million coins, which means that once the number of coins in circulation reaches 21 million, the protocol will stop minting new coins. The ability to create new bitcoins and enter them into circulation is accomplished through a process known as *bitcoin mining*. This same mining process is also used to confirm new transactions and is a critical part of the blockchain ledger maintenance and development algorithm. "Mining" is performed using sophisticated hardware that solves an extremely complex computational math problem. The first computer to find the solution to the problem receives the next block (or issuance) of bitcoins, and the process repeats itself.[16] Cryptocurrency mining is painstaking, costly, and only occasionally rewarding. Nonetheless, mining has a special appeal for certain types of investors who are interested in cryptocurrency given that miners receive rewards for their work with crypto tokens. This may be because entrepreneurial types see mining as a type of 21st-century version of mining for gold.

The original concept behind Bitcoin was that it was intended to serve as an alternative to traditional money with the goal that it would become globally accepted as legal tender, thereby allowing people to use it to purchase goods and services. However, Bitcoin's relative success has been hampered by its price volatility. At issue is the fact that Bitcoin's relative value has fluctuated significantly over time. There are several reasons that account for this, starting with the fact that Bitcoin has proven to be a target for both sophisticated computer hackers and providing a safe haven for digital pirates and money launderers. Consider, for example, the case of Ilya "Dutch" Lichtenstein and his wife Heather Morgan, who were arrested in February 2022. Federal authorities have accused the couple of trying to launder 119,754 bitcoins (the equivalent of $4.5 billion) when they or another hacker breached the crypto exchange Bitfinex in 2016. The hackers operated inside the Bitfinex servers for weeks before attempting the heist. They had been watching other users on the Bitfinex currency exchange buy and sell bitcoins.[17] As a consequence, the Bitcoin heist put a major scare into cryptocurrency investors while simultaneously causing the value of Bitcoin tokens to drop precipitously. As noted earlier, is the issue of trust. Bitcoin (as is true with most cryptocurrencies) is decentralized and does not have a centralized authority controlling it. In order for cryptocurrencies like Bitcoin to have value, there has to be a shared confidence in the promise of what digital currency represents. Part of Bitcoin's perceived value lies in its name recognition since it was the first and best-known of today's cryptocurrencies. The real value, however, is represented by those Bitcoin investors willing to spend real money (millions of Dollars and Euros) in the belief that cryptocurrency represents a unique and valuable form of financial exchange.

NFTs

An NFT (non-fungible token) is a digital asset that represents real-world objects like art, music, in-game items, and videos. They are bought and sold online, using cryptocurrency, and are recorded using blockchain technology. NFTs are like digital passports, because each token contains a unique non-transferable identity to distinguish it from other tokens.[18] NFTs are increasingly becoming a popular way to buy and sell digital artwork. Part of the appeal for NFT digital art is that it allows the buyer to own the original item. Moreover, it contains built-in authentication, which serves as proof of ownership. NFTs are like physical collector's items, only digital. So instead of purchasing an actual oil painting for one's home, the buyer gets a digital file instead. Collectors value the fact that such digital art pieces are considered one-of-a-kind and unique.[19] In 2021, the market for NFT trading was worth an estimated $41 billion. What are some of the kinds of digital NFTs that are bought and sold online? Such examples might include:

- Digital artwork
- GIF image files
- Sports memorabilia and highlights
- Video game assets
- Collectibles (sports cards, Pokémon cards)
- Virtual avatars
- Music

As currency, physical money and cryptocurrencies are considered fungible, that is, they can be traded using the same medium of exchange. In other words, one dollar is equal to one dollar; one Bitcoin is equal to one Bitcoin. Whereas, each NFT contains a unique digital signature that makes it impossible for it to be exchanged or traded as an equal to another. Hence, the term *non-fungible*. The most widely used blockchain for the sale and distribution of NFTs is Ethereum, but there are others as well. To buy and sell NFTs, the user must have a digital wallet and access to a cryptocurrency that allows the user to trade and store such items. Blockchain technology and NFTs afford artists and content creators a unique opportunity to monetize their wares. For example, artists no longer have to rely on galleries or auction houses to sell their art. Instead, the artist can sell their work directly to the consumer as an NFT. This, in turn, allows them to keep more of the profits. In addition, artists can affix royalties so that they will receive a percentage of sales whenever their art is sold to a new owner. This is an attractive feature when one considers that artists generally do not receive future proceeds after their art is first sold.[20] Since NFTs represent an altogether new form of EC trade, the future remains a work in progress. The value factor for an NFT is based entirely on what someone else is willing to pay for it. Therefore, demand will drive the price rather than traditional economic forces that drive investment in stock and real estate.

Interactivity (Network Design Principle 3)

The principle of interactivity suggests the ability to engage in two-way communication. Today, interactive communication is the starting point for all discussions concerning how users interact with the various media and communication devices they use. Much of the research on interactivity concerns how users interact with various communication devices, including computers, smartphones, and video game systems. One method and approach is to view interactivity as a function of the medium itself. This is particularly true when it comes to the development of things such as smartphones and video game systems. Here, the emphasis is on hardware and software devices. More to the point, the interactivity of mediated communication depends on three main characteristics: *speed* (i.e., how quickly a device responds to a user's commands), *range* (i.e., the level of control permitted by the device), and *mapping* (i.e., the degree of correspondence between a user's actions to control the device and how it responds to those actions).

A second method and approach is to look at interactivity from the vantage point of the communication process itself. Interactivity resides in the perceptions and experiences of those who directly participate in the actual communication. This perspective is more closely associated with computer-mediated communication. Interactivity occurs at varying levels and degrees of engagement, ranging from social networking sites to video game participation. Here, the emphasis is on the communication of ideas, information, and shared meaning among two or more persons.

Human–Computer Interface Design

Touch-Tone Telephony

One of the earliest examples of interactive electronic communication (and a technology that is still used today) can be traced back to the beginning use of touch-tone telephony that replaced rotary dial telephones in the 1970s. Touch-tone telephony utilized a concept known as *dual-tone multi frequency*, whereby each button on the telephone handset consists of two frequencies. The original touch-tone provided the basis for interactive capability with a host telephone system or computer.

The goal of touch-tone is to give businesses and other organizations the ability to create a menu structure of services that the user can access by pushing a select number of keys. Consider, for example, calling a vacation cruise line service liking Viking, the user will be prompted by the host computer to first decide if you're a traveler (Press 1) or a travel agent (Press 2). After that, the automated voice will take you through a descending menu structure to determine the type of travel experience you're querying about. It also provides a series of prompts depending on whether you have an existing reservation or are trying to make a new one.

The Computer Mouse

Interactivity has to do with the knowledge transfer between a person and a machine or between a person and a larger set of community users. To fully appreciate the breadth and scope of this idea, one should have an appreciation for the early work in human and computer interface design. In 1963, Douglas Engelbart of the Stanford Research Center pioneered the development of the computer mouse which greatly improved the way in which people interfaced with computers. In 1967, Engelbart applied for and received a patent for a wooden shell with two metal wheels (computer mouse U.S. Patent No. 3,541,541). The patent was issued in 1970. Engelbart described the patent as an "X-Y position indicator for a display system." The device was nicknamed a mouse because the tail (or connection cord) came out of one end.[21]

The computer mouse functions as a pointing device that detects and highlights text and visual displays on a two-dimensional screen. The computer mouse frees the user to a large extent from using a keyboard. It was a simple but masterful form of ergonomic design that greatly improved the way in which people interfaced with computers. The first integrated mouse design for computers was used at Xerox Parc. Apple would later acquire the hardware and software rights to both the computer mouse and graphical user interface design from Xerox. The initial mouse design was both complicated and expensive ($300 per mouse). Steve Jobs then went to the industrial design firm IDEO and contracted with them to come up with a simpler design solution that would later cost $15 per mouse.

Graphical User Interface (GUI)

The development of the GUI icons by Xerox Corporation and later Apple in the 1980s further advanced the cause of human–computer interface design. A GUI offers graphical icons and visual indicators as opposed to text-based interfaces and/or typed command labels to fully represent the information and program selections available to a user. GUI has become a standard feature on all Apple, Android, and Linux-based operating systems.[22] Touch-screen technology came along in the 1980s and has been used in a variety of automated banking and airport flight check-in and ticketing applications. Today, touch-screen capability has become a standard feature found in various kinds of digital appliances, including laptop computers, mobile smartphones, computer tablets, and global positioning navigation systems (GPS).

Speech Recognition

The next and evolving generation of interface software involves speech recognition systems evidenced by the work being done in the military and health-care fields. Speech recognition software allows the user to dictate to a computer or handheld recorder, thus enabling an electronic text version of the spoken words to appear on the user's screen. Each successive generation requires less formatting of the software (i.e., identifying specialized words). Also, the software adapts to the user by keying in on select words and phrases and storing them in its internal memory. A variation on speech recognition systems is voice command systems using Bluetooth technology in cars. Bluetooth represents an industry standard for personal wireless communication devices, referred to as personal area networks. Bluetooth provides a way to connect and exchange information between Bluetooth-compatible devices such as laptop computers, smartphones, and music sound systems using unlicensed short-range radio frequencies (i.e., typically 1–100 meters). Bluetooth simplifies the discovery and setup of services between devices. The voice command system can set up and execute a hands-free cellular telephone call as well as call up music and traffic reports from the vehicle's radio, audio/music control streaming system.

Discussion

The world has become digital and so has the economy. In today's digital economy, the Internet and EC serves as the central hub by which all economic activity occurs. This, in turn, enables such economic activity to be global in scope as well as being available 24/7. The present-day digital economy relies on the selling of goods and services via the Internet. The products and services themselves, however, can be both physical (i.e., household goods, clothing, food, etc.) and digitally based (i.e., music and video streaming, online finance, education, and instructional training).[23] The digital economy brings with it a high degree of exchange efficiency.

At the same time, not all changes in the fast, unfolding digital economy are for the better. Today's digital economy has set into motion a number of unintended consequences. First and foremost has been a significant decline in traditional shopping, specifically department stores and smaller retail outlets.[24] EC has brought a level of convenience and accessibility that traditional bricks and mortar stores cannot match. Online shopping has given shoppers the ability to compare prices and products easily, leading to increased competition while placing pressure on retailers to offer better value for the money.

Browsing in an old used book store for that special find is becoming harder and harder. Gone are the days of interesting and sometimes useful conversations with knowledgeable salespeople at the local music store. Both kinds of retail shops have felt the disruptive effects of exchange efficiency whether it be Amazon, Apple music, or equivalent EC sites. The days of taking photos and placing them in physical albums are no longer the first choice for busy, active working professionals and families. Instead, digital storage options such as one's computer, smartphone, and/or social media account provide simple and direct convenience. Consider further, the young couple sitting across from each other at a restaurant, looking intently at their smartphones instead of each other. Scanning one's phone has become an all-too-easy time-filler for face-to-face communication. Equally challenging are the sometimes dangers of texting and driving, cryptocurrency fraud, and Internet cyberbullying. These are but a few examples of the new digital reality and the hazards that such changes have set into motion. There is no going backwards. But there are ways to use such technologies more wisely.

High Tech–High Touch

In his book *Megatrends*, author John Naisbitt describes the challenge of trying to find the right balance between the material wonders of technology and the spiritual demands of our human nature. He refers to this as the need for "high tech–high touch."[25] Great technology and innovation can be a thing of beauty as evidenced by a well-designed website or virtual reality gaming system. High-touch are the activities that keep us in touch with our basic humanity. They link us to our more authentic self. The effective use of technology and balanced living can be mutually supportive. Creating a high-energy music playlist while running or training hard at the gym provides inspiration to the workout experience. So too is the practical value of carrying a smartphone while engaged in a wilderness hike—just in case. Both examples are high-tech–high-touch in their most essential form.

The lessons of the Covid-19 pandemic forced the world's population to better understand the potential of videoconferencing software for everyday communication whether it be work, family get-togethers, or classroom instruction. Remote working from home has now become an accepted practice in most professional working environments. And while a Zoom videoconference call is no substitute for an actual family get-together, it's the next-best thing when separated by long distance. The Covid-19 pandemic also taught us a lot about the power and potential of online classroom instruction. Online teaching instruction has now become an important staple for university course offerings. What doesn't change, of course, is the high-touch experience of a well-designed class experience taught by a highly motivated and engaged instructor. Nothing takes the place of inspired teaching. This too is high-tech–high-touch. Finally, social media sites like Facebook, Instagram, and YouTube provide a high-tech way of sharing information with one's friends, family, and colleagues, but it remains our special obligation to tell stories that are purposeful and worth telling.

Notes

1 Don Tapscott, *The Digital Economy. Rethinking Promise and Peril in the Age of Networked Intelligence* (New York: McGraw-Hill, 2015), 11–50.
2 Richard Gershon, *Media, Telecommunications and Business Strategy*. 3rd ed. (New York: Routledge, 2020).

3 Joe Lambert, *Digital Storytelling: Capturing Lives, Creating Community*. 5th ed. (New York: Routledge, 2018).

4 Adam Thomas, "What Is Binary?" *Built-in*, 2023, April 4, https://builtin.com/software-engineering-perspectives/binary

5 Steven Shepard, *Telecom Crash Course*. 3rd ed. (New York: McGraw-Hill, 2014), 197–200.

6 Steve Jones, Ron Kovac and Frank Groom, *Introduction to Communications Technologies*. 3rd ed. (New York: CRC Group, 2016).

7 Yue-Ling Wong, *Digital Media Primer*. 3rd ed. (Upper Saddle River, NJ: Pearson, 2016).

8 Anjan Bharadwaj, "Data Compression: What It Is and Why It's Important," *Indeed*, 2023, March 2, www.indeed.com/career-advice/career-development/data-compression

9 Frederick Marckini, "What Is a Software Spider?" *Inc.*, 2022, September 1, www.inc.com/articles/2000/04/18600.html

10 Tom Roston, "The Wikipedia Story," *OneZero*, 2021, January 14, https://onezero.medium.com/an-oral-history-of-wikipedia-the-webs-encyclopedia-1672eea57d2

11 Gershon, *Media, Telecommunications and Business Strategy*. 3rd ed., 181–182.

12 Julia Kagan, "What Is a Digital Wallet?" *Investopedia*, 2022, April 10, www.investopedia.com/terms/d/digital-wallet.asp

13 Satoshi Nakamoto, "Bitcoin: A Peer-to-Peer Electronic Cash System," 2023, https://bitcoin.org/bitcoin.pdf See also, Bitcoin, "Getting Started with Bitcoin," 2023, https://bitcoin.org/en/getting-started

14 Whizy Kim, "Sam Bankman-Fried's Arrest Is the Culmination of an Epic Flame-out," *Vox*, 2022, December 22, www.vox.com/the-goods/23458837/sam-bankman-fried-ftx-sbf-downfall-explained

15 Kate Ashford, "What Is Cryptocurrency?" *Forbes Advisor*, 2022, June 6, www.forbes.com/advisor/investing/cryptocurrency/what-is-cryptocurrency/

16 Euny Hong, "How Does Bitcoin Mining Work?" *Investopedia*, 2022, May 5, www.investopedia.com/tech/how-does-bitcoin-mining-work/

17 Zeke Faux and Chris Burnett, "Don't Forget an Exit Plan," *Bloomberg Businessweek*, 2022, July 4, 22–29.

18 Rakesh Sharma, "Non-Fungible Token, What It Means," *Investopedia*, 2022, June 22, www.investopedia.com/non-fungible-tokens-nft-5115211

19 Robyn Conti, "What Is an NFT?" *Forbes Advisor*, 2023, March, www.forbes.com/advisor/investing/cryptocurrency/nft-non-fungible-token/

20 Conti, "What Is an NFT?" www.forbes.com/advisor/investing/cryptocurrency/nft-non-fungible-token/

21 Walter Isaacson, *The Innovators* (New York: Simon & Schuster, 2014), 274–281.

22 Walter Isaacson, *Steve Jobs* (New York: Simon & Schuster, 2011), 94–99.

23 Klaus Schwab, *The Fourth Industrial Revolution* (New York: Crown-Business, 2016).

24 Tapscott, *The Digital Economy. Rethinking Promise and Peril in the Age of Networked Intelligence*, 11–50.

25 John Naisbitt, *Megatrends* (New York: Warner Books, 1982).

6

THE DIGITAL ECONOMY II

Personalization, Mobility, Virtual Communication, and Convergence

The digital economy involves the full integration of transnational business, nation-states, and technologies operating at high speed. It is a global economy that is being driven by free-market capitalism and the power of intelligent networking. The digital economy stands in marked contrast to many of the basic patterns and assumptions of the Industrial age. The once highly centralized business has given way to the transnational organization that operates in multiple countries throughout the world. Instead of time and communication being highly synchronized, today's working professional lives in a digital world of asynchronous and virtual communication that allows for the international collaboration of projects regardless of time zones, geographical borders, and physical space. We have entered the era of global virtual teams where work is produced across multiple time zones and geographic spaces. The digital economy has become a society of networks. We don't talk with people; we network with them.[1]

Personalization (Network Design Principle 4)

In today's digital economy, we are witnessing the demassification of media and entertainment product made possible by EC and the power of intelligent network design. EC companies are using the Internet to communicate and personalize the information exchange between an EC site (or retailer) and the end consumer. From personalized music playlists on one's smartphone to video-on-demand streaming services, consumers now have the ability to compile, edit, and customize the media they use.[2] More and more companies are tailoring their product and service offerings to meet the unique tastes of the individual. We have entered the era of personalization (see Table 6.1).

DOI: 10.4324/9781003294375-6

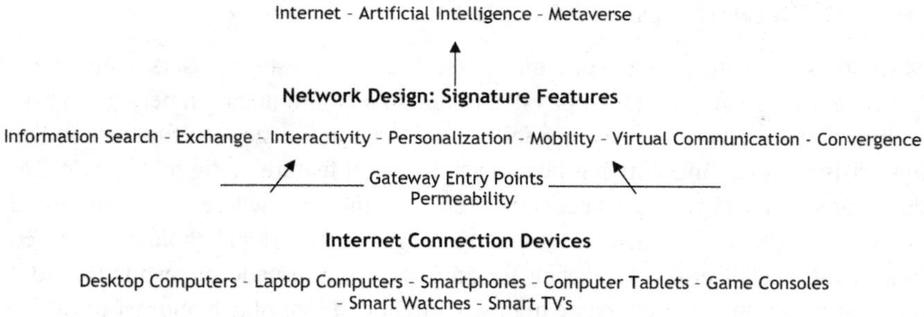

Internet – Artificial Intelligence – Metaverse

↑

Network Design: Signature Features

Information Search – Exchange – Interactivity – Personalization – Mobility – Virtual Communication – Convergence

Gateway Entry Points
Permeability

Internet Connection Devices

Desktop Computers – Laptop Computers – Smartphones – Computer Tablets – Game Consoles – Smart Watches – Smart TV's

FIGURE 6.1 The Digital Economy Business Model

Source: Richard A. Gershon, 2023.

TABLE 6.1 Select Examples of Digital Media and Personalization

• Personalized Website Design and Marketing
• Customized Music Playlists, Spotify, Apple Music
• OTT Video streaming, Netflix, Amazon Prime, HBO Max, Disney Plus
• Digital Video Recording and Personalized TV
• Social Networking, Facebook, Instagram, TikTok, LinkedIn

Micromarketing

Micromarketing (or personalized marketing) involves knowing more about the particular interests and buying habits of one's customers. For marketers, the steady shift from mass to micromarketing is being driven by a combination of technological change as well as strategic opportunity. Advanced portal software permits users to receive personalized information in the form of specialized content (i.e., daily news updates, stock reports, weather, book recommendations, etc.).[3] As an example, Amazon.com routinely sends out information updates to its customers notifying them of newly published books based on information obtained and analyzed from previous purchasing selections. Similarly, both Spotify and Apple utilize a proprietary recommendation software that makes suggestions of possible music selections that the consumer might like based on past selections. These type of digital footprints provide relevant and useful information to the EC service provider about consumer likes and interests. Electronic commerce and personalized marketing have changed the basic relationship between the EC service provider and the customer, challenging marketers to shift their emphasis from persuasion sales to relationship building.[4]

Mobility (Network Design Principle 5)

Mobility is a signature feature of digital lifestyle and suggests that users require flexibility of movement and not be physically tied to a communication network. From architects who require wireless capability in a construction zone to first responders in a crisis situation, mobility has become an essential feature of digital lifestyle. Today's Internet user expects to access the web—anytime, anywhere. Location should never be an obstacle. Consider, for example, the number of stakeholders involved in a disaster relief effort. Preparing for an impending tornado or responding to a multicar collision on an interstate highway might call into play a number of different players, including police, fire and rescue, first responders, hospital emergency personnel, and the news media. An impending crisis situation, by its very nature, creates a situation where rumors and misinformation can pose a threat to safety and security. Mobile and wireless IT allows planners and first responders to maintain continuous communication and better manage the flow of critical information. The information should be fast, immediate, and accessible.[5]

Smartphones

The term *smartphone* describes a new generation of cellular telephones that are highly personalized and features a variety of enhanced information services. The smartphone combines the best elements of exchange, mobility, and convergence. The real start into smartphone design began in 2006 with the introduction of the Apple iPhone. The iPhone set the standard for Internet mobile phone design by using a multi-touch screen with a virtual keyboard and buttons. Since then, companies like Samsung, Google, and others have introduced their own smartphone versions. Unlike, Apple's IOS proprietary operating software, most other companies have adopted the Android *open source* operating software developed by Google. Today's smartphones have built-in functionality that is programmable.

Mobility makes possible a whole host of wireless Internet activities that range from making and receiving telephone calls to securing an airline reservation. Some observers have called it "broadband on the go."[6] The smartphone has become the primary accessory of digital lifestyle. It has become one of our essential possessions; no less important than a set of car keys or a favorite article of clothing. The smartphone allows us to stay in touch with one's friends, family, and work as well as providing mobile Internet access as needed. The smartphone emphasizes the personal aspect of wireless technology by advancing a number of enhanced feature elements that can be seen in Table 6.2.

Global Positioning System (GPS)

GPS is widely used for the purpose of detecting the location of a moving vehicle or a ship at sea. GPS represents a particular kind of mobility, specifically,

TABLE 6.2 Primary Smartphone Applications

 1. Voice Communication
 2. Internet Access
 3. Text Messaging
 4. Email Messaging
 5. Camera and Video Camera
 6. Photo Storage and Display
 7. Music Streaming and Playback
 8. Video Streaming and Playback
 9. GPS Locator, Directional Mapping
10. Digital Wallet
11. News and Weather Apps
12. EC Shopping Apps
13. Calculator
14. Alarm and Wake-Up
15. Calculator

a real-time digital mapping system. In the GPS system, a constellation of 24 satellites circle the earth in near-circular inclined orbits. Each of these satellites circles the earth at medium-range orbit (12,000 miles) making two complete rotations every day. The orbits are arranged so that at anytime, anywhere on earth, there are at least four satellites visible in the sky[7] (see Figure 6.2). The original GPS concept and design was developed by the U.S. Department of Defense and has been available for civilian use since 1994. Other international GPS systems include Russia's GLONASS system, China's Compass navigational system, and the Galileo system used by the European Union.

A GPS receiver is designed to read three or more of these satellites, coordinate the distance to each, and use this information to deduce its own location. This operation is based on a mathematical principle called trilateration. A GPS receiver computes its position by comparing the time taken by signals from three or four different GPS satellites to reach the receiver. By receiving signals from at least three of these satellites, the receiver's position (latitude, longitude, and altitude) can be accurately determined.[8]

The primary benefit of GPS includes travel directions and location accuracy. Whether travelling locally, cross-country, or globally, the user is able to access accurate directions in real time as well as being provided the constant monitoring of his/her vehicle location. GPS has become an essential navigational tool for personal travel, freight delivery, and courier services. Maritime users also benefit from GPS use. Ships at sea depend heavily on GPS for navigating their way across the oceans and major lakes. GPS has become a standard feature in the design console of today's automobiles as well as an essential app found on most user's smartphones. Two of the best-known GPS navigational apps include Google Maps and Waze.

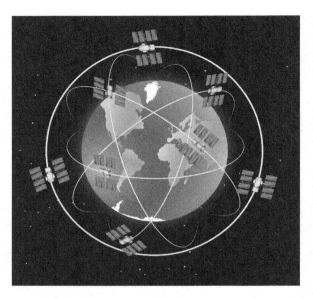

FIGURE 6.2 Global Positioning System (GPS)

Google Maps and Waze

Worldwide, Google Maps and Waze are the two most widely used GPS navigational apps.[9] Both GPS systems are owned by Google. In 2013, Google purchased the Israel-based Waze GPS service for $1.3 billion. This created an opportunity to combine and enhance its own Google mapping service with what promised to be the most powerful GPS automobile service to date. Waze is designed primarily for travel by car. When activated, it plots out the most direct and efficient driving route between the user's starting location and destination point. Waze excels at finding alternative routes around accidents and traffic jams and alerts drivers in advance of road-related incidents. The Waze GPS service is based on real-time location data combined with user-generated information updates. Waze users share information about slowdowns, speed traps, police sightings, and road closures, allowing Waze to update suggested routes in real time. Among its other features, Waze can be used to find restaurants and gas stations along the selected route. It's worth noting that Waze tends to be the GPS service of choice for ride-sharing services like Uber and Lyft.[10]

Google maps, by comparison, is an all-purpose GPS service. Google Maps offers its users walking, driving, biking, and public transportation directions. Google maps, like Waze, provides real-time traffic updates including information pertaining to traffic jams, accidents, and road closures. Google Maps has a built-in *Explore* features that allow users to see events, reviews, photos, restaurants, points of interest, etc. Google Maps also has a *street view* mode to see location points at street level. Google Maps provides detailed information about businesses, landmarks, and popular tourist destinations, making it easy to explore new places. Still to be determined is whether Google Maps and Waze will become a fully integrated GPS service or remain as two highly popular stand-alone services.

Drone Technology and Mobility

Another example of the importance of mobility as a design principle can be seen in the area of drone technology. An unmanned aerial vehicle, commonly referred to as a drone, is a small aircraft without any human pilot, crew, or passengers on board. Drone technology allows journalists to take footage of news events such as volcanic eruptions, war-torn villages, and natural disasters. Because drones are operated remotely, senior editorial staff and journalists see it as a safer and more cost-effective means of video recording, especially in areas considered dangerous (see Figure 6.3).

Drones, in general, have seen growing utilization in a variety of industries that require high arial photography and videography. Examples include:

- Television/film production
- Land surveying and mapping
- Agriculture and forestry
- Environmental monitoring and conservation
- Tourism and travel
- Real estate sales and marketing
- Archeology and cultural heritage

Technological improvements, including enhanced flight time, payload capacity, data gathering, and high resolution photography/video, have significantly

FIGURE 6.3   Drone Technology Design

led to the increased use of drones in various industries. Drones, for example, are being used for the direct delivery of food and medical supplies in support of present-day disaster relief efforts. Drones are small, lightweight, and can be controlled remotely. For journalists, in particular, drones provide the capability to report unique and untold stories in various hard-to-reach conflict zones or natural disaster areas. With the help of remotely piloted technology, journalists can take aerial footage, thereby greatly reducing safety concerns. The use of drone technology, for example, is revolutionizing news coverage in Ukraine, allowing journalists to deliver extraordinary visuals from the sky while providing a unique and engaging perspective. Reporters can now access hard-to-reach areas and capture compelling footage that would have previously been impossible to record. This has proven particularly useful in Ukraine, where various conflict zone areas are off-limits to reporters.[11]

Virtual Communication (Network Design Principle 6)

The term *virtual communication* can be used to describe the artificial space and network linkages connecting a separate and dispersed group of users using various forms of computer and communication technology. From Zoom and Webex videoconferencing software to social media sites like Facebook, Instagram, and YouTube, the common denominator with all forms of virtual communication is the ability to create a simulated environment. The communication, itself, can be both synchronous (real time) and asynchronous (different times). The selection and type of communication technology are based on how much information content the sender wishes the receiver to have. Researchers Daft and Lengel refer to this as *media richness*.[12] The difference in quality and depth varies according to the communication medium.

Virtual Private Network

A *virtual private network* (VPN) is a computer network that uses a dedicated data and public telecommunications infrastructure to provide remote users (or departments) secure access to their organization's network. A VPN can range in size and scale of operation. Such examples might include a major medical hospital that must provide secure health-care information to physicians and other medical professionals located in a variety of clinics and adjoining facilities. A second example might be a transnational business enterprise operating worldwide that must tie together multiple divisions responsible for the organization's varying operations, including research and development, manufacturing, sales, marketing, and strategic decision-making. To that end, various members of a so-called global virtual project team need immediate and secure access to the company's ERM system for a variety of information needs and shared documents[13] (see Figure 6.4).

Virtual Private Networks and the Transnational Corporation

A transnational corporation (TNC) is a nationally based company with overseas operations in multiple countries around the world. Strategic decision-making and the allocation of resources are predicated upon economic goals and efficiencies with little regard to national boundaries. TNC has become a salient feature of our present-day global economic landscape.[14] Through a process of foreign direct investment, the TNC relies on the use of advanced information technology as a way to stay globally connected. At the heart of transnational business operations is the importance of *organizational control* which describes the need for a system-wide method for managing, tracking, and evaluating a TNC's domestic and foreign operations. Organizational control provides the ability to centralize decision-making, thereby giving senior management the tools necessary to plan, allocate resources, and take corrective action to meet changing international conditions. The ERM system and other forms of intelligent networking

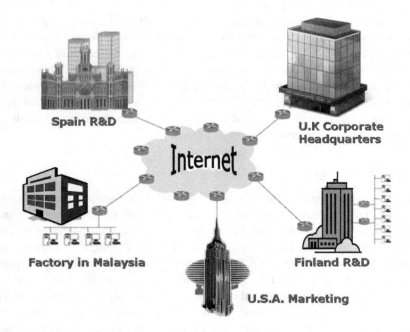

FIGURE 6.4   The Transnational Organization and Virtual Private Network

Source: Richard A. Gershon, 2020.

have become the vital nervous system enabling the TNCs multiple divisions and subunits to function independently while being part of a larger communication network. As a consequence, traditional divisions and departmental hierarchies tend to be flatter, thereby permitting direct communication between and among organizational players.[15]

Virtual Global Project Teams

International project teams are the key to smart, flexible, and cost-effective organizations. A virtual global project team represents working professionals from a TNC's worldwide operations assembled together for both regular international operations and specialized project assignments. They are staffed by working professionals from different countries. More and more, virtual teams are used as part of a larger effort to share international expertise across the entire organization. The virtual global project team offers certain distinct advantages, including shared access to information, collaborative research and design work, reduced travel costs, and so on. Advancements in communication technology and the intelligent network have elevated the work of virtual team to a whole new level in terms of collaborative effort.[16]

At the same time, global virtual teams bring with them a unique set of challenges. Foremost are issues pertaining to trust involving differences of culture, geographic dislocation, complex problem-solving, and the effective collaboration of ideas. Specifically, how does one creatively engage a group of people that one has never physically met and trusting that everyone is equal to the task?[17] The global virtual team presents a unique set of challenges in terms of blending the technical efficiencies of virtual communication with the practical needs of creating a cohesive international project group.

Videoconferencing

One of the standard tools for the virtual global project team is the videoconference. The videoconference provides an electronic meeting format using video images and audio sound. People are typically linked together at two or more locations via an Internet connection. The videoconference permits the exchange of information, data, and/or drawings between two or more people at separate locations. The organizational videoconference has become a standard feature of transnational communication and serves as an alternative to face-to-face meetings. This can include both point-to-multipoint videoconferences using structured conference meeting rooms and smaller project team group meetings.

A group videoconference offers some distinct advantages, including 1) the timely exchange of information, 2) increased productivity, 3) cost savings, and

4) employee training. First and foremost, the group videoconference is about information exchange. This gives the large-scale organization a level of productivity and efficiency that would otherwise be unavailable. The videoconference can link together members of a global project team, thereby eliminating the need for in-person meetings as well as flight, hotel, and meal expenses associated with travel. The group videoconference also contributes to increased productivity as key management people are in the office and not in transit. Today, nearly all desktop, laptop, and tablet computers are equipped with a webcam and microphone. Software applications like Zoom, WebEx, Microsoft Teams, Google Hangouts and Facetime make regular consultations and global project team meetings a fairly routine exercise. In addition, a prearranged webinar can provide organizational employees with a timely method for obtaining professional training and information updates. Typically, the webinar is scheduled ahead of time and involves an information specialist as well as written materials. Videoconferencing and webinars make real-time business communication possible, enabling working professionals the ability to remain productive without the need for extensive travel.

Lessons of the Covid-19 Pandemic

Starting in the spring of 2020, the Covid-19 pandemic disrupted the world's economy by forcing the closing of schools, business, and government agencies throughout the world. But like a natural disaster or war, necessity proved to be the mother of invention. One of the unintended consequences of the Covid-19 pandemic is that it has led to an exponential increase in the use of Zoom and equivalent conferencing software, thereby creating a new comfort level in terms of its use for business, education, health care as well as the general public.

Zoom

Zoom is among the best-known cloud-based videoconferencing services that allow users to virtually meet by video, audio-only or both. Zoom was founded by Chinese-born Eric Yuan, a former corporate vice president for Cisco Webex. He left Cisco in April 2011 with 40 engineers to start a new company, originally named Saasbee, Inc. The company initially had trouble finding investors because many people thought that the business of video telephony was an already saturated market. Zoom was launched in 2013 under the direction of Eric Yuan. Zoom's hosting capability greatly increased over time, and by 2015, the company had ten million users and one billion meeting minutes. By 2017, Zoom was defined as a "unicorn," or a private business that was worth over $1 billion. In 2019, Zoom went public and was valued at $16 billion after the first day of its initial public offering. More than half of the world's Fortune 500 companies reportedly used Zoom in 2019 while the company achieved 227% growth a year later in 2020.

Few companies soared during the Covid-19 pandemic quite like videoconferencing specialist Zoom. The company proved to be a major technology innovator by helping to redefine the principle of video telephony. Nearly overnight, Zoom became the go-to conferencing service for business, education, government, and the general public. Remote working at home became the new norm, and workers needed to be connected with coworkers and clients. Zoom also became the preferred conferencing platform for the everyday user who wanted to stay in touch with both family and friends. Zoom adopted a freemium model that let anyone host a meeting of 40 minutes or less for free. This meant that friends and family could stay in touch during the lockdown regardless of geographic separation whether that be regionally, nationally, or internationally. Zoom made possible a natural economies of scale, whereby the cost of service bore no relationship to the number of users and distance involved. Zoom's success has been astounding, making the company's founder Eric Yuan very wealthy. His total network is estimated to be $5.6 billion.

During the Covid-19 pandemic, the one major challenge facing Zoom was security. The sudden and exponential increased use in Zoom caught the company unprepared. For the first time, the company was faced with an issue known as Zoom bombing. The term "Zoom bombing" refers to a type of cyber-harassment in which an individual or a group of unwanted and uninvited attendees interrupt online meetings over the Zoom videoconference platform. These type of virtual intruders tend to be loud, sometimes obscene, and very disruptive to the meeting process. In response, the company soon developed a set of security protocols that included both then and now — required Registration (or Authentication) as well as passcode entry (or Waiting Room). Zoom now requires that all users either enable a passcode or use the waiting room for meetings.

The Covid-19 pandemic proved to be a major game changer in terms of promoting the everyday use of videoconferencing. Zoom (and equivalent conferencing software) has now become an essential part of remote working from home while enabling the everyday user to stay virtually in touch with one's family, friends, and colleagues regardless of geographic location. Whether it's meetings, conference calls, classroom presentations, or family get-togethers, Zoom has fundamentally changed day-to-day communication. We now celebrate birthdays and attend virtual wakes via Zoom.

Convergence (Network Design Principle 7)

The clear lines and historic boundaries that once separated broadcasting, cable television, telephony, and Internet communication are no more. A natural convergence of industries and information technologies have blurred those distinctions. The term *convergence* means the joining together of media and in-formation technologies to create entirely new forms of communication expres-sion. Digital media has proven to be a major game changer when it comes to the presentation format, display, and storage of information. Digital media allows for the creative handling and transformation of data. Such examples include 1) television/film special effects, 2) Internet website display, 3) social media and enhanced graphics, 4) digital news presentation and display, and 5) video game entertainment systems.

Digital Photography

The digital media revolution owes its beginnings to the many changes that trans-formed the field of photography. Digital photography has many advantages over traditional film. Digital photos are convenient and allows the user to see the results instantly. Digital photography offers the user the ability to customize one's photos, including the ability to edit and engage special effects (i.e., re-touch, color saturation, contrast, cropping, and removal of objects). Moreover, digital photos don't require the costs associated with film and development time. Gone are the days of purchasing rolls of Kodak and Fuji films in preparation for a vacation trip. No longer do users have to take rolls of completed film to the local supermarket or camera store and wait for prints to be developed. Instead, digital cameras allow the user to take multiple shots at no extra cost. They can be stored on a variety of digital devices, including personal computers, flash drives, smartphones, computer tablets as well as being uploaded to a preferred social media site as well as personal/professional website displays.

Today, there are numerous types of digital cameras that allow individuals to capture the events unfolding around them with varying levels of ease and sophis-tication. The digital camera is a requisite part of any smartphone design. All this points to the fact that the transition to digital cameras is no longer about a single product but rather a fundamental shift in thinking regarding visual display, stor-age, and the communication process.[18]

CGI Filmmaking and 3D Special Effects

The special effect scenes that appear in modern-day adventure films involve the blending of live action footage and computer-generated imagery to create environments which speak to the imagination but would be too expensive or impractical to build. Computer-generated imagery (CGI) is the art of creating highly complex fixed or moving images that are used in television, film, video games, advertising, and website display. To a creative filmmaker, nothing is im-possible whether it's monsters rising from the sea to terrorize a Japanese city or space aliens traveling to earth to fight humans. Both CGI special effects and digital animation have become the go-to production techniques in creating adventure and superhero films. CGI makes possible uniquely created scenes and backdrops not seen in the real world. CGI and special effects design is a slow, painstaking process that requires a special attention to detail as well as a deep understanding of human anatomy and movement, building construction, and landscape settings (see Figure 6.5).

(a)

(b)

FIGURE 6.5 CGI Film Characters: Hogwarts School of Witchcraft and Wizardry—(a) Harry Potter; (b) The Incredible Hulk

3D animation refers to the process of drawing/constructing people and objects and making them come to life by creating the illusion that they're moving through a three-dimensional space. These computer-generated people and objects appear on a two-dimensional screen but are crafted to look like a 3D world.[19] Most on-screen special effects begin as 3D digital models. The models are first created as wireframes that establish the underlying structure of the person or object. The next step is for the animator to add realistic surfaces, skins, and textures. Facial features and clothes are moved on key frames. The skilled animator can apply select mathematical algorithms to achieve detailed facial expressions or the effect of someone falling through space. The differences in appearance between key frames are adjusted automatically by the computer in a process known as morphing. The animation is subsequently rendered.[20] Human movement can also be replicated using motion-capture technology. The technology records and captures real-life movement and then transfers it to the computer. This technique was widely used in the making of the James Cameron's 3D movie, *Avatar*[21] (see Figure 6.6).

A Word About the Uncanny Valley

The uncanny valley is a term used to describe the relationship between the human-like appearance of a robotic object and the emotional response it evokes. The creation of a robot (or robot-like appearance) can sometimes engender a feeling of unease or discomfort for the person interacting with the robot. In the field of present-day robotics (and select filmmaking), the goal is to make them appear friendly and lifelike in appearance. But sometimes, the character does not appear to be quite humanlike (or worse appears artificial or menacing), thereby creating the feeling known as the uncanny valley.[22] The almost human "creepiness" phenomenon was first described by the Japanese roboticist Masahiro Mori in a 1970 article titled *Bukimi no Tani Genshō*, which loosely translated means "Valley of Eeriness." In 1978, author Jasia Reichardt coined the term *uncanny valley* for his book *Robots: Fact, Fiction, and Prediction*.[23]

The uncanny valley principle is often used in filmmaking involving stories of malevolent robots or dystopia characters. One of the early examples of this can be seen in the 2004 film *I, Robot* based on the science fiction writing of Isaac

FIGURE 6.6   Avatar: The Way of Water

Asimov. Here, the viewer is treated to the I. Robot character known as Sonny, built with NS-5 higher-grade materials. The film's intention, of course, is to create a feeling of unease with robots and robotic design. *I, Robot* is just one of several films that make robots the main evildoer. Fast forward to the present day, and there are a number of films that make robots (and by extension AI) the malevolent main character of the storyline. A few examples include *The Creator*, *Mission Impossible*, *Dead Reckoning Part 1*, and *Heart of Stone*. In all of these films, the uncanny valley principle is fully present to convey a lack of human warmth as evidenced in Figure 6.7.

In contrast, sometimes the uncanny valley effect is accidental as was the case in the 2019 musical film production of Cats. Here, members of the star-studded cast are dressed up as cats but appear, nonetheless, as feline creepy characters. The blending of heavy make-up and exaggerated CGI effects combined with singing and dance movement made for a sometimes unsettling effect for the viewer. The uncanny valley has important implications for robotic design and video game avatars where getting the right level of facial features are important. One such example can be seen with an AI-powered humanoid robot called Sophia from Hanson Robotics. Sophia has been featured on the cover of *Cosmopolitan* magazine and appeared as a guest on *The Tonight Show* hosted by Jimmy Fallon (see Figure 6.8). But what sets Sophia apart in terms of the uncanny valley is her own self-awareness. In various Hanson Robotic ads, she describes herself as "personification of our dreams for the future of AI." Sophia represents the next generation in robotic design; humanlike in appearance while still engendering a slight, disquieting effect.

FIGURE 6.7 The Uncanny Valley

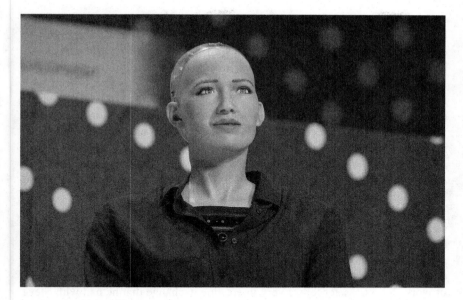

FIGURE 6.8   Sophia: Hanson Robotics

Pixar

Pixar Animation Studios is a computer animation studio originally formed when Steve Jobs purchased a failing Lucasfilm special-effects computer division for $10 million in 1986. Dr. Edwin E. Catmull, who was the head of the Lucasfilm subsidiary, was instructed by George Lucas to find a buyer if he wished to continue his work as an animator. When Dr. Catmull was unable to lure any buyers to acquire the special-effects division, he turned to Apple's Steve Jobs. After some initial hesitancy, Steve Jobs agreed to purchase the Lucasfilm unit.[24] With Steve Jobs acting as CEO of the newly formed Pixar Studios, Ed Catmull, who was vice president of the division at Lucasfilm, was named president.

The main thread to the Pixar story occurs with the hiring of John Lasseter. Starting as a graphic designer for Lucasfilm in 1984, he stayed with the division after it was purchased by Steve Jobs in 1986. John Lasseter was the creative genius behind many of the colorful characters that are featured in Pixar's animated films. If Ed Catmull provided the hands on management at Pixar, it was John Lasseter who instilled the creative vision that became Pixar. Says John Lasseter,

> When I came into this studio, I just loved the heritage of this place. Why I do what I do for a living is because of the films of Walt Disney. When I figured out as a kid that people made cartoons for a living, and that's all I ever wanted to do.[25]

More than any other production studio for its time, it was Pixar that combined computer animation with the special effects lessons of Lucasfilm to create an altogether new approach to film animation. Pixar elevated computer animation to a whole new level using software technology known as Render Man which provides photorealistic renderings of people, objects, and landscapes. Pixar's success began with the 1995 debut of *Toy Story*, which earned revenues of $192 million domestically and $362 million worldwide. From there, Pixar was responsible for producing an ongoing series of animated film hits, including *A Bug's Life* (1998), *Toy Story 2.* (1999), *Monsters Inc.* (2001), *Finding Nemo* (2003), *The Incredibles* (2004), *Cars* (2006), *Ratatouille* (2007), *WALL-E* (2008) *Up* (2009), Coco (2017), Soul (2020), and Buzz Lightyear (2022).

There have been numerous films beyond that including multiple sequels to some of the earlier films. Several of Pixar's films have won Academy awards for best animated feature film including *Finding Nemo* and *Toy Story 3*, which are among the top 50 highest grossing films of all time. In 2006, the Walt Disney Company purchased Pixar for $7.4 billion dollars. Reflecting on Pixar's body of work, John Lasseter tells a very interesting exchange that he had with Steve Jobs.

Steve Jobs and I were very close, and early on when I was making *Toy Story* we started talking and he said, "John, you know at Apple when I make computers, what is the lifespan of this product, two years, three years at the most, and then about five years, they're like a doorstop. But if you do your job right, these films can last forever." I was amazed by that statement, and I was humbled by it too.[26]

Data Security and the Permeability Predicament

Intelligent networks by definition presuppose permeable boundaries, that is, structured entry points that allow users to access and contribute to the overall system design. Permeability means allowing information to flow in and out of the system or organization. The level of permeability varies according to the openness of the system.[37] The biological equivalent would be the human body's ability to interface with the external environment (e.g., breathing, eating, and learning). The intelligent network must adhere to an internal logic (i.e., system protocols) while having the capacity to grow and develop.

Today's digital economy has rapidly grown in size and complexity due to the many contributions of its users ranging from powerful EC sites to the power of social media. The principle of permeability is central to this discussion since the Internet must allow easy access points for its users (e.g., smartphones, desktop computers, and computer tablets). At the same time, permeability also means opening up the system to any number of unwanted influences and outcomes. I call this the *permeability predicament*.[27] The biological equivalent is the human body's susceptibility to various kinds of colds and viruses. It is not by accident that computer professionals use the same word to describe a software system that has become infected. What are some of the unwanted influences that affect network design and critical infrastructure? Such examples might include network security threats, financial fraud, privacy loss, disinformation and cyberbullying to name only a few. The permeability predicament becomes the reason why business and organizations spend enormous amounts of time, money, and effort to offset the problem of permeability.

Network Security Threats

Critical infrastructure such as electrical power, banking and finance, transportation, and government services run on information networks. A network security threat is generally understood to mean unlawful attacks against an intelligent network and the information contained in such networks. Such attacks are directed against critical infrastructure resulting in the destabilization of a network and/or violence against persons and property. The goal of the cybercriminal is to intimidate an organization in furtherance of a political, military, or financial objective. In general, there are four broad categories of security threats to a network:

- Unstructured Threats—These threats primarily consist of random hackers using various tools such as password crackers, credit card number generators, and malicious telephone and email scripts to access a user's account or obtain proprietary information.
- Structured Threats—These threats are more closely associated with industrial or government espionage. Such efforts are more deliberate in design and planning. The goal is to penetrate another nation's computer networks for the purpose of intelligence gathering and/or causing severe disruption. One use of cyberwar is to make a conventional attack easier by disabling an enemy's IT defenses.[28]
- Internal Threats—These threats are typically initiated from a disgruntled employee. The internal threat poses a serious problem to an organization given that the employee may have direct access to sensitive information.
- Denial of Service Threats—The goal is to disrupt or destabilize a third-party proprietary network as part of a personal, political, and/or social cause. Denial of service threats can also be financially motivated in the case of malware attacks.

The challenge of ensuring IT security has become a major requirement for businesses and organizations worldwide. At issue is the fact that the digital economy regularly experiences ongoing data breaches that affect both large and small organizations alike. The social and financial cost to both business and individual users is enormous. Consider, for example, that a major corporation like Equifax or Marriott International risks damage to reputation, including customer confidence in the company as well as its IT security capability. For other companies, the problem translates into lost productivity and operation time. Table 6.3 provides a brief listing of some of the |more high-profile data breaches including the business or organization, date, and the number of compromised/stolen records.

Network Security: Why Is This Important?

To offset the problem of network security, IT managers build into their systems various kinds of network protections. Central to this discussion is the principle of entropy (the second law of thermodynamics), which states that there is a natural tendency for complex systems (including IT systems) to degrade over time. In a communications context, all major information networks will at some point fail in their design and operation. To offset this problem, IT managers need to regularly engage in routine maintenance of the system as well as building

TABLE 6.3 Major International Data Breaches

Business/Organization	Date	Number of Compromised/Stolen Records
Twitter	November 2022	200 million user accounts exposed
LinkedIn	June 2021	700 million user accounts exposed
Facebook	April 2021	530 million user accounts exposed
Microsoft	January 2021	60,000 companies worldwide
Sina Weibo	March 2020	538 million user accounts exposed
First American Financial Corp.	May 2019	885 million file records leaked
Marriott International	November 2018	500 million guest records
Aadhaar (Tie with Alibaba)	January 2018	1.1 billion Indian identify records exposed
Facebook/Cambridge Analytica	April 2018	50–90 million user accounts exposed
Equifax	September 2017	148 million user accounts exposed
Yahoo	2013–2016	3 billion user accounts exposed
JP Morgan Chase	June 2014	76 million user accounts exposed
Home Depot	April 2014	56 million payment card numbers
eBay	March 2014	145 million user accounts exposed
Adobe	October 2013	38 million credit card numbers
Target	November 2013	70 million credit card numbers
Adobe	October 2013	38 million credit card numbers

Source: UpGuard.[29]

redundancy (or information backup) into the design of its operations. The principle of redundancy is at the heart of all critical infrastructure systems including electrical power, transportation, finance, military defense, and government services. Select examples of intelligent networking and critical infrastructure can be seen in Table 6.4.

TABLE 6.4 Select Examples of Intelligent Networking and Critical Infrastructure

- Banking and financial recordkeeping
- Infectious disease and criminal surveillance databases
- Nuclear reactor and power grid operation and maintenance
- Airport traffic control
- University and student recordkeeping
- Bridge, tunnel, and highway operation and maintenance
- Hospitals and medical recordkeeping

Consider what would happen if the financial recordkeeping at American Express was suddenly and irretrievably lost. The enormity of accurately recreating the lost data would fully destabilize the company and have a cascading effect on the world's financial markets, hence the term, *critical infrastructure*. All critical infrastructure networks require a plan for duplicating computer operations (i.e., redundancy) after a catastrophe occurs, such as a fire or earthquake. Redundancy is also important in cases where a company or organization is held hostage by a cyberattack. Consider further, the problems associated with ransomware attacks, that is, cyberattacks on hospitals and school districts where the would-be perpetrator(s) insert a malicious software into the said organization's recordkeeping and restrict user access until a ransom is paid to unlock it. Two of the better-known international cyberattack groups are the Russia-based Conti group and Hive, which extort millions of dollars from these and other types of organizations. In January 2023, the Hive group was infiltrated by the FBI and European law enforcement and has been effectively shut down. Hive, used a "ransomware-as-a-service" model, where its developers sold their ransomware code to other hackers who carried out the actual attacks. They would split the profits with the various criminal hacker groups. This type of arrangement made it harder for law enforcement authorities to trace the identity of the clandestine hacker group.

Discussion

The term *computer virus* (or virus) is commonly used to describe an unwanted network security threat that adversely affects the proper running of a computer system. A computer virus can be defined as a program or piece of executable code that has the ability to replicate itself. The code or list of instructions attaches itself to a sent email or an access point on a social networking site. It then spreads as files are copied and sent from person to person. The computer virus has the ability to hide in the system undetected for days or months until the right set of conditions are set into place. The right conditions can be a certain date or opening a select email file at which time the virus is activated. The essential element of any computer virus is the Trojan or trapdoor. In computer parlance, a Trojan appears to be one thing but does something else. It feigns a kind of ruse, thereby allowing the unauthorized user a backdoor entrance into the system. Afterward, the Trojan can seize, change, or eliminate the user's data altogether. As a form of writing, the computer virus is elaborate, inscrutable, and abstract. Like their close cousins the graffiti artists, virus writers want above all else for their names to be known.

The success of the infamous 2000 Love Bug virus, for example, depended on Microsoft's Outlook Explorer email program, which acted as the carrier, and five lines of embedded code that created an email message with the subject line "I LOVE YOU." Once opened, the worm attached itself to every name in the victim's email address book. When the user saw the subject tagline, "I LOVE YOU," curiosity got the better part of reason, and the victim paid a high price for carelessly downloading the attachment. It took only five days for the I LOVE YOU virus to spread across Asia, Europe, and North America infecting over one million computers. Office email servers were overwhelmed as thousands of I LOVE YOU emails went back and forth, disseminating the virus to more people. The impact was significant hitting such organizations as the United Kingdom's House of Commons, the U.S. Pentagon, as well as companies like Microsoft, Dow Jones News wire service, and Ford.[30] Surprisingly, it didn't take long for cybercrime experts to trace the virus code back to the city of Manila in the Philippines and a young technical student named Onel de Guzman who was attending the AMA Computer College. The college was home to a self-described hacking group, then called GRAMMERSoft. Suspicion focused on de Guzman when it was learned that he had submitted a thesis proposal that contained many descriptor phrases resembling the virus. His instructor rejected the proposal saying at the time, "This is illegal" and "We do not produce burglars."[31] Once apprehended, de Guzman didn't fully understand the level of chaos and destruction that he had set into motion. When asked by reporters what he felt about the level of damage brought about by the damage, he answered "nothing."

Despite the large amounts of evidence gathered against him by investigators in both the Philippines and the United States, de Guzman was never formally charged for the crime. At issue was the fact that the Philippines, like many countries at the time, had no law on the books for which to charge him. While Philippines lawmakers would soon, thereafter, create a set of laws criminalizing computer hacking, it could not be applied to de Guzman retroactively.[32] In the end, de Guzman became something of a cult hero; having proven himself to be a world-class hacker who affected many countries and companies around the world while putting the Philippines on the map. The Love Bug affected more than 45 million computers worldwide and caused an estimated $10 billion worth of damages. The Love Bug virus was an example of the permeability predicament made real. As one of his fellow students commented at the time, "It was wrong, but amazing!"[33]

Intelligent networks, by design, must create open and accessible on-ramps that are available to all users regardless of intention and purpose. In any organization, there are always going to be a select number of people who do not follow the security policies set forth by their IT department. The lessons of the Love Bug are still instructive today. Such individuals will sometimes fall victim to so-called phishing emails, that is, the fraudulent practice of sending email or text messages purporting to be from a reputable business or government organization requesting personal information such as passwords or credit card information. Therein, lies the permeability predicament. With opportunity comes the chance that such vulnerabilities will be exploited. The goal of the cybercriminal is to exploit those vulnerabilities. New computer viruses and online phishing have become an inescapable fact in today's digital economy.

Notes

1 Don Tapscott, *The Digital Economy. Rethinking Promise and Peril in the Age of Networked Intelligence* (New York: McGraw-Hill, 2015), 73–90, See also: Eli Noam, *Interconnecting the Network of Networks* (Cambridge, MA: MIT Press, 2001).
2 Phil Napoli, "The Audience Product and the New Media Environment: Implications for the Economics of Media Industries," *The International Journal of Media Management* 3,2 (2001): 66–73.
3 Richard Gershon, *Media, Telecommunications and Business Strategy*. 3rd ed. (New York: Routledge, 2020), 186–187.
4 Sylvia Chan-Olmsted, *Competitive Strategy for Media Firms* (Mahwah, NJ: Lawrence Erlbaum Associates, 2006).
5 M. Palenchar and K. Freberg, "Conceptualizing Social Media and Mobile Technologies in Risk and Crisis Communication Practices," in K. Cumiskey and L. Hjorth (Eds.), *Mobile Media Practices, Presence and Politics* (New York: Routledge, 2013), 15–29.
6 Gerard Goggin, "The Mobile Turn in Universal Service: Prosaic Lessons and New Ideals," *Journal of Policy, Regulation and Strategy for Telecommunications, Information and Media* 10,5–6 (2008): 46–58.
7 Gershon, *Media, Telecommunications and Business Strategy*. 3rd ed., 173–174.
8 United States Department of Transportation, "Satellite GPS—How It Works," *Federal Aviation Administration*, 2023, www.faa.gov/about/office_org/headquarters_offices/ato/service_units/techops/navservices/gnss/gps/howitworks
9 "Leading Mapping Apps in the United States in 2020," *Statista*, 2022, January 21, www.statista.com/statistics/865413/most-popular-us-mapping-apps-ranked-by-audience/
10 Brett Helling, "Waze vs Google Maps: The Ultimate Showdown," *Ridester*, 2023, January 13, www.ridester.com/waze-vs-google-maps/
11 Marcin Frackiewicz, "How Drones Are Changing the Face of Journalism in Ukraine," *Ts2*, 2023, February 24, https://ts2.space/en/how-drones-are-changing-the-face-of-journalism-in-ukraine/
12 The principle of *media richness*, which builds on the theory of social presence, argues that communication media differ in their ability to facilitate understanding. See: Richard Daft and Robert Lengel, "Information Richness: A New Approach to Managerial

Behavior and Organizational Design," in L. Cummings and B. Staw (Eds.), *Research in Organizational Behavior* (Homewood, IL: JAI Press, 1986), 191–233.

13 Richard Gershon, "Intelligent Networks and International Business Communication: A Systems Theory Interpretation," *Media Markets Monographs*. No. 12 (Pamplona, Spain: Universidad de Navarra Press, 2011).

14 Richard Gershon, "Transnational Media and Business Strategy: Global Messages in the Digital Age," in M. Mahoney and T. Tang (Eds.), *The Handbook of Media Management and Business* (New York: Rowman and Littlefield, 2020), 175–190.

15 Richard Gershon, "The Transnational Media Corporation and the Economics of Global Competition," in Y. Kamalipour (Ed.), *Global Communication*. 3rd ed. (New York: Rowman and Littlefield, 2020), 37–54.

16 Gerardine Desanctis and Peter Monge, "Introduction to the Special Issue: Communication Processes for Virtual Organizations," *Organization Science* 10 (1999): 693–703, Jessica Lipnack and Jeffrey Stamps, *Virtual Teams: Reaching Across Space, Time and Organizations with Technology* (New York: John Wiley & Sons, 1997).

17 M. Maznevski and K. Chudoba, "Bridging Space Over Time: Global Virtual Team Dynamics and Effectiveness," *Organization Science* 11,5 (2000): 473–492, See also, J. Evaristo, "The Management of Distributed Projects Across Cultures," *Journal of Global Information Management* 11,4 (2003): 58–70.

18 Mark Deuze and Mirjam Prenger, "Making Media: Production, Practices, and Professions," in M. Deuze and M. Prenger (Eds.), *Making Media: Production, Practices and Professions* (Amsterdam, Netherlands: Amsterdam University Press, 2019), 13–29.

19 "What Is 3D Animation? Types, Processes and Uses," *The Upwork Team*, 2021, December 21, www.upwork.com/resources/what-is-3d-animation

20 Richard Rickitt, *Special Effects: The History and Technique* (London: Aurum Press, 2006).

21 Lucien Formichella, "14 Groundbreaking Movies that Took Special Effects to New Levels," *Insider*, 2020, January 11, www.insider.com/most-groundbreaking-cgi-movies-ever-created-2020-1

22 Kendra Cherry, "What Is the Uncanny Valley," *Verywellmind*, 2022, November 14, www.verywellmind.com/what-is-the-uncanny-valley-4846247

23 Jasia Richards, *Robots: Fact, Fiction and Prediction* (London: Thames & Hudson, 1978).

24 David Price, *The Pixar Touch* (New York: Vintage Books, 2009).

25 Stephanie Goodman, "Pixar's John Lasseter Answers Your Questions," *New York Times*, 2011, November 1, http://artsbeat.blogs.nytimes.com/2011/11/01/pixars-john-lasseter-answers-your-questions/?_r=0

26 Goodman, "Pixar's John Lasseter Answers Your Questions."

27 Gershon, "Intelligent Networks and International Business Communication: A Systems Theory Interpretation."

28 Richard Clark, *Cyber War* (New York: Harper-Collins, 2010).

29 Kyle Chan, "Biggest Data Breaches in U.S. History," *UpGuard*, 2023, January 5, www.upguard.com/blog/biggest-data-breaches-us

30 James Griffiths, "I Love You: How a Badly Coded Virus Caused Billions in Damages and Exposed Vulnerabilities Which Remain 20 Years on," *CNN Business Report*, 2020, May 3, www.cnn.com/2020/05/01/tech/iloveyou-virus-computer-security-intl-hnk/index.html

31 Seth Mydans, "National Pride Over a Virus in Philippines," *New York Times*, 2000, May 12, www.nytimes.com/2000/05/12/business/national-pride-over-a-virus-in-philippines.html

32 Griffiths, "I Love You: How a Badly Coded Virus Caused Billions in Damages and Exposed Vulnerabilities Which Remain 20 Years on."

33 Mydans, "National Pride Over a Virus in Philippines."

7

ARTIFICIAL INTELLIGENCE

Artificial Intelligence

Artificial intelligence (AI) is concerned with developing computer systems that are able to perform tasks that imitate human intelligence, such as visual perception, speech recognition, analytical problem study, and decision-making. The study of AI owes its beginnings to British mathematician Alan Turing, the intellectual father of the modern computer, who believed that one day machines would be powerful enough that they could think like humans.[1] The term *artificial intelligence* was coined in 1956 by John McCarthy at the Massachusetts Institute of Technology. AI is closely tied to the study of decision theory in mathematics and expert systems in computer science.

Decision theory is concerned with finding the best tools, methodologies, and software to help people and organizations solve problems and make better decisions.[2] The goal of AI is to develop new approaches to reasoning and problem-solving. The field of AI breaks down into five areas. They include 1) intelligent network design, 2) expert systems, 3) natural language processing, 4) robotics, and 5) machine vision.[3] What all AI systems share in common is the ability to reason, problem-solve, and take corrective action based on preprogrammed assumptions and information inputs.

Intelligent Network Design

International business has been transformed by the power of instantaneous communication. The combination of computer and telecommunications has collapsed the time and distance factors that once separated nations, people, and business

DOI: 10.4324/9781003294375-7

organizations. We begin by considering the subject of intelligent networking which provides the technology and electronic pathways that make global communication possible for small and large organizations alike. A major argument of this chapter is that the intelligent network is not one network but a series of networks designed to enhance worldwide communication for business and residential users.[4] What gives the network its unique intelligence are the people and users of the system and the value-added contributions they bring to the system via critical gateway points. We begin by asking the following question. What makes an intelligent network, intelligent? Specifically, what are the defining characteristics and features that comprise the so-called intelligent networks?

The Intelligent Network Defined

Intelligence can be defined as the ability to reason, problem-solve, think abstractly, comprehend complex ideas, and learn. Researcher William Halal describes organizational intelligence as the "capacity of an organization to create knowledge and use it to strategically plan and adapt to its environment."[5] Intelligent networks, therefore, are the systems of communication that organize, transmit, and display information with the goal of improving organizational performance. Intelligent networks are also responsible for providing expert systems capability, natural language processing, robotics, and machine vision for purposes of analysis and decision support. The intelligent network provides three levels of functionality as illustrated in Figure 7.1. They include 1) transmission, display, and storage; 2) AI; and 3) expert systems and machine vision.[6]

The first level can be described as *Transmission, Display and Storage (TDS)*. The role of the intelligent network is to provide the proper switching and routing of information between a sender and an intended audience. This can vary in size and complexity from a satellite television broadcast to a Zoom videoconference

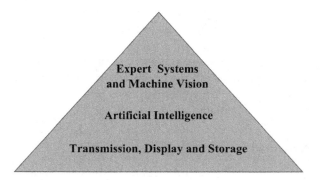

FIGURE 7.1   Intelligent Network: Three-Level Hierarchy

Source: Richard A. Gershon, 2023.

involving a global virtual project team from around the world. In both cases, the goal is to transmit information to an intended audience. The second level can be described as AI; specifically, the simulation of human intelligence processes by machines, especially computer systems. The field of AI is an interdisciplinary branch of computer science concerned with building smart machines capable of performing tasks that typically require human intelligence.[7]

The third level can be described as expert systems. Here the emphasis is on providing the user with critical information for purposes of information gathering, planning, designing, and decision-making. The intelligent network is responsible for providing the organization and its users immediate access to a whole host of internal and external database services that might include investigating infectious diseases (i.e., U.S. Center for Disease Control and Prevention) or pursuing a criminal investigation of a suspected international terrorist (i.e., Interpol, FBI, U.S. Department of Homeland Security, etc.). Depending on how the information is organized and sorted, there is an abundance of information that can provide the user with critical analysis capability.[8] In this same third level is the principle of machine vision which enables the intelligent network to make preprogrammed decisions. The network is designed to make recommendations to the user and/or take corrective action based on established algorithms.

Four Working Assumptions About Intelligent Networks

When engineers discuss the architecture of a network, they are describing how the physical parts of the network are organized, including 1) information pathways (network configurations), 2) terminals (computers, diagnostic equipment, smartphones, etc.), 3) software (AI applications and protocols), and 4) data enhancement equipment (laser printers, display screens, electronic charting systems, etc.). We start with the premise that the intelligent network is not one network but a series of networks designed to enhance worldwide communication for business and individual users alike. Second, what gives the network its unique intelligence are the people and users of the system and the value-added contributions they bring to the system via critical gateway points. Today, the Internet has grown exponentially in size and complexity due to the many contributions of its users ranging from powerful search engines to unique website design as well as the power of social media.

A third assumption is that intelligent networks do not operate in a vacuum. Rather, the use of intelligent networks are part of a greater human communication and organizational decision-making process.[9] Nowhere is this more evident than in the creation of enterprise resource management and just-in-time manufacturing networks designed to aid business process. And fourth, as intelligent networks grow and evolve, they often exhibit self-learning qualities in what can be described as *network evolution*.[10] This is a crucial element in helping to explain what makes an intelligent network, intelligent. More decidedly, it speaks to the importance of AI and the principle known as *deep learning*. By that, we mean the ability of computers to process data in a way that it can recognize complex patterns in pictures, text, sounds, and other data to produce accurate insights and predictions. But equally important deep learning means the ability for the system to self-learn, that is, retain information and past experience for future analysis work, forecasting, and decision-making support.

Expert Systems

An expert system is a computer program that uses AI technologies to simulate the judgment and behavior of a human or an organization that has expertise and experience in a particular field. Expert systems are a combination of technology and computer programs designed to solve complex problems in a highly specialized field at an extraordinary level of human intelligence and expertise. There are two essential parts to an expert system; specifically, the knowledge base which stores information related to the problem being solved and the inference engine which uses that information to provide analysis work. The knowledge base is created by capturing the expertise and experience of multiple human experts, and the inference engine which uses various reasoning techniques to analyze the data and arrive at a corresponding set of solutions and recommendations.[11] Expert systems are intended to complement, not replace, human experts. A good example of an expert system can be seen in the field of air traffic control which is a complex and dynamic process that requires precise decision-making to ensure safe and efficient air operations. Expert systems can analyze data from multiple sources, such as radar, weather and flight plans, to provide real-time decision support to air traffic controllers. These systems can predict hazardous weather condition, reduce air flight congestion, optimize routes, and improve overall airspace utilization.[12] The use of expert systems in aviation has proven to be highly beneficial. They have helped enhance safety, reduce costs, and improve operational efficiency. By leveraging the power of AI and the power of expert systems, they have become invaluable tools in the aviation industry.

Machine Learning

Machine learning is the development of computer systems that are able to learn and adapt by using algorithms and statistical models to analyze and draw inferences from patterns in data. These insights subsequently drive decision-making within business, science, education, and governmental operations. Machine learning allows the user to feed a computer algorithm an immense amount of data and have the computer analyze and make data-driven decisions and recommendations based specifically on the input data. There are three basic functions that machine learning provides. The first is descriptive; specifically, the system uses the data to explain what happened. Second, machine learning is predictive, that is, it provides a forecast of what will happen. And third, it is prescriptive, meaning that the system will use the data and make recommendations in terms of possible course of action. Machine learning can be used for purposes of medical diagnostics, intelligence gathering, and financial forecasting. It powers autonomous vehicles as well as creating value in such applications as chatbots and predictive text, language translation apps as well as Netflix television and film recommendations.[13]

Neural Networks and Expert Systems

A neural network is a type of AI that teaches computers to process data in a way that is premised on the design of the human brain. An artificial neural network (ANN) is a mathematical model that parallels the way the human brain processes information. An ANN is made up of interconnecting nodes or neurons (i.e., programming constructs) that resemble how the human brain functions. Neural networks represent a form of machine learning, whereby it creates an adaptive system that allows computers (and robots) to engage in self-learning. Thus, the ANN is designed to solve complicated problems, summarize documents, or make inferences with greater accuracy.[14] Artificial neural networks are used in the following applications:

- Medical diagnostics: cancer treatment, blood disorders
- Facial recognition in support of travel documentation, criminal investigations, etc.
- Enterprise resource management: schedule planning, tracking customer orders, supply chain management
- Financial predictions by processing historical data of financial instruments
- Automobile diagnostics: designed to troubleshoot car design issues and mechanical faults
- Energy demand forecasting—analyzing peak load times

Facial Recognition

AI is closely tied to the study of decision support analysis where the goal is to provide the user with critical information for purposes of information gathering, planning, designing, and decision-making. AI and decision support analysis require the use of internal and external database information that might be used for predicting hazardous weather conditions, studying population migration patterns, investigating infectious diseases, or pursuing a criminal investigation of a suspected terrorist. Facial recognition represents a way to identify (or confirm) a person's identity using their face. Facial recognition uses a combination of AI algorithms and biometric security software to identify people in photos, videos, or in real-time motion. One such example can be seen in the area of law enforcement where a suspected criminal's photo is matched against a state, federal, or international database containing the name, photo, and police records of known criminals or previously arrested persons.[15] A second example can be seen in the area of social media where a service like Facebook uses facial recognition as the basis for identifying people who appear in a user's digital album while suggesting users "tag" the person with a click, thereby linking the image to that person's account. Facebook has one of the largest repositories of facial recognition photos in the world. Facial recognition is used in a variety of settings for purposes that include:

- Unlocking smartphones
- Law enforcement
- Business and high-tech security clearance
- Airports and customs security
- Social media and photo sharing
- Attendance at special event gatherings

How Does Facial Recognition Work?

Many users are familiar with facial recognition technology as a method for unlocking one's smartphone. In such cases, the facial recognition system simply identifies and recognizes one person as the sole owner of the device while limiting access to others. Another example of facial recognition can be seen in the area of public safety where special cameras are placed on a city street that records the faces of people walking by and matches it to people on a watchlist database. In general, there are three steps to facial recognition.

Step 1: Face Detection

The camera detects and records the image of a face, either alone or in a crowd. The image may show the person looking straight ahead or in a profile position. Facial recognition has become a familiar sight at many airports around the world. An increasing number of travelers now hold biometric passports, which allow them to skip the ordinarily long lines and instead walk through an automated ePassport control to reach their gate and plane faster. Similarly, facial recognition systems are used by customs officials for newly arrived visitors coming into a country.

Step 2: Facial Analysis

The facial recognition system transforms the facial image into a set of digital data points. The numerical code is called a faceprint. The software reads the geometry of

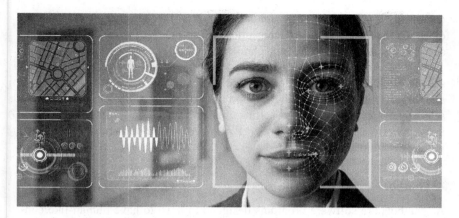

FIGURE 7.2 Facial Recognition Scan

a person's face, including the distance between eyes, the contour of nose, lips, eyes, and ears as well as the shape of an individual's cheekbone. Each faceprint has its own unique set of identifiers (see Figure 7.2).

Step 3: Finding a Match

Once a facial image is captured and analyzed, a prescribed software is used to match the image against a specific information database depending on purpose and application. Examples can range in size and complexity from a company database that contains the identity of company employees to the internationally based Interpol's Face Recognition System which contains facial images received from more than 179 countries which makes it a unique global criminal database. The Interpol face recognition systems is equipped with AI capability that is designed to identify potential criminals even through their appearance might have been altered such as wearing a beard, a change in hair color, or the use of glasses. Facial recognition for the purpose of law enforcement is decision support analysis in its most essential sense.

Natural Language Processing

Natural language processing (NLP) is a subset area of AI that gives computers the ability to understand/recognize text and spoken words. NLP combines computational linguistics; specifically, rule-based modeling of human language with statistical, machine learning, and deep learning models. *Speech recognition* is a term used to describe a computer's ability to process human language, whether it is text or spoken words, with the goal of understanding its full meaning and communication intent. Speech recognition makes it possible to respond to spoken commands while analyzing large amounts of text and spoken text in real time. One of the real challenges in speech recognition is to account for the variation in accents and intonations, regional slang and phrases, as well as people who slur their words.

NLP becomes important when considering the design of personal digital assistants such as Amazon's Alexa, Apple's Siri, and Google's Assistant. Alexa and Siri are capable of providing support assistance when it comes to answering select questions, playing music, setting up timers and alarm settings, and providing support to smart home design. NLP also becomes important when considering the design of an AI Chatbot.

AI Chatbot

AI chatbots are software programs designed to have to have human-like conversations using a process known as natural language processing (NLP). With NLP, the AI chatbot is able to interpret human language as it is written, which enables them to function independently.[16] By that, we mean that an AI chatbot can understand language outside of preprogrammed commands while providing an answer to a user's query based on existing data. This allows the user to generally direct the conversation. AI chatbot design generally comes in two forms. The first is rule-based chatbots, which follow prescribed rules that have been preprogrammed in advance. Sometimes described as a dialog tree, the goal is to simulate a real-life conversation while giving the user a select set of service options such as airline travel, medical diagnosis, fraud protection, insurance, and so on. One advantage of rule-based systems is that they simulate the way people tend to think and reason given a set of known facts and their knowledge about the particular problem or situation. What a rules-based approach cannot do is answer questions that are unrelated to the primary topic. Rule-based chatbots can only offer answers to questions that have already been programmed.

The second type of AI chatbot is AI powered. AI-powered chatbots exhibit what has been described earlier as the ability to self-learn. In practical terms, this means that they can adapt to varying conversations and information inputs. So if a site visitor asks a question, the AI chatbot will analyze the user's intent based on the information query as well as tone and sentiment and then attempt to deliver the best possible answer. One of the key advantages of AI chatbots is that they can quickly review data and make decisions based on their analysis. Part of AI design involves teaching it how to process conversational data as well as understanding the context of a person's words. An AI chatbot responds to questions posed to it by a person using speech recognition as if it were a real person. It responds using a combination of preprogrammed scripts and machine learning algorithms. When asked a question, the chatbot will answer using the most current up-to-date knowledge database that is available to it.

AI powered chatbots are regularly used in business. AI chatbots designed to answer customer questions are available 24/7. This lets retailers confidently service customers globally, regardless of their time zone. And it gives customers what they want most: speed of service, personalization, and fast reply. One of the obvious questions relates to the quality and value of the AI-generated information. How good is the actual information itself?

ChatGPT

One of the better-known AI chatbot design companies is OpenAI. In November 2022, ChatGPT under the direction of CEO Sam Altman launched ChatGPT which may prove to be a game changer in terms of its ability to provide in-depth answers to a wide range of topics. ChatGPT is built on what is called Large Language Model (LLM). These neural networks can process huge amounts of information from the Internet for purposes of information storage and deep learning. AI chatbots like ChatGPT and Bing Chat can provide highly detailed answers to questions. They can be used to provide in-depth answers to research questions. Part of ChatGPT's appeal is it's conversational tone and its liberal use of first-person pronouns that make it appear more human.[17] ChatGPT is being used for a number of applications including:

- Summarizing and paraphrasing any text
- Writing codes
- Translate text
- Write and reply to emails
- Explain complicated topics
- Write papers and reports
- Generate social media posts
- Create songs and poems

At the same time, critics point to the fact that they can make mistakes and provide inaccurate information. A related issue is the ways in which AI-powered chatbots will be used in the future. One concern is the ability of students to plagiarize and use ChatGPT for the purpose of writing papers and essays.[18] Think of it as algorithmic writing. While ChatGPT does not provide perfect writing, AI-powered chatbots are fast becoming an important information tool for the future.

Robotics

Robotics is a branch of engineering that involves the design, manufacture, and operation of robots. The goal of the robotics field is to create intelligent machines that can assist humans in a variety of activities. Robotics can take on a number of different forms. A robot may resemble a human, or it may take the form of a robotic application, such as robotic arm used in car assembly. The stand-alone robot, also known as an autonomous robot, is an intelligent machine that can perform tasks and operate in an environment independently, without human control or intervention. The autonomous robot can vary significantly in size and complexity from self-directed vacuum cleaners on the one end to advanced humanoid robots designed to perform human tasks that involve direct engagement such as talking, walking, answering questions, and more. Two of the better-known examples is Sophia (mentioned earlier in Chapter 5) designed by Hanson Robotics that provides a unique mix of AI and scripting software that allows it to hold a remarkably clear conversation. This, in combination with its life-like appearance and ability to respond to human conversation and gestures makes it unique in the world of robotics. A second example can be seen with the autonomous robot known as ASIMO (Advanced Step in Innovative Mobility), which is a humanoid robot created for search and rescue missions. It can recognize moving objects, postures, gestures, and the surrounding environment as well as sounds and faces, allowing it to interact with humans. ASIMO has two camera eyes in the head which capture visual information that detect the movement of multiple objects and determines distance and direction. ASIMO can differentiate between voices and other sounds that enable it to recognize a group set of participants.

Robotics plays a key role in the field of business process automation, whereby it simulates the role of humans in performing repetitive, rules-based tasks. One such example can be seen with EC logistics and processing centers, specifically stocking inventory, filling orders, and sorting packages for delivery. The robot serves as an automated machine designed to execute repetitive tasks with a high degree of speed and precision. Robots can also take the place of humans in dangerous environments or manufacturing processes or resemble humans in appearance, behavior, and/or cognition.

The branch of the field that deals with how people interact with robots is called social robotics. The study of social robotics is important because it represents a natural progression in human–computer interface design.[19] We empower the robot to perform certain tasks and assignments in our stead. Part of the relationship factor is built on the kinds of communication and information inputs designed between humans and robots. Language plays an important role in how we define that relationship.[20] Giving the robot or digital assistant a name, for example, goes a long way in personalizing that relationship whether it be Hal (2001 Space Odyssey), Siri on an Apple smartphone or Alexa on today's Amazon smart speaker/alarm clock.

Machine Vision

Machine vision in its most essential form is giving computer systems the ability to visually scan its environment and adapt to a rapidly changing set of circumstances. Machine vision in technology gives a computer system the ability to see and make rapid decisions based on what is scanned and observed. Central to this discussion is the importance of adaptation. The term *adaptation* is central to biology, particularly evolutionary biology. Adaptation is part of the natural selection process by enabling a person or an animal to cope with environmental stresses and pressures. Physiological adaptations are systems present in a person that allow the said individual to perform certain biochemical reactions (e.g., sweating, digestion, fight, or flight response). Adaptation, in an AI context, refers to the idea of a system that is preprogrammed to adapt (make decisions, implement procedures) based on well-defined variables. There are two distinguishing features that characterize any and all machine vision systems. First, the AI system must have the ability to scan or perceive its surroundings. Second, the AI system must have the ability to evaluate a situation and initiate an appropriate decision/action. We call this adaptation. As an example, modern aviation relies on an automated flight control management system to control the aircraft. The flight control system can control and automate all phases of a flight operation, including takeoff and ascent, flight guidance (autopilot), descent, approach, and landing. Similarly, commercial flights are equipped with a standard Traffic Alert and Collision Avoidance System (TCAS), which is designed to reduce the incidence of mid-air collisions between aircraft. The TCAS monitors the airspace around an aircraft for other planes and jets and warns pilots of their nearby presence. A second example can be seen with collision avoidance systems on automobiles. For example, a moving vehicle that passes behind a car when it is pulling out of a driveway will cause the car to stop known as Automatic Emergency Braking (AEB).

Self-Driving Vehicles

One example of real-time adaptation can be seen in the design and functioning of a self-driving vehicle. Companies like Tesla, Mercedes-Benz, and Waymo are engaged in the development of self-driving vehicles, whereby the car is designed to do most of the work of the human driver and the actual person functions more as a passenger. The self-driving car uses sensors that monitor traffic flow, oncoming vehicles, pedestrians, cyclists, and other moving objects. Adaptation and inference are key. The self-driving car must be able to safely navigate through constantly changing driving conditions. The car's intelligence center must be able to know its present geographic location as well as destination point. The car's sensors regularly monitor various objects around it according to size, shape, and movement pattern. The self-learning part comes into play in being able to differentiate between a moving vehicle, a cyclist, and a pedestrian. The car's algorithmic software needs to be able to predict what these various objects are going to do next. The software then chooses a safe speed, route, and trajectory line for the car. Therein lies the challenge in terms of the development of self-driving vehicles. It is very difficult to preprogram a car to be able to distinguish between moving objects that appear similar; specifically, different birds taking flights at different elevations and speed.[21] In principle, the self-driving vehicle can make faster calculations and decisions involving complex decision-making and high speeds than humans. But there is no substitute for intuition and experience for a driver in addressing unexpected changes in a varying road environment.

Quantum Computing

Quantum computing is a rapidly emerging field of technology that harnesses the laws of quantum mechanics to solve problems faster and more efficiently than traditional computers. Quantum theory is a branch of physics that explains the nature and behavior of energy and matter at the quantum (atomic and subatomic) level. At the subatomic level, the laws of physics operate very differently from what we see around us. For instance, quantum particles can exist in multiple states at the same time. One such example is the wave–particle duality; specifically that physical light can be both a wave and a particle at the same time.

The main difference between classical and quantum computing is that while conventional computers use only binary digits—0s and 1s, quantum computers employ quantum bits, (or Qubits). The term *superposition* is used to describe a modality, whereby quantum particles are operating in multiple states as represented by a 0 or 1 or a combination of both. This feature allows quantum computers to perform many calculations simultaneously, thereby increasing its processing power exponentially to solve highly complex problems. Quantum computing is intended to support and enhance the capabilities of classical computing.

Classical computing performs successfully if given a clear and well-defined set of program instructions. But when it comes to predicting things, computers can sometimes be inconsistent. Hence, the reason why self-driving vehicles are very difficult to construct. There are too many variables and too many things changing quickly for a regular computer to keep up. Quantum computing is more reliable for complex applications that require handling large amounts of data with a high degree of varying inputs. Quantum computing is well-suited for AI applications such as solving optimization problems, data analysis, and building simulations. The challenge to build quantum computers has turned into something of a global race, whereby both government and business are looking to advance the technology to its highest potential. The future of quantum computing will likely be seen in such areas as:

- Health care and pharmaceutical drug testing
- Space flight predictions and navigation

- Metaverse and virtual reality simulations
- Measuring environmental impact—floods, hurricanes, heat waves, etc.
- Encryption and protection of customer data
- Predicting human population, food shortages, and migration patterns
- Logistics and supply chain robotics

Metaverse

The metaverse is a vision of what many in the media and computer industries believe is the creative next step in virtual reality design; specifically, a shared, highly immersive three-dimensional (3D) space where users can engage in simulated experiences, involving gaming, spaceflight, education, combat, fictional storytelling, and so forth. The principle of metaverse brings together several different types of AI including expert systems, machine vision, and natural language processing. It presupposes a high degree of deep-learning capability. The metaverse virtual world is facilitated by the use of virtual reality and augmented reality headsets.

The Holodeck Principle

Science fiction often provides a useful lens by which to judge the future direction of a promising technology. Film producer/director Steven Spielberg once said that science fiction often provides a "kind of first level alert to think about things to come." One such example can be seen in the design of the holodeck 3D simulator found in the television series Star Trek developed by writer/producer Gene Roddenberry. The 24th-century holodeck can be found aboard all Galaxy-class starships where it provides a space where crewmembers can run training exercises, engage fictional characters inside recreational novels, relax on paradise islands, and hang out with AI-powered approximations of their favorite historical figures.[22] The holodeck manipulates 3D depth perception and spatial awareness to give the user a sense of being in a sprawling, fully explorable environment without running into the holodeck's solid and immovable walls. Let's take a moment to consider three working terms that are central to Metaverse design: virtual reality, augmented reality, and avatars.

Virtual Reality

Virtual reality involves creating a three dimensional space for the user to occupy. A VR game requires a headset and allows the player to step into a 3D environment and engage with his/her surroundings. VR is the consummate form of AI. It represents a natural progression in the applied principles of adaptation, data modeling, and simulation. VR involves constructing illusory realities out of data drawn from a variety of databases. It allows the user to enter into a three-dimensional space and interact with his or her surroundings.[23] The simulated environment can be realistic (e.g., flight simulation and VR surgery) or imagined (e.g., a trip to Mars, playing World Cup soccer). While a video game is played on a two-dimensional screen, VR invites the user to physically enter into a three-dimensional space and engage one's opponent directly. There is a shared common space involving action and reaction to one's movements. The VR environment simulates and reacts to the player's sense of vision, touch, smell, and hearing.

Facebook has become a major player in promoting the metaverse concept. When Facebook renamed itself Meta in 2021, the company was repositioning itself for the future. The quality, color, and realism of the simulated environment begins with the use of a head-mounted display. Facebook was among the first set of companies to design a first generation of VR headset called Oculus. Starting in early 2022, the Oculus Quest VR headset has been renamed Meta Quest, and the Oculus App software has been renamed Meta Quest. In a virtual environment, the visual display must change in accordance with the user's point of view and movement.

A second feature element in metaverse design is the tracking system, which relays the user's position and orientation to the computer. A VR environment must give the user a realistic sense of physical touch. There must be action and reaction to the user's sense of touch and movement. Motion capture is the process of recording the movement of objects and people. In video game design and film-making, motion capture refers to recording the actions of human actors and using that information to animate avatars and digital characters onto a video monitor or screen. Sony corporation, for example, has created a wearable motion-tracking system for metaverse call Mocopi. The new system comprises six colorful sensors that are placed on various points of the body—one on each ankle, one on each wrist, one on the head, and one on the hip. In combination, these body sensors capture human movements in real time and link them to an avatar.

Augmented Reality

Augmented reality (AR) means superimposing an enhanced digital image or auditory sound on an everyday visual display. A simple example can be found when a shopper uses an IKEA or Wayfair furniture app on their smartphone to see what a new couch might look like in the user's living room. Similarly, a shopper can apply a Sherwin-Williams virtual painting app on their computer tablet to see how different color selections would appear in a living room or bedroom wall. The auditory equivalent of AR is an enhanced navigation system such as Waze that superimposes voice directions and electronic mapping as part of the driver's view of the road. Some of the more typical examples of AR in practice include:

- During football games, broadcasters use AR to draw lines on the field to illustrate and analyze plays.

- Military fighter pilots see an AR projection of their altitude, speed, and related data on their helmet visor.
- At historical sites in Italy and Greece, AR can project views of ancient civilizations over today's ruins, bringing the past to life.[24]
- Weather channel studio effects to show the impact of snow, rain, and extreme heat on a photo landscape or electronic map.
- An AR emoji is a virtual character that resembles a person whereby that person can send a text featuring that image via their smartphone to friends and family.

Surgical Theater

Surgical Theater is a California-based start-up company that has created a VR and AR surgical procedure platform designed to instruct doctors and medical professionals when engaging in surgical procedures for the human body. Surgical Theater, using simulation techniques, is best known for its work with the human brain having created a highly detailed VR model. The "theater" concept is based on the long medical history and tradition of training physicians by allowing them to observe active surgery procedures while attending in a theater of the round. The Surgical Theater platform boosts every stage of surgical care, from critical planning, rehearsal, surgery, to patient care. The platform integrates CT and MRI scans as well as advanced postprocessing images of the brain responsible for motor, speech, or visual function. A 3D image of the brain is created that depicts a detailed anatomy of the brain as well as tumors. Physicians and other medical professionals put on a VR headset that immerses them in a digital environment, thereby, enabling the user to move through the virtual space and to interact with brain structures. It allows them to move around inside the patient's virtual brain by examining it from any angle. Such visualization power helps provide surgical training in the following ways:

- Surgeons can plan the entire surgical strategy (opening the human brain, the best path to the location of the surgery) toward a tumor. Surgeons can clearly see boundaries of brain structures and tumors, which are rendered in sharp detail and bright colors.
- Surgeons can choose what kinds of tools and procedures that are most appropriate for removing or treating epileptic tissue, brain tumors, aneurysms, complex arterial venous malformations (AVMs), or other spinal issues.

Surgical Theater and equivalent medical simulation programs help physicians, patients, and families better understand a patient's condition and the surgical procedures that will be needed to help the patient.[25]

Avatar

An avatar is a computer-generated visual representation of a person in both 2D and 3D metaverse worlds. The avatar can be made to look exactly like the person in real life. However, they are more often customized or exaggerated to look like something else. Avatars allow for anonymity between any two people meeting in a virtual world. The avatar enables a person to choose select features or qualities that they wish to represent. Sometimes, its humor, good looks, a menacing expression, and so forth. The technology of virtual reality allows an individual to completely step away from their real-life physical selves. Avatars are typically used in online multiplayer video games such as *World of Warcraft* and *Ever Quest*, which allow users to create custom characters. As the player progresses in the game, his/her character may gain items and experience which allows the avatar to transform and change appearance. Avatars are also used in online community games, such as *Fortnite and The Sims Online*. These avatars can be custom-designed to create a truly unique appearance for each player. Once a user has created an avatar, they become part of an online gaming community filled with other avatars. Players can interact with other avatars and talk to them using text or voice chat. For some people, their Avatar representation becomes a real part of their personal identity.

Metaverse Applications

When we discuss metaverse, what we're really talking about is about enabling the user to enter a 3D working space and simulation for purposes of educational training, business, shopping, entertainment, and leisure.[26] In the area of marketing, metaverse will provide more fully immersive shopping experiences for consumers. Business marketers will be able to create virtual storefronts where clients can browse select goods from the comfort of their homes. An automobile dealership, for example, would allow a prospective buyer to test drive a car or truck simulating a variety of road conditions. A clothing store would allow a shopper to try on an article of clothing to get a more realistic sense of what it might look like—before the actual purchase. Consider further, a travel company wanting to engage prospective customers by simulating a hot air balloon ride over the Eiffel Tower in Paris, France, or the Pyramids of Giza in Egypt.

In the area of education, imagine a Metaverse scenario where a professor specializing in the life and times of Elizabeth I of England can recreate a 3D setting where students can be a part of court life, engage her in discussions on the politics of the times, attend an Elizabethan banquet, or meet with a military commander in preparation for the July 1558 battle of the Spanish Armada. Instead of a lecture, PowerPoint presentation or external reading, the student(s) are invited into a 3D space to engage her Majesty, Queen Elizabeth I directly.

Some of the best work in metaverse (and more specifically VR design is be-ing done in the area of video game systems and design. VR game designers and gaming) will likely pave the way toward a futuristic holodeck concept where the goal is to create fully immersive 3D experiences. At the same time, we're likely to see the development of other types of metaverse examples and applications, including:

- Flight simulation
- Virtual surgery
- History simulations; a tour of ancient Greece or Rome
- Physical health and fitness; simulate a boxing match with Muhammed Ali
- VR soccer, football
- Simulated department store shopping; trying on different types of sports coats, wedding dresses, etc.
- VR travel tours to various international cities
- Hanging out with a favorite author from the past

In the future, business will leverage the metaverse as a way to market and cre-ate highly engaging experiences and entertainment options for their prospective customers. As Microsoft CEO, Satya Nadella says, "The Metaverse is here, and it's not only transforming how we see the world but how we participate in it."[27] The metaverse represents the creative next step in helping to advance tomor-row's digital economy. It will lead to the creation of new business models, new ways of learning, and new ways of doing business.

Discussion

Predicting the future, as any technology futurist can attest, is a risky business. One of the underlying assumptions in technical forecasting is the ability to rec-ognize the natural patterns and trajectories of technology development over time. The seeds of the technology future are in the present. In short, if we want to understand the future, then we have to understand current trends and design practices. Nowhere is this more evident than in understanding the future of AI. AI is both old and new. AI has a decades-long history while still feeling futuristic to many people. Concerns regarding the future of AI are twofold. First, AI has proven to be transformative when it comes to expert systems design, NLP, and machine vision as has already been described. At the same time, there is the fear of the unknown. One of the most widespread fears of AI is a general anxiety of what AI is potentially capable of.[28] This is a recurring theme that dates back many years to a host of films, including 2001: A *Space Odyssey*, *I-Robot*, and *Terminator* to name only a few. People don't like machines that get too smart be-cause we fear what we can't control. At issue is the fact that computing systems could progress to a point where they outstrip their human creators. AI continues to advance at an ever-increasing pace of change in what some researchers describe as the *singularity principle* first identified by Vernor Vinge in 1983 and later popularized by Ray Kurzweil.[29] Technological singularity is the law of accelerating returns not unlike Moore's law.[30] Singularity can be thought of as a theoretical future point of unprecedented technological progress caused by the ability of machines to improve themselves using AI. As technology becomes more cost-effective, added resources are deployed toward its advancement so that the rate of exponential growth increases over time. As Kurzweil points out, "Once machines achieve the ability to design and engineer technology as humans do, only at far higher speeds and capacities, they will have access to their own designs (source code) and the ability to manipulate them."[31] And with such concerns is the issue of superintelligence, whereby AI (or an AI agent) operates independently of humanity.

Other fears and concerns involve the impact that AI might have in creating massive unemployment. The need for skilled working professionals will go away as the use of AI increasingly grows, thereby displacing the human element. There is also the question of trust. Can AI robots and automated processes make the right choices when it comes to critical decision-making? Do computers and algorithmic processes have the intuition and experience in drawing out and developing the right conclusions to a problem? Also important when it comes to trust is the fact that sometimes AI and algorithmic processes make mistakes, and the user doesn't fully understand how or why. These are just a few of the legitimate concerns and uncertainty regarding the future of artificial intelligence.

It is not surprising that more than 1,000 tech leaders including people like Elon Musk (co-founder of Tesla), Steve Wozniak (co-founder of Apple), and others signed an open letter in March 2023 giving their support to a moratorium on developing the most advanced AI systems. In their view, AI presents "profound risks to society and humanity."[32] This was followed by Geoffrey Hinton, one of the patriarchs of the field in AI, who left Google to warn society about the risks of high-end GPT-4 technology. Soon thereafter, Sam Altman, CEO of OpenAI, the company that created ChatGPT testified before a U.S. Senate subcommittee on the need to regulate the future of AI technology. The hearing underscored widespread concerns felt by technologists and government over AI's potential harm. In his remarks, he said, "I think if this technology goes wrong, it can go quite wrong . . . We want to work with the government to prevent that from happening."[33] These momentary protests, of course, will not change the research direction of AI in the years to come. But it does speak to the importance of developing such technology with balanced care and precision. The future of AI technology offers some remarkable opportunities in the areas of expert systems, robotics, machine vision, and metaverse. They show great promise going forward. The future development of such technologies, however, must be done with a clear sense of high-touch purpose so that people retain the proper control and perspective in making good decisions.

Notes

1 Chris Bernhardt, *Turing's Vision, The Birth of Computer Science* (Cambridge, MA: The MIT Press, 2016).
2 John McCarthy, *What Is Artificial Intelligence?* White paper (Stanford, CA: Stanford University Press, revised 2007), www-formal.stanford.edu/jmc/whatisai.pdf
3 Stuart Russell and Peter Norvig, *Artificial Intelligence: A Modern Approach.* 4th ed. (New York: Prentice Hall), 1–5.
4 Don Tapscott, *The Digital Economy. Rethinking Promise and Peril in the Age of Networked Intelligence* (New York: McGraw-Hill, 2015), 11–50, See also: Eli Noam, *Interconnecting the Network of Networks* (Cambridge, MA: MIT Press, 2001).
5 William Hallal, "Organizational Intelligence: What It Is and How Managers Can Use It," *Strategy and Business* 9,4 (1997): 67.
6 Richard Gershon, "Intelligent Networks and International Business Communication: A Systems Theory Interpretation," *Media Markets Monographs.* No. 12 (Pamplona, Spain: Universidad de Navarra Press, 2011).
7 Alyssa Schroer, "What Is Artificial Intelligence?" *Built In*, 2023, May 19, https://builtin.com/artificial-intelligence
8 Richard Gershon, *Media, Telecommunications and Business Strategy.* 3rd ed. (New York: Routledge, 2020).
9 Peter Monge and Noshir Contractor, *Theories of Communication Networks* (New York: Oxford University Press, 2003).
10 Peter Monge, Bettina Heiss and Drew Magolin, "Communication Network Evolution in Organizational Communities," *Communication Theory* 18,4 (2008): 449–477.
11 "What Are Expert Systems?" *Simplilearn*, 2023, February 13, www.simplilearn.com/tutorials/artificial-intelligence-tutorial/what-are-expert-systems-in-ai#what_is_an_expert_system
12 "Expert Systems in Aviation: Enhancing Safety and Efficiency," *AviationFile*, 2023, www.aviationfile.com/expert-systems-in-aviation/
13 Sara Brown, "Machine Learning Explained," *MIT Management—Sloan School*, 2021, April 21, https://mitsloan.mit.edu/ideas-made-to-matter/machine-learning-explained#:~:text=What%20is%20machine%20learning%3F,to%20how%20humans%20solve%20problems
14 "What Is a Neural Network?" *Amazon Web Services*, 2023, https://aws.amazon.com/what-is/neural-network/
15 Richard Gershon, "Facial Recognition—Technical Briefing Paper," *The Digital NavigatorEG*, 2023, www.digitalnavigatoreg.com/_files/ugd/62ba16_fccfb073980a4e-6ebaccdd4fa10eddf7.pdf
16 "What Is a Chatbot?" *IBM*, 2023, www.ibm.com/topics/chatbots#:~:text=Marketers%20use%20AI%20chatbots%20to,Conversational%20interfaces%20can%20vary%2C%20too.
17 Edward Felsenthal and Billy Perrigo, "OpenAI," *Time*, 2023, July 3, 43–46.
18 Stephen Marche, "The College Essay Is Dead," *The Atlantic*, 2022, December 6, www.theatlantic.com/technology/archive/2022/12/chatgpt-ai-writing-college-student-essays/672371/
19 M. A. Goodrich and A. C. Schultz, "Human-Robot Interaction: A Survey," *Foundations and Trends in Human-Computer Interaction* 1,3 (2007): 203–275; See also, Cynthia Breazeal, "Toward Social Robots," *Robotics and Autonomous Systems* 42 (2003): 167–175.

20   Mark Coeckelbergh, "You Robot: On the Linguistic Construction of Artificial Others," *Artificial Intelligence & Society* 26,1 (2011): 61–69.

21   Danielle Balbi, "The Self-Driving Car Promise Is Going Nowhere," *Bloomberg BusinessWeek*, 2022, October 6, www.bloomberg.com/news/newsletters/2022-10-06/the-big-take-how-far-off-is-a-future-with-truly-self-driving-cars

22   A holodeck is a VR facility located on a star ship or star base. The holodeck was first seen in the pilot episode of *Star Trek: The Next Generation* "Encounter at Farpoint." In later episodes, the holodeck is used for research, combat training, as well as entertainment. The holodeck is depicted as an enclosed room in which objects and people are simulated.

23   Todd Brinkman, *Virtual Reality for Main Street* (Lake Placid, NY: Aviva, 2020), 9–32.

24   The Franklin Institute, "What Is Augmented Reality?" 2023, www.fi.edu/what-is-augmented-reality

25   Andrew Zaleski, "Virtual Reality Gets Real in the Operating Room," *Fortune*, 2019, January 9, https://fortune.com/2019/01/09/virtual-reality-surgery-operating-room/

26   Richard Gershon, "Metaverse," *Briefing, The Digital NavigatorEG*, 2023, www.digitalnavigatoreg.com/copy-of-innovation-and-design

27   Satya Nadella, *Linked-In, Comments Related to Metaverse*, 2023, www.linkedin.com/posts/satyanadella_the-metaverse-is-here-and-its-not-only-activity-6861388591730372608-OXsl/

28   Ron Schmelzer, "Should We Be Afraid of AI?" *Forbes*, 2019, October 31, www.forbes.com/sites/cognitiveworld/2019/10/31/should-we-be-afraid-of-ai/?sh=42a3338f4331

29   Vernor Vinge, "Signs of Singularity," *IEEE Spectrum*, 2008, June, 77–82; See also: Ray Kurzweil, *The Singularity Is Near: When Humans Transcend Biology* (New York: Viking Press, 2005).

30   Moore's law describes a long-term trend in the history of computing hardware. Since the invention of the integrated circuit in 1958, the number of transistors that can be placed inexpensively on an integrated circuit has increased exponentially, doubling approximately every two years. The trend was first observed by Intel co-founder Gordon Moore in a 1965 paper. Moore's law is now used as a kind of general metric in evaluating the exponential growth of other digital devices, including processing speed, core memory, and so on.

31   Ray Kurzweil, *The Age of Spiritual Machines: When Computers Exceed Human Intelligence* (New York: Penguin, 2000), 17.

32   Cade Metz and Gregory Schmidt, "Elon Musk and Others Call for Pause on A.I., Citing 'Profound Risks to Society'," *New York Times*, 2023, March 29, www.nytimes.com/2023/03/29/technology/ai-artificial-intelligence-musk-risks.html

33   Cecilia King, "OpenAI's Sam Altman Urges A.I. Regulation in Senate Hearing," *New York Times*, 2023, May 16, www.nytimes.com/2023/05/16/technology/openai-altman-artificial-intelligence-regulation.html

8

SOCIAL MEDIA AND DIGITAL OPINION LEADERSHIP

Introduction

Social media represents a category of Internet-based activity where a virtual community of users share information through the use of individual profiles, personal messages and postings, blogs, commentary, and videos. The operative word is "social" because it involves reaching out and sharing of one's ideas, thoughts, and experiences to a common community of users. Simply put, social media is about the power of networking and relationship building. Social media makes it possible to communicate in real time regardless of time zones, geographical borders, and physical space. The term *virtual communication* can be used to describe the artificial space and network linkages that connect a disparate set of users using various forms of computer and communication technology.[1]

Social media provides a unique set of communication opportunities for its users. First. social media gives its users a public voice that bypasses the traditional media intermediaries, including the regular news outlets as well as corporate and political communication specialists. Social media disrupts the one-way flow of such information by giving the general public an opportunity to comment and react in more direct ways. Dissatisfied audiences can sometimes undermine even the most well-constructed communication campaigns. Second, social media provides business marketers with an altogether new tool for engaging one's audience in a more personalized way.[2] To that end, social media fulfills seven important communication goals (see Table 8.1).

DOI: 10.4324/9781003294375-8

TABLE 8.1 The Seven Communication Goals of Social Media

1. Provides a low-cost platform for enhancing brand awareness
2. Provides a platform for periodic news and information updates
3. Provides an opportunity to meet new friends, colleagues, or clients
4. Makes recommendations based on the experience of friends and acquaintances
5. Provides opportunities to test customer reaction to a product idea or working concept
6. Performs an important gatekeeping role by highlighting select news and video items
7. Can mobilize people to action by providing information on an event, time, and location

Source: R. Gershon adapted from Z. Vukanovic business model.[3]

Provides a Low-Cost Platform for Enhancing Brand Awareness

Social media provides a low-cost platform for enhancing brand awareness. A highly successful brand is one that creates a strong resonance connection in the consumer's mind and leaves a lasting impression. Branding includes a number of key elements, including brand loyalty, brand awareness, perceived quality, and brand associations.[4] Global media brands like Toyota, Disney, and HBO use the power of social media to cultivate brand awareness by developing ongoing relationships with their audiences involving specific television and films, characters, and storylines.

Creates a Platform for Periodic News and Information Updates

Social media creates a platform for giving both companies and individuals alike the ability to give one's audience news and information updates. Television services like NBC (United States), BBC (UK), RTL (Germany), Telecinco (Spain), and NHK (Japan), to name only a few, regularly use social media as a way to engage their viewing audiences with information regarding upcoming programs and/or special event features as well as provide opportunities to comment afterward. Similarly, other business enterprises routinely give their followers news updates concerning product introductions or special event happenings.

Provides an Opportunity to Meet New Friends, Colleagues, or Clients

Social media allows individuals to meet new people as well as strengthen existing relationships. From personal friendships to professional contacts, social media utilizes the power of intelligent networking to make communication easy and accessible.[5] To that end, one of the important features of social media is the ability to add friends and acquaintances to one's contact list. LinkedIn, in particular, has become the digital equivalent of a Rolodex, complete with contact information, résumé, and the power to organize professional contacts. For job seekers, LinkedIn is an essential first step as it allows users to organize information according to various categories like profession, geography, professional skills, university, and so on. For recruiters, it provides the same opportunities in reverse. Both Facebook and LinkedIn use a specialized algorithm that generates a list of potential friends using a friend-of-a-friend reference matrix system (i.e., common index naming points) based on two or more name listings.

Makes Recommendations Based on the Experience of Friends and Acquaintances

Social media facilitates comments and recommendations on a wide variety of topics based on the experience of friends and acquaintances. Marketers regularly look for the person who not only will buy a certain product but will likewise spread the word to their friends. This is word-of-mouth advertising in its purest form. Word-of-mouth electronic communication is more persuasive than general advertising. At issue is a question of trust. Most consumers approach the general advertiser with a certain degree of wariness. After all, it's the advertiser's job to persuade us with claims of a product's superiority. In contrast, our friends will tell it like it is. The sense of raw honesty is far more credible when it comes to a purchasing decision. Whereas the general advertiser is trying to reach the largest audience possible, word-of-mouth communication is more directed toward an audience that is already interested in the product or service being discussed.[6]

Creates Opportunities to Test Customer Reaction to a Product Idea or Working Concept

Social media creates opportunities for a new kind of market research, that is, testing customer reaction to a proposed concept or product idea. The term *crowdsourcing* is used to describe the practice of obtaining needed ideas or feedback by soliciting contributions from an online community of users. From designing ad campaigns to vetting new product ideas to solving difficult technical problems, chances are that people outside one's organization can make useful contributions in terms of providing helpful information or timely feedback.[7] Netflix uses crowdsourcing techniques to improve the software algorithms used for making film recommendations to its customers. Similarly, improvements made to Linux open source software were the result of engineers and other tech professionals who added to the collective wisdom of the software design. In return, most participants simply appreciate having some form of recognition and/or desire to be part of the larger community of users.

Performs an Important Gatekeeping Role by Highlighting Select News and Video Items

Social media aids in the agenda setting process where individuals comment on stories and/or share a news item for general distribution.[8] Given the ease and efficiency of Internet news, readers now go the additional step of commenting and/or passing along a news item that may be of particular interest to a friend, colleague, or family member. In journalism parlance, that means keeping the story alive. Researchers Berger and Milkman found that two features can predictably determine an article's success: how positive the message is and how much it excites the reader.[9] Facebook, in particular, is an important driver to online news sites. It encourages the uploading and distribution of unique specialty news items that are of interest to the user. Many well-established news media sites like *The New York Times*, BBC News, and CNN receive a significant amount of their traffic from Facebook links and referrals. In short, users are especially interested in news stories shared by friends.[10]

Can Mobilize People to Action by Providing Information to Event, Time, and Location

Social media plays a critical role in helping mobilize people to action by providing information about events, times, and locations. The lessons from the 2011 Arab Spring in Tunisia, Egypt, and Yemen demonstrated the important role that social media like Facebook and Twitter (now X) played in helping to mobilize street demonstrations. While Facebook did not create the revolutions that took place in these countries, it did play a major role in helping organize large public demonstrations. The power of instantaneous communication made it possible to mobilize large numbers of people in just days and sometimes hours—simply because someone knew someone else on Facebook, and the word spread from there.[11] Facebook in combination with cell phones, video cameras, blog posts, as well as traditional media outlets like *Al Jazeera*, set into motion a flood of inflammatory information and images. Facebook provided a common space where people were able to watch shocking pictures and sometimes gruesome videos of fellow protesters being brutalized by police and military authorities. Facebook and its numerous special interest sites provided a political platform for people to express their solidarity, both within the country and beyond.[12]

Today, we see the same thing occurring with regard to Russia's invasion of Ukraine. It has set into motion an altogether new and different kind of global reaction. Both government and the business community have been vigilant in their response to the invasion of Ukraine. Add to it, the power of international news reporting, the continuous live streaming of the war, and political commentary via social media make this a story for the digital age.

Virtual Communities

Social media has led to an effective form of audience engagement. One of the more compelling aspects of social media has to do with the various kinds of online relationships that are formed as a result of using social media.[13] A virtual community represents a group of individuals who share a common set of interests and ideas using a specific social networking site. Such virtual communities can include, but are not limited to political advocacy, business, education, religion, technology, and entertainment. One important consideration is social presence theory which describes the degree to which a medium is perceived as conveying the presence of the communicating participants.[14] The social presence of the communicating participants depends on a variety of factors, including the technology platform (i.e., social media, videoconferencing, electronic gaming, etc.), visual displays, facial expressions as well as the full range of verbal and nonverbal cues. Social presence theory has proven to be a fertile ground for those researchers interested in exploring the importance of information exchange and shared meaning.[15] The Internet, for one, brings together people who share a common interest.

Nowhere is the principle of virtual communities more evident than in social networking sites like Facebook, Instagram, YouTube, TikTok, and X. As friends and acquaintances join a virtual community, they become part of a larger social grid that matters to the individual. It creates value to the individual by adding to one's social capital.[16] Since that person's friends are connected to other friends on the network, there is the opportunity to virtually expand one's circle of friends and acquaintances. Each new person and extended link adds value and dynamism to the virtual community. The following five social media platforms are the most widely used internationally. They include Facebook, 2.9 billion users; YouTube, 2.7 billion users; WhatsApp, 2.7 billion users; Instagram, 2.35 billion users; TikTok, 1.67 billion users; and WeChat, 1.67 billion users.[17]

User-Generated Content

The Internet has proven to be the great equalizer by affording its users the opportunity to generate some of the most important and robust content found on the web. The term *user-generated content* (UGC) refers to the idea that the content found on many of today's most widely used websites is created by the very consumers who use it. UGC can include a variety of online content such as postings, blogs, discussion forums, photographs, videos, customer reviews, and so forth.[18]

The blending of smartphones and social media makes the creation and uploading of information ever more easy. Both social media and EC websites strongly encourage its users to input information as well as to comment and react to other user postings. Some of the more notable user-generated content websites can be seen in Table 8.2.

TABLE 8.2 Select Examples of User-Generated Content

1. Facebook
2. Instagram
3. TikTok
4. YouTube
5. Wikipedia
6. Tripadvisor
7. Twitter
8. LinkedIn
9. Craigslist
10. Vacation Rental by Owner
11. eBay
12. Quora

Facebook

Facebook is the world's largest social network, with more than 2.9 billion active users around the world. In a few short years, Facebook has become one of the principal giants of the digital economy challenging companies like Google and Amazon with its vision of the Internet tied together by personal relationships and recommendations. The Facebook experience is built around the people you know. Facebook users flood the social network with their thoughts, commentaries, and photos on a daily basis. While Facebook is first and foremost a social medium, it has also become an important business tool. Facebook has proven to be an essential communication and marketing strategy for those organizations that operate in a world of high-speed information and entertainment. Central to this idea is that social media sites like Facebook provide a low-cost platform with which to market and promote a company's brand. Second, Facebook provides an excellent way to recommend products, services, and ideas based on advice and support coming from someone the user knows.

Historical Overview

The story of Facebook begins with Mark Zuckerberg, who launched his Web 2.0 venture from a Harvard dorm room. Zuckerberg grew up in Dobbs Ferry, New York, and took up writing software programs as a hobby in middle school. His father taught him BASIC and later hired software developer David Newman to tutor him privately. Newman later described Zuckerberg as a "prodigy," adding that it was "tough to stay ahead of him." Zuckerberg later attended Phillips Exeter Academy, where he excelled in classic literature and fencing. His computer skills were noteworthy even then, and he was offered job opportunities at both Microsoft and AOL. He declined both offers and chose instead to attend Harvard University, where he majored in computer science and psychology.[19]

During his time at Harvard, Zuckerberg began coding multiple websites including CourseMatch and Facemash. CourseMatch was a simple online tool used by students at Harvard that recommended which courses to take based on what their friends were enrolled in. Zuckerberg's second and more controversial software program, Facemash, was a rating system that evaluated Harvard female co-eds based on their relative attractiveness. According to the Harvard Crimson, Facemash used photos compiled from the Facebook network of nine residence houses, co-locating two women next to each other at a time and asking the user to choose the "hotter person." To accomplish this, Zuckerberg hacked into the protected areas of Harvard's computer network and copied the houses' private dormitory ID images. The idea of rating one's classmates quickly proved to be a viral sensation and spread among friends and classmates.[20]

Zuckerberg's creation achieved 20,000 page views from more than 400 visitors around campus and was reported to have crashed Harvard's computer network. The site was promptly shut down, and Zuckerberg was reprimanded by Harvard's senior administration. The university initially was prepared to file charges against Zuckerberg for infiltrating the university's online campus directory and for privacy invasion. The charges were later dropped. Shortly thereafter, Harvard classmates Cameron and Tyler Winklevoss brought Zuckerberg in to help finish a new social networking project they were working on. Instead of completing the project, Zuckerberg started a separate website called Thefacebook.com. He registered the domain name in January and launched the website on February 4, 2004. In February 2007, both Zuckerberg and Facebook were the target of a major lawsuit initiated by the Winklevoss brothers and partner Divya Narendra, who claimed that Zuckerberg had taken their idea in the making of Facebook.[21]

The newly launched Facebook was an overnight sensation. More than 1,200 Harvard students had signed up after the first day. By month's end, more than half of Harvard's undergraduate population had a Facebook profile. The diffusion process was immediate. The Facebook network quickly grew to include other Boston universities, later all Ivy League schools, and eventually all U.S. universities. More than a year later, Facebook began to spread worldwide. During this time, the Facebook photos application was implemented, quickly becoming one of the most popular photo-sharing services on the Internet. Facebook's dramatic rise owes a lot to the fact that it began in a college setting where student social activity is both constant and dynamic. Facebook's origins on the campus of Harvard also lent the project an elitist aura that gave it a unique status for early users.[22]

Facebook's early success captured the interest of venture capitalist Peter Thiel, one of the co-founders of PayPal, who provided a beginning investment of $500,000 in the summer of 2004. Zuckerberg had also made friends with Napster entrepreneur Sean Parker, who became the company's first president. Zuckerberg eventually dropped out of Harvard and made the decision to move the company to Palo Alto, California, home to a number of well-known Silicon Valley IT companies. Facebook's meteoric rise gained the attention of some very large media companies, including Viacom's MTV networks as well as search engine giant Yahoo. Both companies offered to purchase Facebook. Zuckerberg rejected both offers, including a $1 billion bid from Yahoo. According to Peter Thiel, Zuckerberg was said to have remarked, "I don't know what I could do with the money. I'd just start another social networking site. I kind of like the one I already have."[23]

By 2008, Facebook was able to claim more than 100 million users. Two years later, that figure grew to nearly 600 million users worldwide. The success of Facebook was evidenced when *Time* magazine selected company founder Mark Zuckerberg as *Time* magazine's 2010 person of the year. Zuckerberg's selection was the result of his having established the world's largest social network.

> For connecting more than half a billion people and mapping their social rela-tions among the (something that has never been done before); for creating a new system of exchanging information that has become both indispensable and sometimes a little scary; and finally for changing how we all live our lives in ways that are innovative and even optimistic.[24]

Facebook Business Model

Facebook, first and foremost, is the world's leading social networking site. It is also one of the most complex intelligent networks ever designed. What gives a network its unique intelligence are the people and users of the system and the value-added contributions they make to the overall system design. This is especially true when it comes to Facebook, which allows individuals the ability to communicate (and present themselves) to one's friends, family, and acquaint-ances. The goal is to make the exchange of information easy and accessible.[25] As Mark Zuckerberg comments, "Our whole theory is that people have real connec-tions in the world. People communicate most naturally and effectively with their friends and the people around them."[26]

Facebook exhibits a kind of dual identity. On the one hand, Facebook is a highly engaging medium of communication for personal expression. On the other, Facebook is a for-profit business that is advertiser driven. From the very beginning, Facebook strategists understood that advertising was going to play a central role in any business strategy going forward. The attraction to advertisers is obvious. Facebook users willingly volunteer enormous amounts of personal data that can eventually be leveraged into targeted advertisements toward the individual user. The challenge for Facebook was how to introduce advertising into the social networking mix without being overly intrusive and, thereby, destabilize the social network's growing momentum. The concern was that highly intrusive ads would impede the user experience. The decision was made to scale back the size and location of banner ads. By opening up one's user profile, what becomes immediately observable are the advertisements that appear along the right side of the screen. The placement of ads is based on the principle of micromarketing, whereby the ads correspond to the stated interests of the user on his/her profile page.[27]

The Facebook computer server is designed to track the regular posting history and status updates of the user. It utilizes a set of highly sophisticated data mining algorithms. Facebook ads are designed not to be overly intrusive. The user is invited to give a thumbs-up (like) or thumbs-down (dislike) to other people's social postings or advertisements. The thumbs-down will permanently remove the ad from future viewing. Alternatively, a thumbs-up (or stated like preference) can change the ad from a simple billboard display into a casual buzz inside the user's news feed and, thereby, into the news feed of the user's friends. A stated like preference becomes part of the conversation among friends, colleagues, and family members. Says Zuckerberg, "The whole premise of Facebook is that everything is more valuable when you have a context about what your friends are doing."[28]

Facebook has been described by its founder and CEO, Mark Zuckerberg, as a "mathematical construct that maps the real-life connections between people. Each person is a node radiating links to other people they know."[29] As friends and acquaintances join Facebook, they become part of a larger social grid that matters to the individual. Each new person and extended link adds value and dynamism to the overall network. Today, Facebook reaches more than 2.9 billion active users around the world.

Mobile Video

Regular video postings on social media sites like YouTube, TikTok, Instagram, and Snapchat have become an important part of social media. Videos have the advantage of capturing viewers' attention for a more direct and extended time. There are multiple ways to view video online, including television, desktop and laptop computers, tablets, and smartphones. The decision, of course, is based on personal preference. However, since smartphones are a part of the user's everyday experience, there is a natural synergy between smartphone use and the ability to view video content.[30] An estimated 40% of all mobile video are seen on smartphones. Among millennials, (born between 1981 and 1996), an estimated 14.9% of this group watch 10–20 hours of videos per week. Smartphones are the #1 device to reach millennials.[31]

YouTube

YouTube was founded by software developers Steve Chen, Chad Hurley, and Jawed Karim in 2005. It has proven to be an absolute game changer when it comes to online video. YouTube was later acquired by Google in November 2006 for $1.65 billion. YouTube has gone from being a repository for amateur video to a powerhouse of highly engaging video presentations for education, business marketing, entertainment as well as the go-to platform for social media influencers. As early as 2007, YouTube launched a mobile front end app that enabled users to upload video via their smartphone. It is interesting to note that *Time* magazine featured a YouTube screen (with a large mirror) on its cover recognizing "You" as its annual Time 2006 Person of the Year. Today, YouTube can rightfully claim an estimated 2.7 billion monthly users. To many observers, the purchase of YouTube is considered one of the best consumer tech acquisitions in the history of media technology. YouTube is responsible for an estimated 11% of annual revenues for Google parent company Alphabet.[32]

YouTube is the quintessential example of user-generated content allowing users to upload videos on a variety of topics and interest. YouTube is the platform of choice for how-to video demonstrations, music videos, short documentary films, educational videos, business marketing videos, movie trailers, social media influencing videos, and so forth. The range of subject matter is all-inclusive ranging from golf tips for amateur players to exploring how geosynchronous communication satellites operate. YouTube has evolved into the world's biggest video search engine, with a sprawling database of clips made navigable by Google's smart algorithms. Google can sell and display various kinds of video ads prior to the start (and during) these video clips. There is a direct tie-in that occurs between a search query on Google and a YouTube video clip listing. YouTube has become the preeminent platform for digital video ads.

Digital Opinion Leadership

In all social systems, there are so-called opinion leaders, that is, select individuals who wield considerable influence on the people and members who comprise such groups. The term *opinion leadership* is a principal idea found in the theory of two-step flow of communication first proposed by researcher's Elihu Katz and Paul Lazarsfeld in 1957. The opinion leader is typically someone who is well respected and embodies the cultural norms of that social system.[33] Opinion leadership has taken its place as one of the signature theories in the field of communication. Fast forward to the present day, and the principle of opinion leadership takes on a whole new meaning within the context of social media. There is no shortage of opinions or consumers willing to comment whether it be social media influencers, blogs, commentary, social media posting, and EC evaluation comments. Today's digital opinion leaders are looking to influence the public conversation on a range of subjects whether it be politics, technology, entertainment, and so forth. The quality of the message can range in size and scope from the professional expert to the amateur observer.[34] There are several important factors that distinguish the genuine expert from the amateur, including identification, professional training, message development, and coordination.[35]

Blogs

A blog is a website that features the opinions and observations of a particular writer or set of writers. Message development in the hands of a skilled professional writer can very directly influence the social conversation. A successful blog helps to build communities with common interests. They tend to focus on a specific set of interests, thereby prioritizing ideas and reaching audiences who are already engaged in a particular issue.[36] News media websites like the *Huffington Post* and the specialty blog have created an altogether new type of opinion leader.[37] The reader sometimes enters the conversation with strongly held views and opinions. The audience composition is relatively homogenous which makes them all the more engaged with the topic. Blogs offer businesses something that has often been lacking in their communication with customers; meaningful dialogue. Devoid of public relations hype and empty promises, business blogs provide an opportunity to reach out in a more personal way, thereby bringing companies and their constituencies together in a way that is more genuine and productive in purpose.

Social Media Influencers

A social media influencer is someone who has the power to affect the purchasing decisions of others because of that person's knowledge, expertise, and/or relationship with their audience. The social media influencer will typically make posts about a select topic using one of several different social media formats, including blogs, podcasts, and video presentations. If done well, a social media influencer can persuade others to consider a product purchase based on their recommendations.[38] When an influencer posts content, even if that content is sponsored, he/she is building a loyal audience of followers. This is the main reason why advertisers hire influencers. They want access to their audience.[39] Social media influencers can also play an important role when it comes to the launch of a new product or service.

A social media influencer's audience depends largely on the topic or area of expertise. There are different ways to gauge the level of influence, most typically, according to audience size and/or by the type of information content. We start with so-called mega-influencers. They typically have a vast number of followers on their social networks. While there are no hard and fast rules, mega-influencers have more than one million followers on at least one social media platform. Many mega-influencers are often celebrities who have gained their fame as a result of their work in sports, film, music, and so forth. The use of celebrity endorsement has a long history in the field of adverting. Social media influencers are a natural extension of that same principle. At the same time, there are multiple mega-influencers who developed their own brand and following simply by creating a unique video message style and approach.

The second category of social media influencers are macro-influencers. They typically have followers in the range between 40,000 and one million followers. The macro-influencer is often an online journalist, commentator, or professional advisor who provides regular commentary on their area of expertise. The third category are micro-influencers who are everyday people who are known for their knowledge about some specialty area. This group of influencers make regular posts about a select topic on their preferred social media channels and generate large followings of engaged people who pay close attention to their views. Most micro-influencers have an audience ranging between 1,000 and 40,000 followers. These type of experts include journalists, academics, industry experts, and professional advisors.

Ratings Systems and Customer Comments

A third kind of digital opinion leader is the power of e-commerce rating systems and consumer comments. The Internet has proven to be the great equalizer by affording its users the opportunity to generate some of the most important and robust content found on the web. The Internet and e-commerce sites like eBay, Amazon, Tripadvisor, and Bookings.com (to name only a few) offer consumers practical and applied ways to evaluate the quality and worthiness of a potential purchase. Who better than one's friends, peers and customers to recommend a particular product or service, albeit, digitally using a rating system or customer comments section.

Tripadvisor

Tripadvisor is a travel website providing directory information and consumer reviews of hotels, restaurants, and destination sites throughout the world. Tripadvisor was founded in 2000 by Stephen Kaufer, Langley Steinert, Nick Shanny, and Thomas Palka. Tripadvisor is fully dependent on user reviews of their hotel stays. In 2004, TripAdvisor was purchased by Interactive Corporation (IAC), parent company to Expedia. In August 2005, IAC spun off its travel group of businesses under the name Expedia. On its website, Tripadvisor provides its readers with a standardized rating system for hotels as well as a customer comments section. The reviews provide the basis for an overall rank-ordered rating system of hotels within a given city. In addition, Tripadvisor provides it readers with both professional photographs (supplied by the hotel) and user-generated photos.[40]

Tripadvisor has become an indispensable part of the social fabric of the traveling process. As writer Linda Kinstler, describes it,

TripAdvisor is where we go to praise, criticize and purchase our way through the inhabited world. It is, at its core, a guestbook, a place where people record the highs and lows of their holiday experiences for the benefit of hotel proprietors and future guests. But this guestbook lives on the Internet, where its contributors continue swapping advice, memories and complaints about their journeys long after their vacations have come to an end.[41]

A successful rating by Tripadvisor has become an essential marketing tool for hotels wishing to court international visitors. Therein lies the real power and appeal of Tripadvisor; the ability to provide firsthand observations and experience from those travelers who have stayed at a certain hotel now under consideration by a prospective visitor. In simple terms, consumers trust each other more than they do hotel advertising. The quality and volume of customer reviews matter. Some studies show that often, when guests explore Tripadvisor, they primarily consider the first 5–8 properties listed. Also important are negative reviews. If there are enough negative reviews about a hotel, that information can prove to be an important difference-maker for prospective visitors considering that hotel. Accordingly, most top-tier hotels have dedicated staff whose job it is to respond to online negative reviews.

Tripadvisor is free to users, and the website is supported by an advertising business model. Tripadvisor is used by an estimated 463 million international travelers each month. The Tripadvisor site provides access to more than 702 million reviews and opinions per year on hotels, restaurants, and things to do, making it the largest travel website in the world.[42] Tripadvisor is an example of digital opinion leadership in its most essential form.

In the travel industry, Tripadvisor is considered the gold standard when it comes to customer ratings and information for hotels, restaurants, and excursions. At the same time, there are some observable problems with the service that are rarely discussed. One such issue is the problem of fake Tripadvisor reviews. Tripadvisor has on occasion been the subject of select news reports that have sometimes proven embarrassing such as a homeless shelter in the UK that was promoted and listed as one of the country's top hotels. Similarly, a 5-star Michelin ranked restaurant in Italy was found not to exist at all. However, the bigger, more ongoing problem are fake Tripadvisor reviews for well-established businesses and restaurants. The importance of customer reviews and comments has made the Tripadvisor a place where the occasional hotel owner and marketing staff will post high-praise evaluations of themselves while attacking their competitors with poor ratings and comments. Since each Tripadvisor review counts equally, the number of cumulative positive or negative reviews can be an important difference maker in terms of the overall evaluation of the hotel. A September 2019 investigation found that among 250,000 reviews, 15% were found to be fake.[43]

Tripadvisor uses a specially designed review algorithm to evaluate the reviews. Given the millions of reviews that are posted, quality control can sometimes be a problem. For example, a select percentage of reviews come from the same person; that is, a user who creates an account to singularly praise or criticize a particular hotel or restaurant experience. There have also been numerous reports of negative reviews being deleted, especially if a business is a Tripadvisor advertiser or engages in pay-per-click marketing campaigns with the company. The company does not want to hurt a potential advertiser or revenue source. In October 2021, Tripadvisor finally published a transparency report. The company officially acknowledged that about 9% of reviews are fraudulent or biased, requiring them to be removed. It is a global problem where fake reviews were found in 131 countries.[44] In response, Tripadvisor has become more proactive in removing or rejecting reviews that are believed to be fake or in violation of its own community standards policy.[45]

X (Formerly Called Twitter)

X is an online social networking service that enables users to send and read short 280-character text messages, called tweets. X provides an immediate electronic gateway for the millions of registered users who wish to comment or express a viewpoint. Registered users can read and post tweets, but unregistered users can only read them. X enables people to exercise a basic human impulse; the ability to communicate with large numbers of people at a time. But before there was X, there was a company called Twitter, which was the brainchild of Jack Dorsey who as a kid growing up in St. Louis was fascinated with dispatch routing systems. Dorsey was taken with the short and punctuated emergency communication used by police, fire, and rescue as well as commercial enterprises such as taxis.[46]

Dorsey first came up with the idea that became Twitter while attending New York University. His experience using instant messaging prompted him to wonder whether it was possible to combine the immediacy of instant messaging with the mobility of an online dispatching system. He later approached Odeo business partners Biz Stone, Evan Williams, and Noah Glass with his idea. At a daylong brainstorming session, Dorsey introduced the idea of an individual using a Short Message Service (SMS) to communicate with a small group of users. The name Twitter reflects chirps from a bird, that is, short bursts of information. Twitter was launched in July 2006 and became its own company in April 2007. Since then, the service has achieved worldwide popularity. X is one of the Internet's ten most widely visited sites. X gives the user a powerful electronic platform by which to "inform, amuse or outrage" other users.[47]

As a social network, X revolves around the principle of followers. On X, the pound sign # (or hash) turns any word or group of words that directly follow it into a searchable link. The hashtag allows the user to organize content and track discussion topics based on those keywords. Clicking on that link enables the user to comment. Similarly, the @ sign followed by the user name is used for replying to other users. When the user chooses to follow another X user, that user's tweets appear in reverse chronological order on the user's main X page. If the user follows 12 people, he/she will see a mix of tweets scrolling down the page: music recommendations, political commentary, football results, and so on. A word, phrase, or topic that is tagged at a greater rate than other tags is said to be a trending topic. Trending topics become popular either through a deliberate effort by users and/or because a major event breaks into the public conversation space. This is made easier by the fact that X works well with mobile phones. X's popularity and general use tends to spike during prominent events whether it's a World Cup Soccer match, a political/entertainment scandal, or commenting on the death of a public figure. The X platform has been adopted by a number of major health organizations, including the World Health Organization (WHO), the Center for Disease Control (CDC), and the National Institute for Health (NIH). X provides a unique platform to convey health messages as well as medical alerts using the power of social media. In 2015, the original Twitter got rid of the 140-character count limit in direct messages and replaced it with a 10,000 character limit. Direct messages lets the user have private conversations about social events, news, and memes that are talked about on X have also been expanded and are now capped at 280 characters.

X Today

X has ridden this momentum to become one of the most important companies in the field of social media. Twitter has become an all-consuming habit for those working or interested in politics, entertainment, and sports around the world. What X has lacked in profits it has more than made up for in influence. X is frequently the go-to social media platform when it comes to fast and emerging news events, the passing of well-known celebrities, political and social commentary as well as scandal. It has become an open microphone for celebrities and private citizens alike. Among politicians and celebrities, no one understood how to utilize (and sometimes weaponize) that influence better than Donald Trump. His bid to become President was greatly aided by harnessing hate and mean-spirited comments via his @realDonaldTrump feed. Throughout his Presidency, Twitter became one of the main platforms for expressing his political views and policies as well as commenting about or criticizing those he dislike. Two days after the January 6th insurrection, President Trump was banned from the Twitter platform. He has since been reinstated by X CEO, Elon Musk.

Elon Musk and Twitter

In April 2022, technology innovator Elon Musk announced his intention to buy Twitter. Prior to that announcement, Musk had begun steadily buying shares of the company which made him the company's largest shareholder with a 9.1% ownership stake. He was invited to join the company's board of directors which he subsequently declined. On April 14, Musk made an offer to purchase the company, which Twitter's board initially opposed. He then offered to purchase Twitter for $44 billion that was later accepted. As part of that effort, Musk indicated a plan to introduce new features to the platform, promote greater free speech, make the platform's algorithms open source and combat spambot accounts.

In July, Musk began wavering in his decision and announced his intention to cancel the acquisition arguing that Twitter had not accurately represented itself prior to the agreement. To most observers, Musk was having second thoughts and was looking for a way out. Twitter's board of directors then filed a lawsuit against Musk, arguing that he was in breach of the purchase agreement. A trial was scheduled for the week of October 17. Weeks before the trial was set to begin, Musk reversed his decision and announced that he would move forward with the acquisition. The deal closed on October 27, 2022 with Musk immediately becoming Twitter's new owner and CEO. Upon taking over, Musk promptly fired several top executives, including CEO Parag Agrawal, CFO Ned Segal, and policy head Vijay Gadde. General council Sean Edgett was present for the transition but was later fired having been escorted out of the building.

The transition in leadership has been described as nothing short of chaotic. Reception to the buyout has largely been negative where Musk has become the center of attention rather than the company he purports to lead. Since taking over, Musk initiated several changes to Twitter including the laying off of half of the company's workforce. He has fired thousands of employees, implemented ill-advised policies, and angered even some of his most loyal supporters. At least 1,200 full-time employees have subsequently resigned from the company after

Musk issued several ultimatums demanding a commitment to an "extremely hardcore" work environment. In short, he asked the staff to choose between working intense long hours or losing their jobs.[48]

Like Donald Trump, Elon Musk knows how to use X to make himself the center of attention. Musk's continuous and sometimes irreverent tweeting has been the source of widespread criticism while at the same time making him the second-most-followed person on X. If free speech was one of the goals for the X platform, it has been the opposite for the X workplace. Dissenting opinion or criticism have led to swift dismissals. With fewer workers and falling revenues, Musk has seen a decrease in the equity value of X and a sizable portion of his own personal wealth. Worse still was the sudden increase in the level of hate speech that now appears on X. Slurs against gay men and antisemitic posts referring to Jews or Judaism increased sharply after Musk took over the site. Said Imran Ahmed, the chief executive of the Center for Countering Digital Hate, "Elon Musk sent up the Bat Signal to every kind of racist, misogynist and homophobe that Twitter was open for business."[49]

Musk now claims that "hate speech impressions" are down by a third from the immediate time he took over. As CEO, Musk released what are called the Twitter Files, which exposed select examples of the platform's involvement with federal agencies to target and suppress certain accounts. The Twitter Files revealed that the company's previous leadership was disproportionately censoring content from users with right-of-center political beliefs.

Among the more recent changes that have occurred under Musk's watch was the decision in April 2023 to rename the Twitter brand with the letter X as in X.com. Throughout its 10 plus year history, Twitter has been recognizable for its blue and white bird logo. To "tweet" someone was fully a verb and became part and parcel of social media culture. The new X brand is a symbol that has a long history signifying both cool and the unknown in both technology and math as in X Men, the X in Algebra, X marks the spot, Generation X, and of course for Musk his other major property Space-X. Elon Musk has declared he wants to transform X into an all-inclusive app that people can use for social media, news, payments, and other applications.

Discussion

Social media has become an integral part of today's digital lifestyle. Social media is about relationship building, specifically, the ability to create and share information with a virtual community of users.[50] Social media depends on user-generated content. From Facebook to YouTube, social media involves sharing information through the use of individual profiles, contact information personal messages, blogs, commentary, and videos. These and other platforms have significantly affected the way people and organizations communicate. What makes social media different, when compared to other forms of electronic communication, is the fact that it has greatly expanded our virtual network of family, friends, and colleagues while operating in real time.

As the public's time and attention have become more fully focused on Internet use, business marketers have taken a special interest in monitoring a user's search history as well as social media activities. The term *media analytics* is used to describe a form of analysis that tracks audience engagement, content usage, and other meaningful metrics to provide media companies with the insights they need to better understand their customers. Social media platforms provide a place for organizations to gain real-time insights into their audience's tastes and preferences. It is done with the intention of improving product offerings and service performance.

Social media channels have become an essential part of any digital marketing strategy. Social media provides a space by which to build brand awareness. It represents 21st-century word-of-mouth communication, albeit, digitally. Research into electronic word-of-mouth communication suggests that it is seen as a reliable source of information which can significantly affect the perceived value of an organization's brand image. Stated differently, social media has the power to more directly engage a prospective customer to a company's product and service offerings.[51] In the past, word-of-mouth communication was difficult to track in terms of potential effectiveness. It was difficult to scale in terms of measurability. All this has changed.

Social media has also leveled the playing field for would-be entrepreneurs and journalists. In today's digital media environment, it is not uncommon to see a consumer-produced YouTube video achieve the type of audience viewership once available only on television. The same can be said for social media influencers who have learned how to produce engaging video that has redefined digital storytelling, resulting in video messages going viral while building a substantial million plus audience following. We have also seen multiple examples of well-crafted news and information blogs that now have monthly subscriptions larger than *Time* Magazine and *Business Week*. Social media provides an entry point for the highly committed entrepreneur, entertainer, and journalist who has a well-crafted message. As Ray Allen, former player for the National Basketball Association writes, "You don't need a corporation or a marketing company to brand you now: you can do it yourself. You can establish who you are with a social media following."[52]

Notes

1 Karen Freberg, *Social Media for Strategic Communication: Creative Strategies and Research-Based Applications*. 2nd ed. (Thousand Oaks, CA: Sage, 2022), 3–22.
2 Zoetanya Sujon, *The Social Media Age* (Thousand Oaks, CA: Sage, 2021).

3 Richard A. Gershon, *Media, Telecommunications and Business Strategy*. 3rd ed. (New York: Routledge, 2020), 195–198; See also: Zvezdan Vukanovic, "New Media Business Model in Social and Web Media," *Journal of Media Business Studies* 8,3 (2011): 51–67.

4 Freberg, *Social Media for Strategic Communication: Creative Strategies and Research-Based Applications*, 57–82.

5 Mikotaj Piskorski, "Social Strategies That Work," *Harvard Business Review*, 2011, November, 117–122.

6 Jonah Berger, *Contagious: Why Things Catch On* (New York: Simon & Schuster, 2013).

7 Keith Quesenberry, *Social Media Strategy*. 2nd ed. (New York: Rowman & Littlefield, 2019), 211–217.

8 Agenda setting involves the ability of the news media to focus public attention on certain issues. First proposed by Maxwell McCombs and Donald Shaw in 1972 in *Public Opinion Quarterly*, the authors suggest that the traditional news media sets the public agenda in terms of what is to be considered newsworthy. The stories that the media covers can often shape public attention and opinion in terms of what is important in day-to-day news affairs.

9 Jonah Berger and Katherine L. Milkman, "What Makes Online Content Viral?" *Journal of Marketing Research* 49,2 (2012): 192–205.

10 Agnes Urban and Tamas Bodoky, "The Impact of Facebook on News Consumption," in M. Friedrichsen and W. Mühl-Benninghaus (Eds.), *Handbook of Social Media* (Berlin, Germany: Springer, 2013), 805–818.

11 Richard Gershon, "Facebook: A Business Perspective on the Power of Intelligent Networking and Social Media," in M. Friedrichsen and W. Mühl-Benninghaus (Eds.), *Handbook of Social Media* (Berlin, Germany: Springer, 2013), 375–389.

12 Jose Antonio Vargas, "Spring Awakening," *New York Times*, 2012, February 19, www.nytimes.com/2012/02/19/books/review/how-an-egyptian-revolution-began-on-facebook.html?_r=0

13 Meghan Mahoney, "Social Media," in M. Mahoney and T. Tang (Eds.), *The Handbook of Media Management and Business* (New York: Rowman and Littlefield, 2020), 323–338.

14 John Short, Ederyn Williams and Bruce Christie, *The Social Psychology of Telecommunications* (New York: John Wiley & Sons, 1976).

15 K. Ning Shen and M. Khalifa, "Exploring Multidimensional Conceptualization of Social Presence in the Context of Online Communities," *International Journal of Human-Computer Interaction* 24,7 (2008): 722–748. See also: A. Ramirez and S. Zhang, "When Online Meets Offline: The Effect of Modality Switching on Relational Communication," *Communication Monographs* 74,3 (2007): 287–310.

16 N. Ellison, C. Steinfield, and C. Lampe, "The Benefits of Facebook Friends: Social Capital and College Students' Use of Online Social Network Sites," *Journal of Computer Mediated Communication* 12,4 (2007): 1143–1168.

17 Company reports and "Most Popular Social Networks," *Statista*, 2023, January, www.statista.com/statistics/272014/global-social-networks-ranked-by-number-of-users/

18 "What Is User Generated Content?" *Nosto*, 2021, January 27, www.nosto.com/blog/what-is-user-generated-content/

19 Jose Antonio Vargas, "The Face of Facebook," *The New Yorker*, 2010, September 20, 54–63.

20 David Kirkpatrick, *The Facebook Effect* (New York, Simon & Schuster, 2010).

21 Harvard classmates (and brothers) Cameron and Tyler Winklevoss brought Zuckerberg in to help finish a new social networking project that they were working on.

Instead of completing the project, Zuckerberg started a separate website called Thefacebook.com. Before the Winklevoss brothers could take action, Facebook had already been launched and became an overnight sensation. The brothers filed a lawsuit against Facebook accusing Zuckerberg of using their idea from the original project. Eventually, an out-of-court settlement was reached for a reported 1.2 million shares in Facebook stock (then worth $300 million).

22 Kirkpatrick, *The Facebook Effect.*
23 Issie Lapowski, "Happy Birthday Facebook: A Look Back at 10 Years," *Inc.*, 2014, February 40, www.inc.com/issie-lapowsky/happy-birthday-facebook.html
24 Richard Stengel, "The 2010 Person of the Year," *Time*, 2010, December 27, 43.
25 Gershon, "Facebook: A Business Perspective on the Power of Intelligent Networking and Social Media," 375–389.
26 Laura Locke, "The Future of Facebook," *Time*, 2007, July 17, https://content.time.com/time/business/article/0,8599,1644040,00.html
27 Gershon, "Facebook: A Business Perspective on the Power of Intelligent Networking and Social Media," 375–389.
28 Brad Stone, "Sell Your Friends," *Bloomberg Businessweek*, 2010, September 27, 63–72.
29 Jena McGregor, "Most Innovative Companies," *Businessweek*, 2007, May 14, 60.
30 Xiaoquan Zhang, Rob Upchurch and Buddy Love, "Mobile Media," in M. Mahoney and T. Tang (Eds.), *The Handbook of Media Management and Business* (New York: Rowman and Littlefield, 2020), 339–354.
31 "Weekly Time Spent with On-Line Video," *Statista*, 2023, March 12, www.statista.com/statistics/611750/millennial-time-spent-with-online-video/
32 Lucas Downey, "Google's Incredible YouTube Purchase 15 Years Later," *Investopedia*, 2021, September 12, www.investopedia.com/google-s-incredible-youtube-purchase-15-years-later-5200225
33 Elihu Katz, "The Two-Step Flow of Communication: An Up-To-Date Report on a Hypothesis," *Public Opinion Quarterly* 21,1 (1957): 61–78; See also, Elihu Katz and Paul Lazarsfeld, *Personal Influence* (New York: Free Press, 1957).
34 Castulus Kolo, Florian Haumer and Alexander Roth, "Formal Professionalization of Early-Stage Social Media Influencers," *Attitudinal Drivers and Their Relation to Personality Traits the International Journal on Media Management* 24,3 (2022): 137–163.
35 Gershon, *Media, Telecommunications and Business Strategy*. 3rd ed., 199.
36 Andreas Kaplan and Grzegorz Mazurek, "Social Media," in A. Albarran, B. Mierzejewska and J. Jung (Eds.), *Handbook of Media Management and Economics*. 2nd ed. (New York: Routledge, 2018), 273–300.
37 The *Huffington Post* is an American online news website and blog founded by Arianna Huffington, Kenneth Lerer, Andrew Breitbart, and Jonah Peretti. The site offers news, blogs, and original content. It covers politics, business, entertainment, popular culture, and lifestyle. *The Huffington Post* was launched on May 10, 2005. In 2012, *The Huffington Post* became the first commercially run digital media enterprise in the United States to win a Pulitzer Prize.
38 Freberg, *Social Media for Strategic Communication: Creative Strategies and Research-Based Applications*. 2nd ed., 193–222.
39 Brittany Hennessy, *Influencer: Building Your Personal Brand in the Age of Social Media* (New York: Citadel Press, 2018), 51–75.
40 Stephen Kaufer, "TripAdvisor," in J. Livingston (Ed.), *Founders at Work* (New York: Apress, 2007), 361–375.
41 Linda Kinstler, "How TripAdvisor Changed Travel," *The Guardian*, 2018, August 17, www.theguardian.com/news/2018/aug/17/how-tripadvisor-changed-travel

42 "Where Is TripAdvisor Going?" *Review 42*, 2022, January 18, https://review42.com/resources/tripadvisor-statistics/

43 "TripAdvisor Is Failing to Stop Fake Hotel Reviews," *The Guardian*, 2019, September 6, www.theguardian.com/travel/2019/sep/06/tripadvisor-failing-to-stop-fake-hotel-reviews-which

44 TripAdvisor, *Transparency Report*, 2021, October, www.tripadvisor.co.uk/TransparencyReport2021

45 Emily Walsh, "TripAdvisor Found Nearly 1 Million Fake Reviews Submitted," *Business Insider*, 2021, October 29, www.businessinsider.com/tripadvisor-found-nearly-1-million-fake-reviews-in-2020-2021-10

46 Jean Burgess and Nancy Baym, *Twitter: A Biography* (New York: New York University Press, 2020).

47 Paul Levinson, *New Media*. 2nd ed. (New York: Pearson, 2013).

48 Zoe Schiffer, Casey Newton and Alex Heath, "Extremely Hardcore," *The Verge*, 2023, January 17, www.theverge.com/23551060/elon-musk-twitter-takeover-layoffs-workplace-salute-emoji

49 Sheera Frenkel and Kate Conger, "Hate Speech's Rise on Twitter Is Unprecedented, Researchers Find," *New York Times*, 2022, December 2, www.nytimes.com/2022/12/02/technology/twitter-hate-speech.html

50 Mahoney, "Social Media," 326–327.

51 Quesenberry, *Social Media Strategy*. 2nd ed., 14.

52 Matthew Royce, "Ten Memorable Quotes About Social Media," *Knowledge Enthusiast*, 2022, March 3, https://knowledgeenthusiast.com/2022/03/03/10-memorable-quotes-about-social-media-that-make-you-think/

9

THE DIFFUSION OF INNOVATION AND PRODUCT LAUNCH STRATEGY

Introduction

In 1962, communication scholar Everett Rogers wrote the first edition of his seminal work *Diffusion of Innovations*. This book is considered a classic in the field of communication and has subsequently gone through multiple editions and updates since that time. Diffusion of innovation is a set of theories that seek to explain how new ideas and technologies diffuse through a specific population.[1] It further considers the rate of adoption, that is, the speed at which some members of a social system accept, reject, or delay an innovative change or practice. Anyone purporting to effect change, whether it be an educator, health-care professional, or marketing specialist needs to understand the rate of adoption process. While the basic principles of diffusion of innovation have stayed the same since Rogers first introduced the concept, what's different today is the speed at which new product launches and introductions are diffused into the public sector. Terms like *diffusion, communication channels*, and *members of a social system* take on a whole new meaning when we consider them in light of today's digital economy. In this chapter, we consider two important questions. First, how does an understanding of diffusion of innovations theory help advance a successful product or service launch? And second, how does an understanding of diffusion of-innovations theory help overcome user-resistance issues when it comes to new product introductions and service?

Diffusion of Innovation

Rogers defines *diffusion* as "the process by which an innovation is communicated through certain channels over time among the members of a social

DOI: 10.4324/9781003294375-9

system."[2] Rogers' definition contains four elements that are present in the diffusion process. They include 1) innovation, 2) communication channels, 3) time, and 4) members of a social system.

Innovation

Rogers (1995) defines innovation as "an idea, practice or object that is perceived as new by an individual."[3] As noted earlier, there are two kinds of innovation, namely sustaining technologies versus disruptive technologies. A sustaining technology (or incremental innovation) has to do with product improvement and performance. The goal is to improve on an existing technology or service by adding new and enhanced feature elements.[4] Incremental innovation is important because it provides steady and necessary improvements in product design while demonstrating a commitment to brand enhancement. In contrast, a disruptive (or breakthrough) technology represents an altogether different approach to an existing product design and process. It redefines the playing field by introducing to the marketplace a unique value proposition.[5]

Communication Channel

A communication channel is the means by which messages get from one individual to another. Mass media channels like television are more effective in generating information about new product innovations, whereas interpersonal channels of communication are more effective in forming and changing attitudes and thus can directly influence the decision to adopt or reject a new idea. Today, the combination of the Internet and social media has fundamentally changed the method and speed at which information is conveyed to a social group or organization. Social media sites like Facebook, Instagram, and YouTube have taken on increasing importance with "like" buttons as well as ongoing opportunities to comment on the launch of a new product or service.

Over Time

Over time refers to the length of time involved in the innovation and decision process (i.e., how quickly does someone adopt the use of a new communications technology). Consider, for example, the difference in the rates of adoption between the telephone and the Internet. Following its introduction in 1876, the telephone took approximately 71 years to reach 50% of all U.S. households. In contrast, the Internet achieved the same penetration rate in only ten years. As a general proposition, both technologies are examples of interactive communication and have allowed humankind to surpass the limits of physical space. But the rate of diffusion is markedly different given the more than 120 plus years that

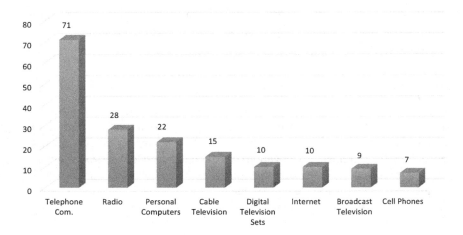

FIGURE 9.1 Diffusion Rate of Major Media and Telecommunication Technologies in the United States

Source: Consumer Electronics Association, Statista, National Cable and Telecommunications Association, MIT Technology Review.

- One challenge in determining the diffusion rate of a certain technology is identifying the actual start date, specifically, the invention date from the general introduction of the technology into the mainstream public use.
- A second challenge with respect to the Internet is differentiating between public access to the Internet versus actually having it in the home. The number 10 represents Internet access in the American home.

---

separate the two technologies.[6] Figure 9.1 illustrates the diffusion rate, that is, the number of years it took for major media and telecommunications technologies to achieve a 50% penetration rates in all U.S. homes.

Members of a Social System

In principle, members of a social system refer to any group of people linked together on the basis of geography, community, work setting, culture, and religion. The social system can vary in size and scope from a small rural village in Vietnam to a level-one hospital trauma center Cleveland, Ohio. Today, of course, digital media and the power of intelligent networking have expanded the definition of social system to include virtual communities where like-minded people share common interests whether it be political, social, religious, or professional.

A Facebook users group such as the Austin (Texas) Musicians Meetup Group or the Jeep Owners of America (Louisville, Kentucky) are their own social system, albeit digital.

The Innovation/Decision Process

In his research, Rogers (1995) discusses the decision-making process through which an individual becomes familiar with a new product or service and later makes the choice to adopt, reject, or delay its use. According to Rogers, there are five stages. They include 1) knowledge, 2) persuasion, 3) decision, 4) implementation, and 5) confirmation.[7]

Knowledge

The starting point is knowledge, whereby a person becomes aware of an innovation and related ideas as to how it functions. The source of that information can be a friend, colleague, or family member. Likewise, the source of that information can also be traditional media such as television, newspapers, and magazines. Alternatively, a person's increased knowledge can be the direct result of acquiring information via the Internet, including EC sites, social media, and list-serve information postings.

Persuasion

The goal of the innovator is to persuade his/her audience as to the merits of the proposed innovation. The consumer, in turn, forms a favorable or unfavorable attitude toward the innovation based on this and other sources of information. One important consideration is the importance of opinion leadership. As noted in Chapter 8, an opinion leader is someone who wields considerable influence on those people who comprise a social group. The social group can be religious, political, professional, entertainment, sports, and so forth. The opinion leader is typically someone who is well respected and embodies the cultural norms and tendencies of that social group.[8] Fast forward to the present day, and the issue of persuasion takes on a whole new meaning when we consider the role of *digital opinion leaders* within the context of social media. From well-scripted blogs and commentary to social media influencers, they each have the power to persuade.

Decision

Decision is about making a choice. For the user, this means making a decision whether to adopt, reject, or delay a potential product purchase. Part of what affects the decision stage is the issue of user resistance. The term *user resistance* refers to anything that may cause a person to hesitate or not go forward with the product adoption or purchasing decision. It follows that after a decision is made, one has to complete the transaction. In digital parlance, this means going online, executing the order, and completing the task. It should be noted that most EC sites give the prospective shopper the opportunity to reconsider their purchasing decision with automated questions such as the following: Are you sure you want to complete this order?

Implementation

Implementation refers to adopting a new product and putting it into practice. This can include everything from pressing the send button on an EC transaction to allowing oneself to register (or sign up) for Covid-19 inoculation as part of a nationwide health-care initiative.

Confirmation

After making a decision and implementing the change, people sometimes need a certain degree of reassurance that they've made the right decision. Confirmation refers to the process of validating one's decision. Depending on the product or service, this can include everything from immersing oneself in the newly acquired product (i.e., taking the car out for a drive, uploading multiple apps on to one's newly purchased smartphone). For others, confirmation may take the form of posting an announcement on Facebook or Instagram. Confirmation also means integrating the new product or service into an ongoing routine.

Rate of Adoption

The term *rate of adoption* refers to the length of time required by someone to consider and adopt the use of a new technology or service.[9] Some users of communication and information technology are technology enthusiasts. They are naturally curious, experimental, and want to be among the first to adopt a new product offering. In contrast, there are others who are more cautious in their approach to the adoption of a new technology or service. The rate of adoption can be defined as the "relative speed at which members of a social system adopt an innovation."[10] It can be depicted as a standard bell curve with innovators and early adopters at the front end and laggards (or late adopters) at the back end of the curve. There are five general categories of adopters, including: 1) innovators, 2) early adopters, 3) early majority, 4) late majority, and 5) laggards (see Figure 9.2).

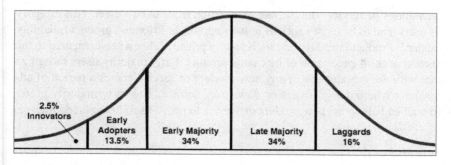

FIGURE 9.2 Innovation Diffusion Curve

Source: Rogers, 1962, p. 150.

Innovators

Innovators are technology enthusiasts. They are the first to adopt a new technology or service. Innovators represent a fairly elite set of users whether we measure them in terms of education level, income, or occupation. They have a higher degree of risk tolerance since the potential investment in the said technology or service may fail.[11] The commitment, therefore, is not trivial when it comes to a new product launch or major change in design. The motivation for making such purchase decisions can be for business and research, but likewise, it can be based on genuine interest and enthusiasm for the product. And for some individuals, the decision can be a statement about social status. Innovators tend to have greater financial resources with which to pursue their personal and professional interests.

Early Adopters

Early adopters comprise the second fastest category of individuals who adopt an innovation. Such individuals are typically younger in age and have advanced education as well as greater financial resources. Early adopters tend to be people with high prestige positions, including doctors, lawyers, scientists, engineers, and educators. They like having the newest technology or service when it becomes available.[12] At the same time, they tend to be more discerning in their adoption choices than innovators. Early adopters are often considered opinion leaders within the groups or organizations that they participate in. In sum, there is a positive correlation between socioeconomic status and early adoption.

Early Majority

The early majority represents a large segment of the general public. Early majority adopters are genuinely interested in acquiring the newly introduced technology or service. But the rate of adoption tends to be slower. This category of users tend to be more cautious in their approach. Price and product reliability matter.[13] Product introductions are typically priced higher when compared to the second or third generation of that same product. Early majority users recognize that with the introduction of any new product or service comes a period of adjustment where design issues or flaws may surface. The early majority prefer to wait and allow the new product or service to prove itself in the marketplace.

Late Majority

Individuals in this category tend to be more resistant to change when it comes to new technologies and services. Late majority individuals will adopt an innovation well after the product introduction. They display a high degree of skepticism about the product or service. They are quite content to make do with their current technology or service. In some cases, the resistance factor is due to a lack of interest (i.e., too complicated, not needed, content with what I've got, etc.), whereas in other instances the reason can be attributed to a lack of financial resources.

Laggards

Laggards are the last to adopt an innovation. Such individuals are typically older and more resistant to change. They don't see the practical need for making the change until a friend or family member prompts them to think about making one. Late adopters are more reluctant to spend money on new technologies. They tend to place a greater emphasis on the value of family and tradition. Researchers Knowles and Hanson make the point that many older adults play the age card citing social concerns as the basis for their non engagement with new technology.[14] Categorically, late adopters have less discretionary income and tend to be more resistant to change. Both late majority and laggards tend to exhibit little interest in the way of opinion leadership.

Product Launches and Introductions

In his book, *Crossing the Chasm*, author Geoffrey Moore reconsiders Rogers' rate-of-adoption model by arguing that there is a chasm between the early adopters of a product (visionaries) and the early majority. Moore believes that both groups operate with a different set of expectations in terms of the product adoption process. The early adopters (or visionaries) represent a unique group of people who possess the insight necessary to see the possibilities of an emerging technology. The visionary has the right temperament and personality to engage the rest of their organization to buy into an untested project idea. As a group, visionaries are highly motivated. They want to achieve a business or product design goal that makes a difference. Visionaries, in most cases, are willing to take risks with what at the beginning is an unproven technology to achieve breakthrough improvements in productivity and customer service.

In contrast, the early majority (or pragmatists) share some of the visionary's enthusiasm for new technology and what it can do. At the same time, they are driven by a strong sense of practicality. Pragmatists are less risk tolerant because they have seen enough examples of highly touted new technologies that eventually fail in the marketplace. Pragmatists are driven by a keen sense of performance and cost. They want to see an established track record before investing substantially. In identifying the differences, Moore writes:

> Visionaries are the first people in their industry segment to see the potential of new technology. Fundamentally, they see themselves as smarter than their opposite numbers in competitive companies—and, quite often, they are. Indeed, it is their ability to see things first that they want to leverage into a competitive advantage . . . Pragmatists, on the other hand, deeply value the experience of their colleagues in other companies. When they buy, they expect extensive references, and they want a good number to come from companies in their own industry segment.[15]

There is a natural chasm (or divide) that separates early adopters who are willing to try new technologies and the early majority who tend to be much more cautious. The chasm represents the time period during which a product launch will take place. It is during this time interval that a product rollout will either succeed or fail.

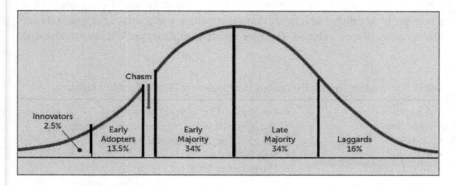

FIGURE 9.3   Crossing the Chasm: The Difference Between Early Adopters and Early Majority

Source: Geoffrey Moore, 2014.

In Moore's view, both category of users are essential to a successful product launch. But they each require a different strategy and approach.[16] Moore explains that many technologies elicit strong enthusiasm in the beginning stages but later fail to obtain wider adoption. There are several reasons that help to explain why a product sometimes fails to gain sufficient traction and later fails in the diffusion process.

Why New Product Launches Sometimes Fail

New product launches often fail because of a lack of preparation. A product launch that is riddled by design flaws or failures in delivery execution will generate confusion as well as prove costly in terms of people, time, and resources. When such problems do occur, they are often linked to the project team and the individuals responsible for product development and delivery. Too often, companies are so focused on meeting delivery schedules that they postpone the difficult task of knowing how to market and sustain product delivery weeks and months after the initial launch. This is especially true for global product launches, where regional teams need to be in place to ensure a successful product introduction. The success of a product launch can be undermined by shifting responsibilities throughout the development and delivery process.

Managing a successful product launch requires a clear, disciplined approach to product growth. For that reason, it's important to think of the product launch as a process rather than a singular event. In the absence of a well-defined leadership structure (and coordinated effort), tasks and responsibilities such as sales, customer service, delivery, and training are not effectively aligned toward an achievable outcome. A product launch failure represents a failure in execution.[17] The history of media and telecommunication is replete with examples of companies that learned the hard lessons of a failed product launch (see Table 9.1). In a manner of speaking, several of these companies and product designs were unable to cross Moore's chasm. The user resistance factors proved insurmountable.

TABLE 9.1 Product Launch Failure and the Problems of Being First to Market

• Amazon	• Fire Phone, Fire tablet in phone form
• Apple Inc.	• The Apple Newton, personal digital assistant
• Google	• Google Glass, head-mounted display
• Microsoft	• Spot Watches
• Sony Corporation	• The Betamax VCR
• Time Warner, Inc.	• The Full Service Network, enhanced cable network
• Walt Disney Company	• Euro Disney "Paris" theme park
• TIVO	• Digital Video Recording prototype
• News Corporation Ltd.	• My Space, social networking site

Why Products Fail

A product launch can fail for a number of reasons. They include 1) product viability, 2) unsustainable business model, 3) product design flaws, and 4) timing and the vagaries of the marketplace.

Product Viability

Sometimes, a product is compelling, but there is no market for it. The proposed product launch is steeped in the *Field of Dream's* belief that if you build it, they will come. A major issue in technology-driven environments is the tendency of the research and development team to drive the technology design without giving consideration to the market itself. Sometimes, the solution requires an insightful senior manager who is prepared to ask tough questions like, "Who will buy this and at what price?" A telling example can be seen when Sony Corporation was involved with the design specifications for its original compact disk.

Early Designs for the Sony CD

Sony President Norio Ohga, a former student of music, was enamored with the possibilities of digital recording. In 1975, he designated a small group of Sony engineers to give the laser disc top priority. In the spring of 1976, the team of audio engineers proudly presented Ohga with an audio laser disc 30 centimeters wide (approximately the size of an LP record). It was capable of providing the listener with three hours and 20 minutes of digital sound. Ohga was not pleased. As author John Nathan writes, "for their pains, they received a withering lecture on the folly of engineering for its own sake and the importance of developing a business sense."[18]

A new product concept needs to be clear to the consumer in simple easy-to-understand ways. The consumer must be able to grasp the immediate benefits of acquiring the product or service. If the product requires a lot of explanation and individualized training, it will flounder in terms of consumer acceptance. In the best sense, a successful product launch clearly shows how the product/service will satisfy an unfilled need.

Unsustainable Business Model

A successful product launch requires a business model that is sustainable over time. The business logic has to be clear and maintainable. According to researchers Osterwalder and Pigneur, a business model describes the rationale of how an organization creates and delivers value to both the end consumer and itself.[19]

Regardless of how innovative a company might be, if the resource/infrastructure demands are too costly, the product launch will falter. It sometimes happens that a product or service concept is right in principle but is far ahead of the curve in terms of practical application. Being first to market can sometimes be a major challenge as there are a number of technical, financial, and regulatory challenges that must be overcome to be successful.

Webvan

In 1997, Louis Borders, a successful book retailing entrepreneur, saw an opportunity to modernize American grocery retailing. Borders believed that automated warehouses combined with computerized scheduling would provide the basis for a virtual supermarket. It was a very compelling idea for the busy, working professional. It could mean fewer weekly trips to the grocery store and/or waiting in long lines at the checkout counter. Webvan was launched in June 1999, in the San Francisco Bay area. The company offered customers access to 24/7 online grocery shopping via the Internet. The company promised to deliver orders within a 30-minute window. Webvan represented the quintessential EC company of the future.

Louis Borders was able to attract financing from a number of capital investment firms, including Benchmark Capital, Sequoia Capital, and Goldman Sachs. One important consideration in determining business model sustainability is revenue in relation to capital investment and margins. Webvan's initial capital investments were huge. The company's 300,000-square-foot distribution centers would require a highly sophisticated supply chain management (SCM) system. To be successful, Webvan would need a large number of customers spending considerable sums of money per order or the company would have to achieve significant distribution efficiencies. Supermarket retail stores work on very thin sales margins. For starters, Webvan lacked the buying power of Wal-Mart, Kroger, and other large grocery chains. Without the savings realized by its competitors, Webvan was unable to keep its food costs low.[20] The challenge, therefore, was whether customers would be willing to pay more for convenience. If not, then savings would have to be realized by achieving cost-efficiencies in distribution. And then, of course, there were the intangibles. Would consumers trust Webvan to select and deliver fresh produce? If a certain food item was unavailable, how much would it affect the week's dinner menu?

By the end of 2000, Webvan's San Francisco customer list had grown to some 47,000 households, with fourth-quarter sales totaling $9.1 million. But customer orders averaged only $81, far less than the $103 Webvan's plans required. As noted earlier, Webvan needed either huge sales volumes or significant operating efficiencies to make its business model work. What became apparent is that the process of fulfilling customer orders was particularly expensive. In a regular supermarket setting, the customer does this work at no cost to the retailer. Webvan charged a $4.95 delivery fee for orders under $50, which later increased to $75 in November 2000, as delivery expenses exceeded budgets. In time, it became clear that cost-effective grocery delivery can work only in densely populated areas that don't require expensive and complicated distribution systems. One can achieve business sustainability, if it's a matter of having a minimum paid worker packing groceries and riding elevators in a tightly populated area. All this changes when distribution costs involve running trucks to the suburbs and paying delivery drivers $25 to $35 an hour.

By July 2001, after just two years in business, Webvan had spent most of its $1.2 billion in outside capital investment. In the meantime, the pressure to grow fast caused the company to launch equivalent direct-to-home grocery delivery in other cities, including Seattle, Chicago, and Atlanta with plans to expand further. Each city's capital requirement was well over $50 million in start-up costs.[21] While on the surface Webvan appeared to be a burgeoning EC company, the reality is that it was a very traditional company with a highly complex infrastructure and associated set of costs. In practical terms, Webvan was susceptible to razor-thin profit margins, high warehouse costs, an expensive fleet of vans, and distribution requirements that proved unsustainable. Webvan closed its doors on July 9, 2001.

Being the first to introduce a new product or service is not always an advantage. There is a learning process, as in the case of Webvan, that required the company start-up to overcome multiple logistical, financial, and technical challenges. The takeaway lessons from Webvan proved highly instructive for future companies wishing to engage in direct-to-home grocery delivery. In time, of course, new direct-to-home grocery delivery services would prove highly successful, including Walmart + InHome grocery, Instacart, Shipt, and Amazon Fresh to name only a few.

Product Design Flaws

A product that is introduced before it's ready can create a whole host of problems for the sponsoring company. There is nothing worse to a manufacturer's reputation than to be subjected to a product recall because of a design flaw in the planning and design process. Such design flaws were either not taken into account or ignored prior to the product launch. In the case of software launches, the problem translates in having to issue multiple software upgrades and patches, thereby undermining public confidence in the company and its product design. Computer manufacturer HP, for example, was willing and ready to compete with the Apple iPad when it released its own HP Touchpad in 2011. The product launch of the HP Touchpad tablet was a huge event with expensive advertising. However, it soon became clear that HP had rushed the release of its product with a poor operating system and lots of bugs. Stores soon faced excess inventory and were forced to slash prices. HP eventually discontinued the Touchpad and took a loss of hundreds of millions of dollars.

Timing and the Vagaries of the Marketplace

Despite a company's best planning efforts, a new product launch is sometimes subject to the vagaries of the marketplace. This is the proverbial joker in the deck; "we didn't see it coming." A failure to fully understand consumer tastes, the emergence of rival technology, or the anticompetitive behavior by one's rivals can undermine the best-laid plans. The ability to design and implement a strategy quickly is essential in a global, fast-paced business environment. Being first to market is both an opportunity and a problem. On the one hand, being first to market can prove to be an important strategic advantage as evidenced by the successful debut of Home Box Office, the Apple iPhone, and Netflix. In each case, the said companies were able to traverse Moore's chasm and establish a sizeable lead in their respective market before the next, nearest competitor was able to grab a foothold. On the other hand, being first to market is not without some risks as evidenced by the Webvan example. A company that tries to introduce a product, (including a possible change in technical/industry standards) before the market is ready, can wind up spending a lot of time and money and ultimately fail.

TiVo

TiVo is a digital video recorder (DVR) that was developed by Jim Barton and Mike Ramsey and introduced to the public at the Consumers Electronic Show in 1999. TiVo provides an on-screen guide of scheduled television programs, whose features include the ability to record selected programs for later viewing. The value proposition for the consumer is the ability to record one's favorite television programs for later viewing, including the ability to skip over commercial TV ads.[22] TiVo includes a *wish list* function that allows users to find and record shows that match their interests by title, category, or keyword. TiVo soon proved to be the quintessential disruptive technology. At issue was the fact that the traditional broadcast advertising business model was now being challenged by a technology that would enable viewers to effectively skip over commercials. TiVo and the principle of digital video recording sent shock waves throughout the industry.

What distinguished TiVo from the previous generation's VCR recording technology was that it was software based, enabling the user to simultaneously record, playback, and fast forward television programs. The second key attribute was the program guide itself which drove the function of the machine.[23] TiVo made a name for itself following its initial product launch by selling its devices at reduced cost while making up the difference in subscription fees. For TiVo to work, the company had to work in concert with multichannel television service providers like cable television, satellite TV, and later telephone-based IPTV systems. For a time, TiVo functioned as a stand-alone service with a steadily increasing monthly subscription fee. Over time, Americas' multichannel television service providers began to offer a stripped-down version of TiVo. In doing so, they effectively bypassed the need for TiVo making the latter a redundant service. This, in turn, begs the obvious question, why would a consumer elect to pay for TiVo when he/she can obtain the same basic recording functions from a cable operator at a reduced cost? The problem was made worse by the consumer shift to Over-the-Top video streaming technology that has greatly reduced cable television subscriptions. Today, digital video recording has become a mainstream service feature offered by all multichannel television service providers leaving TiVo unable to share in the success of the market it once helped create.[24]

Creative Destruction in the Digital Age

Change is never easy. Change is especially difficult when a start-up company (and technology) is poised to displace a well-established business. The launch of a new product or service routinely triggers suspicion and user resistance by those immediate industries and people who are directly affected by its introduction.

User Resistance

User resistance is the lack of willingness to try a new product, technology, or service. For the product innovator, it's important to understand the reasons why users are sometimes resistant to the introduction of a new product or service (or product change). Such reasons can include 1) the fear of change, 2) a lack of trust, and 3) wanting to stay with what's familiar. It is important to note that user resistance in one area does not necessarily translate into other areas.

Fear of Change

People often fear what they don't know how to do. This is particularly true when it comes to information technology. There are numerous documented examples of workers employed by traditional manufacturers where long-standing employees are resistant to the idea of learning new IT skills that will enable them to do their jobs better. At issue is the fear of being unable to keep up. In some cases, the requirements for change may mean having to learn certain types of math and/or basic programming skills that appear to be beyond the comprehension of the employee. The fear of change also applies to users who are challenged by the unfamiliar. Sometimes, the simple downloading of software can be a major barrier for the non-technically inclined person. The fear of making a mistake can paralyze the learning process. The airlines recognized this when they introduced self-check-in at airports in the late 1990s. To offset user resistance, airline personnel were stationed nearby to walk customers through the check-in line.

Lack of Trust

This issue is particularly true when it comes to e-commerce transactions. For some users, the entering of personal data (i.e., social security and credit card information) can be very challenging. Such users fear that the system will not execute the transaction correctly and that a mistake may occur. Or there is a fear that such information is susceptible to a data breach. In February 2020, for example, the personal information involving an estimated 10.6 million users who stayed at MGM Resorts hotels were posted online to a hacking forum. The leaked information included full names, phone numbers, dates of birth, home addresses, and phone numbers. This, of course, is a user's worst nightmare. Another example can be seen in the 2013 highly publicized computer hacking of consumer credit card data at Target department stores in the United States. The data breach that affected Target cost the company an estimated $148 million in lost sales as well as recovery costs. For these and other companies, revenue loss was nothing compared to the loss in customer confidence.

Wanting to Stay With What's Familiar

People are often creatures of habit. They tend to stay with what's familiar to them. This is particularly true when it comes to information technology. A typical example is the person who becomes fully comfortable with a certain type of phone, computer, or home entertainment system. They will go to extraordinary lengths to preserve the current setup and not be forced to change or upgrade to the next generation version or software update. When a software company releases a new version or update, it's done with improving the users' experience in mind, but that improvement is only realized if users actually apply the update.

For the user, the intended benefits are not always clear and in some cases may make the device slower or less responsive because the existing operating system is unable to fully support the change.

The Sharing Economy

Start-up companies like Vacation Rental by Owners, Uber, and Airbnb are examples of what some observers have called *the sharing economy*. Such peer-to-peer networks allow users to harness the power and immediacy of the Internet with the goal of monetizing primary assets (i.e., cars, homes, apartments/spare bedrooms).[25] The sharing economy is made possible by the fact that while we may distrust strangers, we totally trust people. The trust factor becomes practical and real when everyday users can access the ratings/comments section found in EC services like Tripadvisor, eBay, and Amazon to name only a few.[26] And for some, the sharing economy is more trustworthy than government or large business. It is not surprising, therefore, that start-up companies like Uber and Airbnb have become a lightning rod for criticism by challenging the well-established business models of the taxi and hotel industries respectively. Cities throughout the world are grappling with how to handle the world of technology-enabled digital services.

Uber

Uber is a mobile transportation network company based in San Francisco, California, that connects passengers with drivers of vehicles for hire and ride-sharing services. Uber was founded as UberCab by Garrett Camp and Travis Kalanick in 2009. Uber was premised on a single idea: "What if you could request a ride from your phone?" The Uber mobile app service was officially launched in San Francisco in June 2010.[27] Users are equipped with a mobile app that provides real-time information of drivers for hire. Cars are reserved by sending a text message or by using a mobile app. Using the app, customers are provided a brief profile of the driver, overall ratings, as well as track their reserved car's location. Once the ride is secured, the cost is automatically charged to a credit card on the user account. The Uber global ride-sharing app proved to be a major game changer by disrupting taxi and limousine services worldwide.

Ten years after its founding, Uber went public on May 9, 2019. Uber's IPO was one of the most highly anticipated of the year, and the company was valued as high as $120 billion by Wall Street investors. Best efforts aside, Uber made history with the biggest first-day dollar loss in U.S. history. Since then, Uber has steadily become profitable evidenced by its continued growth internationally.

The Uber ride-sharing services can be found in 72 countries around the world. It should be noted that in 2017, Uber's corporate culture became the focus of public attention for having created a hostile and sexist work environment and became the focus of a company-wide investigation. CEO Travis Kalanick was forced to resign, along with more than 20 other employees.

That said, Uber has proven to be a major game changer in terms of re-defining ride-sharing services. The popular ride-sharing service has directly affected the worldwide taxi industry by offering lower prices, faster and more quality service, as well as a higher degree of transparency in terms of choosing drivers and determining fares. Uber provides convenience and is cashless. Instead of chasing down a taxi on a street, or calling and waiting for a car service, users can hail a car from any location and have it arrive in minutes. This, in turn, has forced the taxi industry to take on some of these same features for the benefit of its customers.

Airbnb

Airbnb was founded by Brian Chesky, Joe Gebbia, and Nathan Blecharczyk in San Francisco in August 2008 where they became one of the first peer-to-peer services that specialized in housing accommodations. The founders were traveling to a conference in 2007 but couldn't pay for their housing, so two of the founders decided to rent out part of their apartments to help pay for the cost of the trip. This sparked their idea. What if you could rent out your apartment or room to the public listing such information on the Internet or one's mobile phone? Airbnb allows users to access the company's website, create a profile listing, and then rent out a spare bedroom or an entire apartment. The profile includes a brief description of the lodging facility, recommendations by other users, reviews by previous guests, as well as a response rating and private messaging system.

As Airbnb has become more fully established, there has been a steady shift in the reasons why people rent room space online. Initially, a large segment of Airbnb users were tourists in foreign cities who wanted a more authentic and less expensive form of lodging in a local neighborhood setting. More of today's bookings now include business travelers as well as conference attendees. Many of Airbnb guests like being within walking distance to an area's better restaurants and main attractions. Airbnb makes it possible to rent a room, a home or even a castle for a night or longer. According to Airbnb's latest data, the company has more than 5.6 million listings worldwide representing 220 countries including an estimated 100,000 plus cities and towns.[28]

Digital Diffusion Meets User Resistance

In the years following Uber's launch, thousands of European taxi drivers have engaged in public protests against Uber in cities across the continent, including London, Paris, Berlin, and Madrid. Their complaint centers on the fact that private taxi services like Uber do not adhere to the same licensing requirements, tests and costs that regular taxi drivers are expected to follow. While most major countries and cities have adapted and accommodate Uber (and equivalent ride-sharing services), some countries have imposed different kinds of regulations and bans. As an example, the Uber ride-sharing service is not allowed in Belgium. Whereas, in countries like Ireland and Greece, Uber service is available, but the only drivers who perform such services are licensed taxi drivers.

Similarly, Airbnb has also come under a lot of scrutiny given the fact that room and apartment sharing services effectively bypass the need for hotel lodging. Critics of Airbnb point to the fact that it is an unregulated industry where the host apartment may not be committed to the basics of the hospitality industry. They are quick to point out that so much depends on the unique situation and readiness of the host in terms of furniture, level of cleanliness, security, and so forth. It can sometimes happen the person renting an apartment might find themselves in a place lacking in the most basic amenities, including little or no furniture, no linens and towels, and so on. The Airbnb user evaluation system has gone a long way to offset this problem.

The opposite problem is equally true. Sometimes, an unruly guest can cause a lot of problems for the host, but more importantly it is the building owner who is ultimately responsible for a guest who misbehaves. Cities like San Francisco, London, Paris, Barcelona, and New York have specific ordinances regarding the subletting of apartments for short-term use. Many smaller communities and neighborhoods, likewise, have concerns about neighbors who sublet a house or apartment for short periods of time. The concern centers on noisy, temporary guests entering and leaving at all hours of the day, loud music, smoking on porches, or finding garbage cans overflowing when they leave. In some cases, people who rent out space on Airbnb are facing fines and restrictions by various city planning and housing authorities.

The sharing economy has set into motion a unique value proposition for the consumer based on cost and convenience. Start-up companies like Uber and Airbnb are facing user resistance on a number of fronts, including entrenched business interests and outmoded regulatory systems that are unable to keep up with the pace of change. The scale of protests underscores the extent to which the Internet and digital lifestyle are challenging two of the world's most regulated industries. Such are the growing pains of these new emerging industries in today's fast-paced digital economy.

The Tipping Point

Much has been written about the profound effect of the *tipping point*, the moment at which a product innovation catches fire—spreading wildly through the population. Writer Malcolm Gladwell identifies three key factors that are central in determining whether a particular product idea will expand into wide scale popularity. Gladwell's discussion includes 1) the stickiness factor, 2) law of the few, and 3) the power of context.[29] The stickiness factor is an intangible but very important idea. Does the proposed idea elicit curiosity and fascination? Consider, for example, the idea of creating a theme park built around a magic kingdom or city of tomorrow with period architecture, design, and characters. One important feature of any great innovation is that it begins with a compelling idea. To use the colloquial, "it takes our breadth away."

The law of the few contends that every great innovation needs a chief spokesperson and advocate. Gladwell describes such individuals as "Mavens, Salesmen and Connectors."[30] They become the champion for the new product concept. Part of that effort involves making the right connections with various designers, marketers, and outside investors who will help advance the product launch. When Steve Jobs pitched the iPhone at the 2007 Macworld exposition, he wanted to engage the audience in the iPhone's stickiness factor. Similarly, OpenAI's Sam Altman has had to elicit support for the launch of the company's ChatGPT AI natural language processing tool. In both cases, Steve Jobs and Sam Altman served as the salesmen and connectors for their respective product introductions.

Gladwell defines the term *context* very broadly, discussing the implications of how timing and circumstances are a major consideration in whether a new product idea will be successfully received. Is the public ready? Diffusion of innovation depends on the readiness and receptivity of the group, neighborhood, or community. In 1964, AT&T test marketed a first-generation video telephone service called *Picturephone*. It was introduced at the 1964 New York World's Fair as well as Disneyland in California. The public was invited to place calls between special exhibits at both locations. In 1970, AT&T's commercial Picturephone service debuted in downtown Pittsburgh. The company's senior leadership was fully convinced that a million Picturephone sets would be in use by 1980. It never happened. The general public was not ready to accept this otherwise highly intrusive medium of communication into the privacy of one's home. People did not want to be on display. The context for using video was not there. In contrast, today we routinely engage in international Zoom and Webex calls via our laptop computers and smartphones. Organizations regularly schedule videoconferences and webinars for the purpose of sharing information. And the posting of pictures and videos on social media has become a daily occurrence. In sum, context is everything. We have become a video savvy generation of users.

Discussion

The launch of a new product or service requires a unique type of storytelling. In launching a new product or service, the astute marketer recognizes that one important essential for any product launch is to show how the soon-to-be product or service will make a difference in the lives of the user. Specifically, how will the product, service, or idea prove beneficial to the user and/or provide a solution to a legitimate problem?[31] The focus should be on promoting one or two product features (or issue ideas) that people really care about. The message should be simple, clear, and compelling. Digital storytelling is greatly aided by the power of digital opinion leaders. If done well, digital opinion leaders can legitimize and speed up the diffusion process. Nowhere is this more evident than when a product or an idea goes viral on the Internet.

The Tipping Point and Going Viral

Viral marketing is the Internet version of word-of-mouth communication. It involves creating a website, posting a message on one or more social media sites, and/or uploading a video. The message becomes so infectious that consumers will want to pass it along to their friends. Because the content comes from a friend, the receiver is more likely to pay attention and use it to make informed purchasing decisions while passing it along to others voluntarily. Viral marketing often uses existing social networks, such as Facebook, Instagram, Twitter, and YouTube, as conduits.[32] What's central to this discussion is the speed at which an idea, commentary, mobilizing effort catches fire due to the power of social media and intelligent networking.

Intended Versus Unintended Consequences

The diffusion of new technology brings with it both intended and unintended consequences in the marketplace. From a business standpoint, the intention is rationale and is in keeping with a firm's larger business mission. Product designers and business strategists are hopeful that a successful product launch will result in wholesale product adoption among intended consumers as well as increased revenues and market share. These represent the intended consequences of product diffusion.

In contrast, the unintended consequences of product diffusion represent a set of results that are wholly unexpected. Sometimes, the results are immediate and can be easily seen. Sometimes, the unintended consequences of a new product introduction are long term and take a while for the public to discern. The example often used by sociologists is the development of the automobile in the 20th century. In a matter of decades, the automobile went from being a luxury good of the wealthy elite to the preferred, everyday method of passenger travel in most developed countries. The steady diffusion of the car introduced sweeping changes in daily life. While mass-produced automobiles represented a revolution in mobility and convenience, the long-term consequences have been significant, including the development of the modern suburb, where people choose to live and work, commuting, traffic, increased roads and highways, as well as environmental impact. A second example can be seen with the launch of smartphone technology. The widespread diffusion of smartphones in the early 21st century set into motion the obvious benefits of mobile voice communication as well as the convenience of being able to access the Internet anytime and anywhere. Over time, however, the public became more fully aware of some of the less favorable aspects of smartphone technology ranging from mobile phones going off in movie theaters and restaurants to the dangers of texting and driving.

The introduction of a new technology is the consummate triggering event that can cause any number of intended and unintended consequences in the marketplace, hence, the term *creative destruction*. One of the accompanying rules of creative destruction is that once a technology has been fully introduced, there is no going backward. There is no disinventing what one already knows how to do. Consider this the fallacy of nuclear disarmament (i.e., there may be a reduction in arms, but the core knowledge remains permanent). This is not unlike the same type of questions and challenges now facing the field of AI. There is no separating the intended goals from the unintended consequences. The power of innovation still comes down to quality design and the power of a good idea. Therein, lies the opportunity and challenge.

Notes

1 Everett Rogers, *Diffusion of Innovations* (New York: Free Press, 1962).
2 Everett Rogers, *Diffusion of Innovations*. 5th ed. (New York: Free Press, 2003), 5.
3 Rogers, *Diffusion of Innovations*. 5th ed., 11.
4 Clayton Christensen, *The Innovator's Solution* (Boston, MA: Harvard Business School Press, 2003).
5 W. Chan Kim and Renée Mauborgne, *Blue Ocean Strategy* (Boston, MA: Harvard Business School Press, 2005).
6 H. Chen and K. Crowston, "Comparative Diffusion of the Telephone and the World Wide Web: An Analysis of Rates of Adoption," *Proceedings of the WebNet '97— World Conference of the WWW*, Internet and Intranet, Toronto, Canada (1997): 110–115.
7 Everett Rogers, *Diffusion of Innovation*. 4th ed. (New York: Free Press, 1995).
8 Elihu Katz, "The Two-Step Flow of Communication: An Up-to-date Report on a Hypothesis," *Public Opinion Quarterly* 21,1 (1957): 61–78; See also, Elihu Katz and Paul Lazarsfeld, *Personal Influence* (New York: Free Press, 1957).
9 Rogers, *Diffusion of Innovation*. 4th ed.
10 Everett Rogers, *Diffusion of Innovation*. 3rd ed. (New York: Free Press, 1983), 21 & 23.
11 Rogers, *Diffusion of Innovation*. 5th ed., 282.
12 Rogers, *Diffusion of Innovation*. 5th ed., 282–283.
13 Rogers, *Diffusion of Innovation*. 5th ed., 282–283.

14 Bran Knowles and Vicki Hanson, "The Wisdom of Older Technology (Non)users," *Communication of the ACM* 61,3 (2018): 72–77.
15 Geoffery Moore, *Crossing the Chasm*. 3rd ed. (New York: Harper Business, 2014).
16 Moore, *Crossing the Chasm*.
17 Donald Sull, Rebecca Homkes and Charles Sull, "Why Strategy Execution Unravels," *Harvard Business Review*, 2015, March, pp. 58–66.
18 John Nathan, *Sony: The Private Life* (New York: Houghton-Mifflin, 1999), 138.
19 Alexander Osterwalder and Yves Pigneur, *Business Model Generation* (Hoboken, NJ: John Wiley & Sons, 2010), 14.
20 In the United States, margins of 2–3% are considered healthy; 1% is not uncommon. John Mullins, *The New Business Road Test* (New York: Pearson Education, 2003), 118–122.
21 "Where Webvan Failed and How Home Delivery 2.0 Could Succeed," *Tech Crunch*, 2013, September 18, https://techcrunch.com/2013/09/27/why-webvan-failed-and-how-home-delivery-2-0-is-addressing-the-problems/
22 Richard Gershon, *Media, Telecommunications and Business Strategy*. 3rd ed. (New York: Routledge, 2020).
23 Mike Ramsey, "Tivo," in J. Livingston (Ed.), *Founders at Work* (New York: Apress, 2007), 191–204.
24 Scott Olster, "Why Did the iPod Win and TiVo Lose?" *Fortune*, 2011, April 27, https://fortune.com/2011/04/27/why-did-the-ipod-win-and-tivo-lose/
25 Christopher Koopman, Matthew Mitchell and Adam Thierer, *The Sharing Economy and Consumer Protection Regulation: The Case for Policy Change* (Arlington, VA: Mercatus Center, George Mason University, 2014).
26 Joel Stein, "Baby You Can Drive My Car," *Time*, 2015, February 9, 32–40.
27 Dan Blackstone, "Uber," *Investopedia*, 2021, September 19, www.investopedia.com/articles/personal-finance/111015/story-uber.asp
28 Jean Folger, "Airbnb," *Investopedia*, 2021, December 31, www.investopedia.com/articles/personal-finance/032814/pros-and-cons-using-airbnb.asp
29 Malcolm Gladwell, *The Tipping Point* (New York: Little Brown and Company, 2000).
30 Gladwell, *The Tipping Point*.
31 Lorraine Marchand, *The Innovation Mindset* (New York: Columbia University Press, 2022), 20–26.
32 Gershon, *Media, Telecommunications and Business Strategy*. 3rd ed.

10

BUSINESS AND INNOVATION FAILURE

The Challenges of Reinvention

Introduction

This chapter looks at modern media and information technology (IT) and the problems associated with preserving market leadership. We begin by asking the question: What is business failure? At first glance, business failure is typically associated with bankruptcy or poor financial performance. But at a deeper level, business failure is also about the proverbial "fall from grace." A company that once dominated an industry no longer finds itself the market leader.[1] Worse still, the very same company is faced with a public perception that it has lost all relevancy in an otherwise highly competitive business and technology environment. The term *business failure* refers to a company that is unable to achieve profitability and can no longer continue its operations. The consequences are very real both symbolically and financially. The company's fall from grace is best illustrated by a dramatic downturn in the company's stock value.[2] But more importantly, it means the discontinuation of a once-successful product line and the loss of jobs for thousands of employees who were once part of the company's name and business mission.

In this chapter, we consider five reasons that help to explain why some companies succumb to business failure. They include 1) the tyranny of success, 2) organizational culture, 3) executive leadership failures, 4) risk-averse culture, and 5) disruptive technology. A major argument is that the warning signs of a troubled business often exist for long periods of time before they combine with enabling conditions to produce a significant business failure.[3] Special attention is given to the Eastman Kodak Company and Blockbuster Video, who

DOI: 10.4324/9781003294375-10

knew they were at risk of failing well in advance of their eventual decline. This chapter will also consider the challenges associated with business reinvention. Specifically, we consider the following question: Why do good companies fail to remain innovative over time? We start with the premise that even highly successful companies are susceptible to innovation failure. The Sony Corporation provides a good illustration of a company once known for being a worldwide leader in innovation and technology and the challenges associated with preserving market leadership.

The Tyranny of Success

Past success can sometimes make an organization very complacent; that is, they lose the sense of urgency to create new opportunities.[4] Author Jim Collins makes the point unequivocally when he writes that, "good is the enemy of great."[5] Companies, like people, can become easily satisfied with organizational routines. They become preoccupied with fine-tuning and making slight adjustments to an existing product line rather than preparing for the future. They are engaged in what MIT's Nicholas Negroponte once described as the problem of "incrementalism." Says Negroponte, "incrementalism is innovation's worst enemy."[6] The history of business is filled with examples of past companies where senior management failed to plan or react quickly enough to sudden changes in the marketplace. Such companies do not anticipate a time when a substitute product (or changing market conditions) might come along and dramatically alter the playing field.

- **Author's Note**: The information contained in this chapter is based on two previous chapters that were part of an edited works collection titled:

  Richard Gershon, "Innovation Failure: A Case Study Analysis of Eastman Kodak and Blockbuster Video," In A. Albarran (ed.), *Media Management and Economics Research in a Transmedia Environment*. (New York: Routledge, 2013). 46–68.

  Richard Gershon, "The Sony Corporation: Market Leadership, Innovation Failure and the Challenges of Business Reinvention," In Fu Lai Yu & Ho-Don Yan (eds.), *Handbook in East Asia Entrepreneurship*. (London, UK: Routledge, 2014). 225–239.

Nokia

At the start of the 21st century, Finland-based Nokia Corporation was a global leader in mobile cell phone manufacturing. Nokia was said to have one of the most valuable brands in the world. At the height of its success, the company could rightfully claim an international market share of over 40%. While Nokia's journey to the top was swift, its subsequent decline was equally fast culminating in the sale of its mobile phone business to Microsoft in 2013. Let's consider for a moment the challenges associated with the tyranny of success.

Changing Market Conditions

For years, Nokia relied on the mass market production of its cell phones. Each generation of Nokia cell phones proved incrementally better than previous versions. In 2007, the successful launch of the Apple iPhone ultimately proved to be a real game changer in terms of smartphone design and underscored the importance that the blending of voice and data (not voice alone) was the future of communication. Nokia was slow to react to this news and sudden change in the marketplace. Not only did Nokia fail to recognize the growing importance of smartphone design, it also underestimated the complexity and time requirements necessary to make the transition to smartphone development and manufacturing.

The problem can be explained, in part, by the fact that Nokia was by and large an engineering company. Nokia's development process was largely dominated by hardware engineers; whereas software developers were marginalized. The company's engineers were experts at building physical devices but not the programs that make those devices work.[7] In contrast, Apple's leadership saw the integration of hardware and software as being equally important. They encouraged product design teams that were multidisciplinary in method and approach. As strong and well-respected as the Nokia brand was, the constancy of technology change should have made them better prepared. Instead, Nokia was a victim of its own past success. Nokia overestimated the strength of its brand and believed they could arrive late to the smartphone game and still succeed. Nevertheless, brand strength is not enough. When companies fall behind, consumers are quick to punish them.

Executive Leadership and Strategic Decision-making

Between 2001 and 2005, Nokia's then CEO Jorma Ollila was becoming increasingly concerned that the company's rapid growth had brought about a loss of agility and entrepreneurialism. In his efforts to recreate the once highly innovative Nokia, a number of management decisions were made. This included the reorganization of several important leadership roles into what has been described as an organizational matrix system. This set into motion the departure of several important members of the company's executive team. In practical terms, Nokia's leadership matrix system proved cumbersome. Tensions within matrix-type organizations are common as different groups with varying priorities and performance criteria are required to work collaboratively. Mid-level executives often lack the training and experience to know how to strategize, put organizational priorities first, and collaborate. Each product line group was responsible for profit and loss while competing among each other for organizational support and resource allocation.[8]

The problem was made worse by the company's unwieldy Symbian IT operating system. Symbian was a cumbersome device-centric system that stood in marked contrast to the principle of unified organizational IT platforms and the ever-increasing application software being developed globally. Symbian caused routine delays in product launches requiring a new set of codes to be developed for each phone model. By 2009, Nokia was using 57 different versions of its operating system. The limitations of the Symbian IT system had become fully pronounced, and it was clear that Nokia had missed the worldwide shift toward application software being pioneered by Apple. In retrospect, Nokia was a victim of its own past success. The company suffered and failed to transition to the new era of smartphone design.[9]

Organizational Culture

Organizational culture (or corporate culture) refers to the collection of beliefs, values, and expectations shared by an organization's members and transmitted from one generation of employees to another.[10] Organizations (even large ones) are human constructions. They are made and transformed by individuals. Culture is embedded and transmitted through both implicit and explicit messages such as formal statements, organizational philosophy, adherence to management orthodoxies, deliberate role modeling, and behavioral displays by senior management.[11]

But what happens when organizational culture stands in the way of innovation? What happens when being tied to the past (and past practices) interferes with a company's ability to move forward? The combination of past success coupled with an unbending adherence to management orthodoxy can seriously undermine a company's ability to step out of itself and plan for the future. Suddenly, creative thinking and the ability to float new ideas get caught up in a stifling bureaucracy. Sometimes, what passes for management wisdom and experience is inflexibility masquerading as absolute truth.[12]

AT&T

The breakup of AT&T in 1984 was a watershed event in the history and development of telecommunications in the United States. This is admittedly an old story but a good example of how organizational culture stood in the way of progress. The AT&T divestiture, and the subsequent competition that followed, ushered in a whole new era in telecommunication products and services for business and residential users, including 1) customer-owned telephone sets; 2) choice of long-distance carriers; 3) personal computers; 4) mobile cellular telephony; and 5) the Internet, to name only a few examples. Throughout most of its one hundred-year history, AT&T never had to concern itself with the effects of competition in the marketplace and such things as marketing its services to the public. Theirs was a guaranteed market. AT&T controlled 80% of the U.S. local telephone market and virtually all of the nation's long-distance operations.

Following the divestiture agreement, one of the company's most pressing issues was how to address the organization's own internal culture. The management at AT&T understood the external challenges. The problem was how to overcome the company's institutionalized bureaucracy dating back to the days of Alexander Graham Bell. The culture was sometimes irreverently referred to as "carpetland." As journalist Leslie Caulie writes,

> Literally a century in the making, the culture was so omnipresent that it even had its own nickname: the Machine. It was an apt moniker. Almost impenetrable to outsiders, the Machine was a self-perpetuating mechanism that was loath to change . . . Process was a big part of the Machine's artistry. At AT&T's operational headquarters in Basking Ridge, New Jersey, meetings could ramble on for weeks or even months. It was not uncommon for AT&T execs to have meetings to talk about meetings. Ditto for memos about memos . . . The Machine steadfastly resisted change and embraced those who did the same.[13]

Starting in the decade of the 1990s, AT&T was faced with competitive challenges on a number of fronts including competitive services from the Regional Bell Operating Companies (RBOCs) Verizon and SBC, as well as the rapid rise of cellular telephony. Long-distance telephony was fast becoming a commodity and was no longer the highly profitable, sustainable business as was originally intended. Talented employees who attempted to test the boundary waters of AT&T's organizational culture were met with such well-worn corporate phrases as "that's not the AT&T way." It was only a matter of time before AT&T was sold off in pieces to the highest bidder. In January 2005, SBC, the second-largest RBOC in the United States agreed to acquire AT&T business and residential services for more than $16.9 billion. The proposed deal seemingly marked the final chapter in the 120-year history of AT&T; the first great American company of the information age and the original model for telecommunications companies worldwide. The phoenix did indeed rise from the ashes. In 2006, SBC would rename itself the new AT&T.

Executive Leadership Failures

Leadership is a process that involves influence and the art of directing people within an organization to achieve a clearly defined set of goals and outcomes. Successful leaders know what they want to accomplish in terms of organizational outcomes. The challenge for a company occurs when the executive leader makes questionable or bad decisions that hurt the long-term success of the business enterprise. A related problem occurs when the executive leader loses perspective on his/her own role within the organization. In time, the executive leader becomes bigger than the company itself. They become an example of what Jim Collins describes as the "celebrity leader."[14] Such individuals feel, by virtue of their position, intelligence, or compensation, that they are in charge of every key decision that is made on behalf of the business enterprise. Sometimes it works. But sometimes it does not because the people who are responsible for executing strategy have a better understanding of what's happening on the ground. Fellow managers and board members are less likely to challenge the strategic vision of a charismatic leader out of respect for the CEO's past success and/or by not wanting to appear contrary. Over time, the celebrity leader tends to isolate themselves from others and makes unilateral decisions without seeking the input from the company's senior management team. The celebrity leader becomes more concerned with their own ideas and reputation rather than securing the company's future.[15]

Risk-Averse Culture

Successful businesses with an established customer base find it hard to change. There is a clear pattern of success that translates into customer clients, predictable revenue, and public awareness for the company's brand and the work that has been accomplished to date. The adage "why mess with a winning formula" slowly becomes the corporate norm. There are no guarantees of success when it comes to new project ventures. The difficulty, of course, is that playing it safe presents its own unique hazards as was seen in the case of Nokia. Even well-managed companies can suddenly find themselves outflanked by changing market conditions and advancing new technologies. At the same time, forward-thinking companies recognize the need to develop new business opportunities.

RadioShack

RadioShack is a set of U.S. electronics stores founded in 1921 by two London-born brothers, Theodore and Milton Deutschmann. The brothers set up shop in Boston, and their audience and appeal were ham radio enthusiasts. They chose the name RadioShack, which is a colloquial reference to a small section of a ship that houses onboard radio equipment. By 1962, the company had become a leading distributor of electronics equipment in the northeast United States. The next year, Texas-based Charles Tandy, who ran a chain of leather stores, bought the company for about $300,000. He moved the company to Fort Worth, Texas. Over the next four decades, RadioShack carved out a unique niche in retailing by appealing to hobbyists and consumers wanting to purchase low-cost, easy-to-find electronics parts. RadioShack stores tended to be small, managed by a knowledgeable staff, and were found everywhere throughout the United States.[16]

RadioShack grew from 100 stores in 1966 to well over 7,000 in 2006 and were found in eight countries, including Australia, Belgium, Canada, China, France, Malaysia, Mexico, and the UK. A typical RadioShack location housed a variety of equipment including batteries, coaxial cables, cordless soldering irons, portable CD players, small stereo speakers, and the like. In time, RadioShack would be the go-to place for gadgets including CB radios during the 1970s. The company designed and manufactured the TRS-80 computer, one of the first prototype PCs ever built. RadioShack also became the place where computer enthusiasts modified their own computer.

During the decade of the 1990s, RadioShack began to sell cell phones and serve as a retail distributor for some of the emerging cell phone carriers. RadioShack's early success with wireless phones didn't last. If ever there was a company that fell victim to changing market conditions, it was RadioShack. In time, all the major cell phone carriers began to operate their own retail locations. The cell phone (and later smartphone technology) would eventually have a downward cascading effect on other parts of RadioShack's business, including answering machines, GPS, camcorders, and so forth. Rather than staking a claim in either computers or cell phones, RadioShack sold its cell phone manufacturing business and phased out its computer business in 1993. The field of consumer electronics retail sales was also changing. RadioShack faced stiff competition from several major box store retailers of the time, including Best Buy, Circuit City, Office Depot, and Staples, which carried similar types of electronic parts equipment. And from a consumer's perspective, the stores appeared to be outdated and expensive.

Last, RadioShack fell victim to the devastating effects of EC. Companies like Amazon and dedicated computer companies such as Dell and HP made

RadioShack's bricks-and-mortar approach both expensive and redundant. The RadioShack name and brand were well-positioned to be at the center of the communications revolution. But in the end, the company proved too risk-averse and was unable to reinvent themselves strategically.

Disruptive Technology

A disruptive technology is the quintessential game changer. Disruptive technologies, by their very definition, set into motion a whole host of intended and unintended consequences in the marketplace. As noted earlier, once a technology or service has been introduced, there is no going backwards. Over time, tastes, preference, and technology change. Innovative companies keep abreast of such changes, anticipate them, and make the necessary adjustments in strategy and new product development.[17] The question may be asked: If strategic adjustment and innovation are such basic elements, why then don't more companies succeed at it? Harvard researcher Clayton Christensen makes the argument that even the best managed companies are susceptible to innovation failure.[18] In fact, past success can sometimes become the very root cause of innovation failure going forward. Ironically, the decisions that lead to failure are made by executives who work for companies widely regarded as the best in their field.

The Innovator's Dilemma

Christensen (1997) posits what he calls the innovator's dilemma, namely that a company's very strengths (i.e., successful product line, consistent profitability, and growth) now become barriers to change and the agents of a company's potential decline.[19] Successful companies are highly committed to serving their existing customers and are often unable (or unwilling) to take apart a thriving business in favor of developing an unproven new technology or service. Worst still, the start-up of a new technology or service requires expensive retooling and whose ultimate success is hard to predict. In time, such companies lose because they fail to invest in new product development and/or because they fail to notice small niche players who enter the market and are prepared to offer customers alternative solutions at better value. The anticipated profit margins in developing a future market niche can be hard to justify given the high cost of entry, not to mention the possible destabilization of an otherwise highly successful business. Therein, lies the innovator's dilemma.

The Innovator's Dilemma and Product Life Cycle

Product life cycle theory was first proposed by Raymond Vernon (1966) and explains the evolution of a product development from the point of its introduction

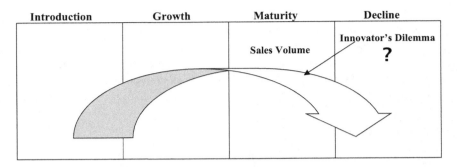

FIGURE 10.1   The Innovator's Dilemma and Product Life Cycle

into the marketplace to its final stages of decline. The theory of product life cycle has evolved over the years and has come to include a series of four stages, including 1) introduction, 2) growth, 3) maturity, and 4) decline.[20] After a product or service is launched, it goes through the various stages of a life cycle and reaches a natural decline point. Part of the innovator's dilemma is to know when in the course of the product life cycle to innovate (see Figure 10.1). The decision to innovate represents a strategic choice to discontinue (or phase out) a mature product in favor of an untested one. The decision to innovate has to occur well before the product hits its decline phase to allow sufficient time for development. This was clearly evident with respect to both Nokia and RadioShack. This means that the critical decision has to occur during the very time when the product is mature and realizing its highest profits. The downside risk is that the manufacturer may get it wrong and thereby destabilize an otherwise highly successful product line.

The history of media and telecommunications is filled with examples of companies faced with the innovator's dilemma. It is worth noting that many companies that are highly regarded as innovative can momentarily lose their innovative edge only to rebound at a later time (i.e., IBM, Disney, Apple, Nintendo, etc.). In sum, few companies are able to remain consistently innovative across time. We now consider two case study examples of companies that bring together the many contributing factors that lead to business failure. They include the Eastman Kodak company and Blockbuster Video Inc.

The Eastman Kodak Company

The Eastman Kodak Company is a pioneering company in the field of photography. The company was founded by George Eastman in 1889 and is headquartered in Rochester, New York. Kodak is best known for a wide range of photographic and imaging equipment. Throughout most of the 20th century, Kodak was singularly the most important company in the production and sale of film equipment.

The company's visibility and dominance were evidenced by the phrase "Kodak moment," which became part of the public lexicon of terms to describe a personal event worthy of being recorded for posterity.[21] On January 19, 2012, the 131-year-old company filed for bankruptcy. It was several years in the making, but Kodak steadily faltered beneath the wave of advancing digital media technology.[22]

The Start of Kodak

Founded in 1880 by George Eastman, Kodak became one of the United States' most recognized brand names, helping to establish the market for film and instamatic cameras which the company dominated for the better part of the 20th century. Eastman did not invent photography. He did, however, make it accessible to the public at large. As writer Neil Genzlinger points out,

> Before Eastman, photography was like portrait painting. Subjects would sit prim and still while a photographer wielding a bulky camera, glass plates and assorted chemicals caught the moment. The moment, though, had to last some seconds to allow for exposure, and the life captured by these early photographers was one without spontaneity.[23]

Eastman's work led to the creation of the *Kodak* camera. The Kodak was a fairly expensive camera in the beginning stages of its design. It would eventually give way to the *Brownie* family camera designed by Kodak's Frank Brownell. Throughout the years, Kodak has led the way with an abundance of new products and processes, including the introduction of *Kodachrome*, which set the stage for color photographs. Kodachrome became the color film standard throughout the 1950s and 1960s. In the 1960s, Kodak also introduced the *instamatic camera*. The company achieved $1 billion in sales in 1962. By 1976, Kodak captured the majority of the U.S. film and camera market (90% and 85%, respectively). Kodak's photofinishing process quickly became the industry standard for quality.[24] As a result, a major focus of the company was on its massive filmmaking plant. Traditionally, most of the company's CEOs had a strong manufacturing background.

The External Challenges: Rivalry With Fujifilm

Starting in the 1970s, Kodak was faced with a number of foreign competitors, most notably Fujifilm of Japan, which undercut Kodak's prices. In the beginning, Kodak did not take the competitive threat seriously. That complacency proved costly when the company passed on the opportunity to become the official film sponsor of the 1984 Summer Olympics in Los Angeles. That decision gave Fuji high visibility, sponsorship rights, and a permanent foothold in the U.S. film market. Soon thereafter, Fuji opened a film plant in the United States, cut prices, and aggressively marketed its film product. Kodak was rightly criticized for being slow to react and for underestimating its rivals.[25] Kodak also found itself at odds with its chief camera rival, the Polaroid Corporation. In October 1990, Kodak found itself on the losing end of a major patent infringement initiated by Polaroid. The company was forced to pay Polaroid $909.4 million for infringing on seven of Polaroid's instant photography patents. That decision forced Kodak out of the instant photography business.[26]

The Shift to Digital Cameras

As early as 1981, Kodak recognized that a shift toward digital camera technology was underway. That year, Sony Corporation announced the launch of a new digital camera called Mavica. Kodak had some prior experience with digital cameras having developed an early prototype design in 1975. Throughout the decade of the 1980s, Kodak introduced more than 50 products that were tied to digital photography and the storage of images. Yet the company was unable to successfully commercialize them.[27] At the same time, Kodak was fully committed to traditional film technology and processing. By the 1990s, the onset of digital photography started to erode the demand for conventional film and processing, thereby affecting Kodak's business.[28]

The Advantages of Going Digital

Digital photography has many advantages over traditional film. Digital photos are convenient and allows the user to see the results instantly. Digital photos don't require the costs associated with film and development time. Digital cameras enable the user to take multiple shots at no additional cost. They can be stored on a variety of digital devices as well as being uploaded on to the Internet. All this points to the fact that the transition to digital media was not just about a single product but rather, a major shift in technology and mindset in terms of how photos should be taken and stored.[29] Digital photography proved to be the ultimate disruptive technology. It was only a matter of time before traditional film processing would become obsolete.

Executive Leadership Challenges

Between 1983 and 1993, Kodak underwent seven organizational restructurings. In 1993, Kay Whitmore (a Kodak insider) stepped down as CEO and was succeeded by George Fisher. Fisher was recruited from Motorola where he had successfully revitalized that company. As Kodak's newly appointed CEO, Fisher began steering the company to embrace a digital future. Fisher clearly recognized that the organizational culture at Kodak had to change. The importance of digital media and communication had to be understood and embraced at all levels of the organization. The challenge, however, would prove formidable. While

Kodak recognized the importance of digital media to its future, company executives could not imagine a world without traditional film.[30] Specifically, they wanted to engage the process in its own way while staying within the confines of its Rochester, New York headquarters. This was ultimately a recipe for failure. The creativity demands for producing digital media are so vastly different than traditional photography. Kodak's leadership was not prepared to impose the kind of disruptive changes on the organization that would have been required.[31]

Kodak eventually settled on a combination strategy, whereby they created a separate digital and applied imaging division while still preserving its core capabilities in traditional film. By 1993, Kodak had spent $5 billion to research and develop digital cameras and imaging equipment. While Kodak had the right intentions, the company's middle management resisted the move toward digital photography. At issue were the high costs associated with developing new production facilities as well as a genuine concern that such changes might result in a loss of jobs. In the meantime, Kodak continued to miss critical target dates and experienced multiple setbacks in research and development.

Business Reinvention

The year 2001 proved to be an important cutover point. The company experienced a significant drop in film sales. CEO, Daniel Carp (Fisher's successor), continued the process of moving the company into digital cameras. They began by introducing the Easy Share family of digital cameras. By 2005, Kodak became the number one digital camera manufacturer in the United States with sales having risen 40% to $5.7 billion. Their success was short-lived. Despite an impressive start, Kodak's digital camera line became quickly copied by a host of Asian competitors that could produce equivalent cameras at lower cost. Digital cameras soon proved to be a low-profit margin item. To stay competitive, Kodak found itself losing money on every digital camera sold. Consumer electronics companies like Sony, Panasonic, and Canon could afford to be patient and lose money on select line items because they had hundreds of other products to offset potential losses. Not so for Kodak which had a limited product line. The final coup de grace came with the onset of cell phones equipped with cameras. In the beginning, at least, the cell phone camera represented the dumbing down of picture-taking since the quality was not as good as a camera. That said, a younger generation of users were willing to sacrifice picture quality for the sake of convenience. Today, digital cameras have become a lot more sophisticated in design and are a standard feature on all smartphone and tablet devices.

Adjusting to Marketplace Realities and Bankruptcy

By 2011, Kodak's financial reserves had reached a critical stage. The company had $5.1 billion in assets and nearly $6.8 billion in debts. Its biggest group of unsecured creditors were bondholders represented by the Bank of New York Mellon who were owed $658 million. Kodak filed for Chapter 11 protection in January 2012. The company closed 13 manufacturing plants and 130 processing labs while reducing their workforce by 47,000 employees.[32] In a final effort to stabilize their finances, Kodak hired the asset management firm, Lazard Ltd. to sell 1,100 of its digital imaging patents. This proved too little—too late. Kodak failed to generate enough potential interest, driven in part by fears of the company's deteriorating financial health. In the end, George Fisher was unable to transform Kodak into a high-tech growth company. Fisher's belief in the future of digital communication lacked urgency and did not permeate all levels of the organization. Nor were his successors Daniel Carp (2000–2005) and Antonio Pérez (2005–2012) any more successful. The price of Kodak shares decreased from around $25 in 2005 to less than one dollar by September 30, 2011. It was emblematic of the fall of a once-great American company.

Blockbuster

Blockbuster Inc. was an American-based videotape, DVD and videogame rental service. Blockbuster was founded by David Cook who used his experience with managing large database networks as the foundation for Blockbuster's retail distribution model. At its peak in 2009, Blockbuster had an estimated 7,100 retail stores in the United States with additional locations in 17 countries worldwide. Blockbuster employed over 60,000 employees in the United States and worldwide. The company was headquartered in McKinney, Texas. The Blockbuster business model would eventually prove unsustainable given the Internet and the rise of EC video rental services like Netflix. Blockbuster would sustain significant revenue losses in later years. The company filed for bankruptcy just shy of its 25th anniversary on September 22, 2010.[33] In April 2011, Blockbuster was acquired by satellite television service provider Dish Network at an auction price of $233 million and the assumption of $87 million in liabilities and other obligations.

The Start of Blockbuster Video

The first Blockbuster store opened in October 1985 in Dallas, Texas. Shortly thereafter, the company founder David Cook opened several additional stores and later built a $6 million warehouse in Garland, Texas that could service them all. The key to Blockbuster's early success was the convenience and ease of renting film entertainment for consumer use. Another important factor to Blockbuster's early success was their timely access to recently released feature films combined with films on VHS geared to the neighborhood demographics of its local retail outlets. In 1987, Waste Management President, Wayne Huizenga and his business partner John Melk paid Cook $18 million for a controlling interest in the new upstart company. Together, they used the lessons from their experience with Waste Management to build Blockbuster into a global enterprise. Huizenga took the company public in 1989 and aggressively transformed it from a $7 million business with 19 stores to a $4 billion global enterprise with more than 3,700 stores in 11 countries.[34]

Viacom Acquires Blockbuster Video

Despite Blockbuster's success, Huizenga felt that it was only a matter of time before technology advancements would directly challenge Blockbuster's bricks and mortar approach. Blockbuster was the right technology for the time. It was a 20-year interim technology that provided a practical solution in meeting the needs for home television viewing. As early as 1994, Wayne Huizenga understood the limitations of Blockbusters' business model and strategy. He sold the company to Viacom. His concerns were shared by any number of observers throughout the industry. On the immediate horizon was cable television and its promise of video-on-demand service. Less obvious was the future of e-commerce and the disruptive technologies made possible by the Internet. One of those disruptive technologies would take the form of a unique business process innovation and a company called Netflix.

The Start of Netflix

Netflix is an online OTT video streaming service. Netflix was founded by Reed Hastings in 1997 during the emergent days of e-commerce when companies like Amazon and Dell Computer were starting to gain prominence. It began as a subscription-based DVD rental service. Hastings made the important decision not to duplicate the Blockbuster business model but rather to utilize the Internet and the power of intelligent networking for enabling customers to place video rental orders online. Netflix then offered its customers a great value proposition, namely two to three DVDs per week (depending on the service plan) for a fixed monthly price. In practical terms, Netflix offered its subscribers greater value when compared to a traditional video rental store which charged by the individual DVD rental unit.[35] Second, Netflix also offered its subscribers greater convenience in the form of "no late fees." Third, a big part of Netflix's success was the direct result of personalized marketing which involved having more direct knowledge and viewing habits of its customer base.[36] This, in turn, enabled the company to use its proprietary recommendation software to make future viewing suggestions to its customers. A common complaint with Blockbuster was the problem of limited inventory and having to rent an unfamiliar movie and being dissatisfied with the viewing experience later on. The Netflix software recommendation system, on the other hand, made suggestions of other films that the consumer might like based on past selections and a brief evaluation that the subscriber was asked to fill out. Netflix proved to be the ultimate game changer by transforming the DVD rental business through the use of business process innovation and its e-commerce technology platform.[37]

Blockbuster Fails to React

Blockbuster had more than sufficient time to react to the competition and revise their business model. As early as 2001, Blockbuster was in a position to strategically reposition itself. The company could have possibly acquired Netflix or modified its strategy by duplicating many of the same EC efficiencies that Netflix's business model had already demonstrated. Alternatively, it could have opened kiosks (i.e., similar to RedBox) and begun closing stores. This would have reduced capital costs and improved convenience. Instead, Blockbuster chose to ignore the competitive threat posed by Netflix. They were doing quite well for the moment and didn't want to destabilize an otherwise successful business enterprise (i.e., the innovator's dilemma). In practical terms, Netflix was allowed to go unchallenged for six years before Blockbuster launched their own EC service in 2004. By then, Netflix had brand recognition, three million customers, and a strong business momentum.[38] In a bid to slow the competition, Blockbuster introduced a flat monthly fee and later eliminated late fees as well. Subscriptions did increase but not enough to offset the $300 million loss the company absorbed by eliminating late fees. The combined strategy wound up costing the company an estimated $400 million.[39] Critics point to the fact that then CEO John Antioco should have taken the Netflix threat more seriously and acted sooner. Blockbuster's business complacency coupled with a failure to appreciate the power of e-commerce would prove costly in securing the company's long-term future.

Blockbuster's Executive Leadership and Activist Board

In 2004, Viacom (which still owned 80% of the company) chose to sell its stake in Blockbuster and took a $1.3 billion charge to reflect the declining value of the business. Later that same year, a second major change occurred that affected the company's organizational dynamics when activist investor Carl Icahn bought nearly $10 million shares of Blockbuster stock. Shortly, thereafter, Icahn began giving interviews to the press and writing letters to Antioco as well as shareholders claiming that Blockbuster had spent too much money on developing its online business and eliminating late fees. He was critical of Antioco's attempted merger strategy and claimed that the CEO was making too much money. Icahn proceeded to launch a proxy fight.

For Antioco and his management team, a set of contentious directors meant having to constantly justify and explain each business decision. To the public,

Blockbuster's evolving business strategy seemed fragmented and disjointed, evidenced by an inconsistent policy involving late fees. Blockbuster was a company in trouble. The problem was made worse by the fact that Antioco and the company's board of directors were at serious odds with one another. Icahn routinely battled with Antioco about how to revive the company. Antioco wanted to keep the company independent while Icahn wanted to sell it to a private-equity firm.[40]

In December 2006, the situation came to a head over executive compensation. The Board decided to significantly reduce Antioco's bonus compensation. Antioco chose to negotiate a severance deal with Blockbuster rather than accept the reduced bonus amount. Set against the backdrop of some highly intense corporate infighting, the board approved the hiring of Jim Keyes, who was the former head of 7-Eleven. He had a difficult assignment that included quelling the unrest at Blockbuster while trying to develop a strategy for the future. Unfortunately, the hiring of Jim Keyes was too little—too late. By now, it was clear to everyone that Blockbuster was in a slow death spiral. In the end, Blockbuster video failed because the company chose not to change. They were too slow in reacting to the competitive challenges posed by Netflix and Redbox. This, in combination with a highly contentious board of directors, proved to be a toxic mixture. Reflecting on Blockbuster's Chapter 11 filing, former CEO John Antioco (2011) concludes:

> The day the company's failure will hit me hardest is probably when my own neighborhood store closes.[41]

Sony Corporation: The Challenges of Business Reinvention

Sony Corporation is a leading transnational media corporation in the production and sale of consumer electronics, music, film entertainment, and video game technology. Throughout its 75 plus year history, the Sony name has become synonymous with great innovation. During that time, Sony introduced a number of firsts in the development of new communication products. Words like *Walkman*, *Compact disk*, and *Play Station* have become part of the global lexicon of terms to describe consumer electronics. Such products were truly revolutionary for the time and set into motion the beginnings for today's digital lifestyle.[42]

Historical Overview

Sony Corporation was founded by Masaru Ibuka in the months following Japan's defeat during World War II. In September 1945, Ibuka left the countryside, where he had sought refuge from the bombings, and returned to the war-torn capital of Tokyo to begin a new business. Shortly thereafter, Ibuka established the Tokyo Tsushin Kenkyujo (Tokyo Telecommunications Research Institute).

In the beginning, the new start-up company was nothing more than a few individuals who occupied a small space on the third floor of the Shirokiya department store in the Nihonbashi district of Tokyo. It became the workshop for Ibuka and his newly founded group. During its initial start-up, Ibuka's shop was primarily in the business of radio repair.[43] After reading an article in the *Asahi Shimbun* newspaper, friend and colleague Akio Morita wrote to Ibuka who replied at once. He urged Morita to come to Tokyo and join him in the start-up of this new business venture.[44] At the time, Ibuka was 38 and Morita was 25. Both were knowledgeable and enthusiastic engineers. And both understood the importance of what new technology meant to post-war Japan and the future of their newly created company. Ibuka and Morita officially incorporated their new business start-up as the Tokyo Tsushin Kogyo (Totsukou) or the Tokyo Telecommunications Engineering Corporation on May 7, 1946. The company's name was officially changed to Sony (derived from the Latin word "sonus" for sound) in January 1958.

Sony's Entry Into World Markets

Most companies do not set out with an established plan for becoming a major international company. Rather, as a company's exports steadily increase, it establishes a foreign office to handle the sales and services of its products. Early on in his tenure, Akio Morita demonstrated the kind of business skills that allowed him to successfully enter into foreign markets. He did not initially have a global strategy in mind. Morita tended to operate in those markets that he believed were important and where Sony's products would be readily accepted. The United States and Europe represented a first step in realizing that objective. Throughout its history, Sony has achieved a number of firsts in product design and innovation, including the Trinitron television set (as well as the more recent *OLED* 4K and 8K ultra high-definition television sets), the portable videotape recorder, the Sony Walkman (portable music player), the joint Sony/Philips compact disk (CD), the Sony television studio camera and monitor, and the Sony PlayStation video game system to name only a few examples.

The Challenges of Business Reinvention

Starting in 2005, Sony experienced the beginning of a decade-long decline in major product development. For the first time in its history, Sony was faced with a public perception that it was losing its competitive edge. Sony's financial performance proved highly inconsistent in the years thereafter. Nor did the company maintain the technological leadership position that it once held in the past. Sony's decade-long decline was the result of a number of self-inflicted wounds. What went wrong is a story of missed business opportunities, repeated failures to take necessary risks, and disastrous corporate infighting. In time, Sony found itself being challenged on a number of technology fronts by a host of international rivals that included South Korea-based Samsung and LG as well as U.S. companies Apple, Google, Amazon, and Microsoft. This, in combination with a failure to develop timely, innovative products, made Sony's competitive business environment punishingly difficult.[45]

Executive Leadership Failures

Some of Sony's business challenges can be traced back to the leadership of Nobukei Idei, who introduced an altogether new management philosophy. Under Idei's tenure, Sony underwent a corporate reorganization that was built on what the company called its five pillars of operation. This included 1) electronics, 2) entertainment, 3) financial services, 4) game, and 5) Internet services. The objective was to transfer day-to-day management responsibility from Sony's Tokyo headquarters to the company's foreign operations. To that end, Sony's headquarters was reorganized into two areas called the Global Hub (GH) and the Electronics Headquarters. The purpose of the GH was to develop corporate wide strategy and to promote strategic intragroup alliances among the five pillars of business operations. The organizational model was described as "integrated/decentralized management."[46]

At the time, Sony officials believed that to be more globally competitive the company had to promote greater responsibility and autonomy in the field. The Sony manager was expected to rely less on corporate headquarters and display more individual initiative. In time, the integrated/decentralized management approach would set into motion a number of unintended consequences. One such consequence was a decline in collaboration and timely sharing of information between divisions and departments. Executives at the time complained privately of recalcitrant managers who refused to share information or work with other divisions. Sony's top management privately acknowledged that Sony was then dominated by proud, territorial engineers who often shunned cooperation. The Japanese refer to it as "tatewari." For many such engineers, ceding intellectual territory and cost-cutting were considered the enemy of creativity.

The integrated/decentralized management approach made it difficult for Sony's executive leadership team to wield authority over the company's many subsidiaries and divisions. At issue, was the fact that CEO Idei and his senior administrative staff found it difficult to interfere with individual company decisions, especially when they were making money. Such companies and divisions were becoming increasingly risk-averse. They came to rely on dependable products that could be tapped for quick, reliable profits. Instead of planning for the next generation in product design there was a strong tendency toward products with a proven track record (i.e., the innovator's dilemma). As an example,

Sony's audio and video divisions were highly profitable during the beginning years of the 21st century. Both divisions felt no pressing need to develop digital technology.[47] The TV business began responding only after it began suffering huge losses in 2003 due to South Korean rivals Samsung and LG. Suddenly, the company found itself in catch-up mode rather than being the industry leader that it should have been.

Streamlining Business Operations

Nobuyuki Idei also made the controversial decision to streamline and downsize the company. A number of Sony executives and engineers were given early retirement options. There was a substantial brain drain of veteran and middle-aged engineers and technicians. Several played a critical role in helping to advance Sony's past success. Many found employment elsewhere; specifically, in Korea, working for companies that would one day become some of Sony's most challenging competitors. As one observer wryly noted: "Korea and Taiwan immediately welcomed the exiting Sony techies with open arms. It was better than industrial espionage—Samsung could openly buy the technology that Sony had developed simply by rehiring their best and brightest."[48] One story is very apocryphal of the problem.

> When an investor pointed out that Sony's operating profits on electronic products were roughly 2–4 percent and that Samsung was making similar products at a 30 percent profit margin, Idei hushed him by reportedly saying, "They make the parts for our products. We put them together. It's the difference between a steel maker and an automobile maker. We make the automobiles."
>
> The investor apparently countered, "Well, I've got news for you-the people you laid off from the car plant are now working at the steel mill, and soon the steel mills will be building cars with your technology."[49]

Sony—Television Set Design

The loss of many of Sony's top engineers in 2000–2001 left behind a younger group of engineers and technicians who were more risk-averse and less willing to experiment. Sony was engaged in a default strategy, whereby it was playing not to lose rather than to win. Sony's approach to the design and manufacture of high-definition television sets is highly illustrative of this problem. Rather than advancing new and original research in the area of digital television set design, the company chose instead to extend the life of its analog-based Trinitron CRT (and later WEGA TV). The company's senior leadership team did not want to give up the immediate profits that

WEGA generated because it contributed to the company's overall profitability. That kind of short-term thinking would eventually cause Sony irreparable damage.

Despite having been a pioneer in television set design (including Sony's early prototype work in high-definition TV), the world's population was now buying LCD plasma TVs from South Korea-based Samsung and LG. They proved to be less expensive, well designed, and the difference in quality was not significant. Samsung would eventually surpass Sony in terms of market capitalization. Samsung had become a master of business process innovation. They fully embraced the principles of fast and efficient, low-cost television manufacturing.[50]

Sony's Internet Strategy

Sony's Internet strategy was problematic from the start. One such example can be seen in the area of music. In 2001, Apple introduced its iTunes music service. A year later, the company launched its iPod portable music player, which in time captured 65% of the portable music player market. In 2007, Apple debuted its iPhone which fully eviscerated Sony's one-time dominance in the portable music area. Apple, for its part, was fully focused on the user experience. Stated differently, hardware was not enough. Apple products like the iPhone and iPad enabled users to experience information and entertainment on multiple levels including one or more combinations of text, audio, and video. This was the idea of convergence made practical and real. Sony failed to grasp the importance of user experience in terms of being able to customize one's music and video playlist. By leveraging the power of the Internet and digital distribution, Apple let music lovers browse and download a song or album in a fraction of the time it had previously taken to record music onto a Sony Walkman tape or compact disk. Moreover, Apple took a page out of Sony's playbook by redefining the principle of portability in a whole new way by allowing music owners to place an entire music collection onto a simple device that could fit into one's coat pocket. Sony was caught flat-footed. It was adhering to an old industrial model where the emphasis was on reliable, stand-alone products sold in great quantity.[51]

Lengthy Development Times and Missed Opportunities

The combination of changing technology and shifting consumer demands makes speed-to-market paramount today. Yet companies often can't organize themselves to move faster. More to the point, companies that are highly compartmentalized can become immobilized when it comes to fast turn-around times given the entrenchment of existing departments and area silos. Sony's Internet strategy was problematic from the start. First and foremost, Sony was slow to develop a fully integrated common platform to deliver music, movies, and games. One by one, every major product category where Sony held a market lead—from portable music players (Walkman) to music recording devices (the compact disk) to video game systems (PlayStation)—eventually felt the punishing effects of disruptive Internet technology. Given the company's multiple business silos, there was a lot of internal resistance from various divisions in terms of surrendering control over their individual operations. This, in turn, resulted in a lack of coordination that seriously impaired Sony's product innovation and development times. There was a preoccupation with organizational process rather than end results.

To remedy this problem, Sony appointed Kazuo Hirai as its new CEO in April 2012. When Hirai took the helm at Sony, its TV business had been losing money for eight straight years running. There was an immediate need to rebuild the company's highly prized electronics business if the company as a whole was to be restored. This process involved steep cuts in the company's workforce which amounted to a loss of 30% of its employees. One of Hirai's first initiatives was to advance a new corporate strategy known as *One Sony*; the goal of which, was to think and operate in a more unified way. Hirai visited Sony's factories and research and development centers around the world, listening to what his professional staff had to say. During those conversations, he identified with the Japanese word "*kando*," which means "deeply moved." In that sense, he recognized that *kando* hearkens back to Sony's past where the company's original charter underscored the importance of freedom and open-mindedness and where sincerely motivated engineers could take their technical skills to the highest level.[52]

Sony: Business Reinvention and the Future

Today's Sony has undertaken a major organizational change to meet the company's future. Sony plans to sharpen its focus by directing its attention toward being excellent in a few specialized areas. The company will focus its energies in several important areas including 1) electronics, 2) gaming technology, 3) entertainment, 4) CMOS image sensing, and 5) financial services. In April 2018, Kaz Hirai was succeeded by Kenichiro Yoshida as the company's new CEO. During Sony's Corporate Strategy Meeting FY2020, CEO Yoshida emphasized the importance of *kando* by greatly expanding the company's Internet presence in all areas of its business operations. At a deeper level, Yoshida and his predecessor Kaz Hirai are reminding both employees and the general public that Sony (better than most companies) understands the importance of shaping the user experience and making an emotional connection. Says Yoshida, "People are at the Core of the Sony Group's business portfolio.

> Sony's purpose is to "fill the world with emotion through the power of creativity and technology." [53]

Despite its past challenges, Sony is an example of a company that has learned to reinvent itself. The company is steadily rediscovering the entrepreneurial side of its business enterprise while sharpening its focus going forward. This can be seen in terms of the development of a more diverse product line as well as increased and steady profitability for the years 2017–2023. Overall, Sony has regained its position as a media tech leader ranking in the top 60 of Forbes' most valuable companies and #47 worldwide business brands.[54]

Discussion

It can be said that the warning signs of a troubled business often exist for long periods of time before they combine with enabling conditions to produce a climactic business failure. Author Jim Collins refers to this as "the silent creep of impending doom."[55] The business failures at both Kodak and Blockbuster share one thing in common. Each failed to recognize the early warning signs of advancing technological change.

Kodak

Kodak was paralyzed by an organizational culture that was highly resistant to change. While Kodak had the right intentions, the company was not prepared to make the costly changes needed to fully embrace the business of digital media and information technology. When a business is confronted with a highly disruptive technology, senior management has to be a catalyst for change at all levels of the organization.[56] Although Kodak recognized the external threats, the company's organizational culture prevented them from moving forward. Rosabeth Kanter makes the point that Kodak was very Rochester-centric and never really developed an innovation presence in other parts of the world that were developing leading-edge media technologies. Instead, Kodak adhered to a kind of old-line manufacturing mentality.[57] They were in the film business plain and simple. It was, after all, what made them profitable in the past.

Blockbuster

In retrospect, it seems clear that the practice of driving to a store to rent a movie was a business process destined to fail as the Internet became more of a factor in the world of e-commerce. For years, business analysts and professional observers have recognized that Blockbuster was a flawed business model that would be difficult to sustain in the wake of advancing technology. As early as 1994, Wayne Huizenga understood the limitations of a bricks-and-mortar approach when he sold Blockbuster to Viacom Inc. Ten years later, Viacom CEO Sumner Redstone came to the same conclusion when he sold his 80% stake in the company as well.

Both Huizenga and Redstone operated at a time when the conventional wisdom and smart money was on cable television and its highly touted video-on-demand service. Despite many attempts, video-on-demand television in its early stages of development never fully caught on. All this, of course, changed with the development of the Internet and the power of e-commerce.

For Blockbuster, disruption came in the form of a company called Netflix. The situation at Blockbuster was further complicated because of failures in executive leadership coupled with a highly contentious board of directors. The standoff between CEO John Antioco and the company's board resulted in business strategy gridlock and a public loss of confidence in the company. Both Kodak and Blockbuster were highly successful companies that once dominated their respective markets. Their previous strengths and one-time success ultimately laid the groundwork for their eventual decline. Each was susceptible to the innovator's dilemma. In the end, the requirements for change proved too formidable an obstacle.[58]

Sony

Throughout its history, the Sony name has been synonymous with great innovation. During the decades of the 1980s and 1990s, Sony had an astonishing ability to be at the forefront of the next technological challenge. From the original Sony Walkman to the PlayStation video game system, Sony could do it better, faster than any of its nearest competitors. Sony was the company that stirred the consumer's imagination. All this changed with the successful emergence of Samsung and Apple at the start of the 21st century. Suddenly, Sony found itself being challenged by a set of rivals in two very different ways. Samsung proved to be the organizational master in fast and efficient (almost military-like) production. Samsung focused on becoming a superior manufacturer. The company learned how to operate in the highly volatile world of commoditized products.[59] In contrast, Sony's organizational culture became steadily more bureaucratic over time, and its business units tended to operate as independent silos which made strategic planning and resource allocation very inefficient. Sony's challenges were the result of missed opportunities, risk avoidance, and organizational failures to make everyone accountable to the larger Sony mission.

Sony's other major rival has been Apple Inc. which focused public attention on the importance of the user experience. Apple products like the iPhone and iPad provide users with the capability of experiencing information and entertainment on multiple levels including one or more combinations of text, audio, and video. By leveraging the power of the Internet and digital distribution, Apple let music lovers browse and download a song or album in a fraction of the time it had previously taken to record music onto a Sony Walkman tape or compact disk. Moreover, Apple took a page out of the Sony's playbook by redefining portability in a whole new way by allowing music owners to place an entire music collection onto a simple device that could fit into one's coat pocket. Sony was caught flat-footed. It was adhering to an old industrial model where the emphasis was on reliable, stand-alone products sold in great quantity.[60]

Under the leadership of Kaz Hirai and Kenichiro Yoshida, the new Sony is steadily reinventing itself. The company is rediscovering its entrepreneurial side by aligning with the company' founding principles with its emphasis on *kando*. Sony benefited in some measure from the 2020–2022 global pandemic as the world's population was forced to stay at home and where there was an increased need for music, television, and gaming entertainment. All companies, big and small, go through periods of business reinvention. It goes with the territory of being a smart, creative company. What has not changed is the Sony name which is still greatly respected around the world. Sony has now come full circle and stands at the crossroads of its future.

Notes

1 Richard Gershon, "Innovation Failure: A Case Study Analysis of Eastman Kodak and Blockbuster Video," in A. Albarran (Ed.), *Media Management and Economics Research in a Transmedia Environment* (New York: Routledge, 2013), 46–68.
2 Richard Gershon, "The Sony Corporation: Market Leadership, Innovation Failure and the Challenges of Business Reinvention," in Fu Lai Yu and Ho-Don Yan (Eds.), *Handbook in East Asia Entrepreneurship* (London: Routledge, 2014), 225–239.
3 Jim Collins, *How the Mighty Fall* (New York: Harper Collins, 2009).
4 Michael Tushman and Charles O'Reilly, *Winning Through Innovation* (Boston, MA: Harvard Business School Press, 1997).
5 Jim Collins, *Good to Great* (New York: Harper Collins, 2001), 16.
6 Nicholas Negroponte, "Incrementalism Is Innovation's Worst Enemy," *Wired*, 1995, April, 188.
7 James Surowiecki, "Where Nokia Went Wrong," *The New Yorker*, 2013, September 3, www.newyorker.com/business/currency/where-nokia-went-wrong
8 Yves Doz and Keeley Wilson, *Ringtone: Exploring the Rise and Fall of Nokia in Mobile Phones* (Oxford: Oxford University Press, 2017).
9 Yves Doz, "The Strategic Decisions that Caused Nokia's Failure," *Insead Knowledge*, 2017, November 23, https://knowledge.insead.edu/strategy/the-strategic-decisions-that-caused-nokias-failure-7766
10 Edgar Schein, "The Role of the Founder in Creating Organizational Culture," *Organizational Dynamics* 11 (1983): 13–28.
11 Joseph Pilotta, Timothy Widman and Susan Jasko, "Meaning and Action in the Organizational Setting: An Interpretive Approach," in *Communication Yearbook 12* (New York: Sage, 1988), 310–334.
12 Gary Hamel, "The What, Why and How of Management Innovation," *Harvard Business Review*, 2006, February, 72–87.
13 Leslie Cauley, *End of the Line: The Rise and Fall of AT&T* (New York: Free Press, 2005), 116–117.
14 Collins, *Good to Great*.
15 Richard Gershon, *Media, Telecommunications and Business Strategy*. 3rd ed. (New York: Routledge, 2020), 221–222.

16 Steven Solomon, "A History of Misses for RadioShack," *New York Times*, 2014, September 16, http://dealbook.nytimes.com/2014/09/16/for-radioshack-a-history-of-misses/?_r=0
17 Richard Gershon, "Media Innovation: Three Key Strategies to Business Transformation," in A. Albarran, B. Mierzejewska and J. Jung (Eds.), *Handbook of Media Management and Economics*. 2nd ed. (New York: Routledge, 2018), 241–258.
18 Clayton Christensen, *The Innovator's Dilemma* (Boston, MA: Harvard Business School Press, 1997).
19 Christensen, *The Innovator's Dilemma*.
20 Raymond Vernon, "International Investment and International Trade in the Product Cycle," *Quarterly Journal of Economics* 80,2 (1966): 190–207.
21 Gershon, "Innovation Failure: A Case Study Analysis of Eastman Kodak and Blockbuster Video," 46–68.
22 Michael DeLaMerced, "Eastman Kodak Files for Bankruptcy," *New York Times*, 2012, January 19, http://dealbook.nytimes.com/2012/01/19/eastman-kodak-files-for-bankruptcy/?_r=0
23 Neil Genzlinger, "Television Review: He Changed Photography and Transformed Society," *New York Times*, 2000, May 22, www.nytimes.com/2000/05/22/arts/television-review-he-changed-photography-and-transformed-society.html
24 "Kodak's Legacy," *New York Times*, 2012, January 19, https://archive.nytimes.com/www.nytimes.com/interactive/business/kodak-timeline.html?ref=cameras#/#time188_6043
25 Thomas Finnerty, *Kodak v. Fuji: The Battle for Global Market Share*, White Paper (New York: Pace University—Lubin School of Business, 2000), https://pdgciv.files.wordpress.com/2007/05/tfinnerty2.pdf
26 "Kodak's Legacy," *New York Times*.
27 Henry Lucas and Jie Mein Goh, "Disruptive Technology: How Kodak Missed the Digital Photography Revolution," *Journal of Strategic Information Systems* 18 (2009): 46–55.
28 Kaitlyn Tiffany, "The Rise and Fall of an American Tech. Giant," *The Atlantic*, 2021, July/August, www.theatlantic.com/magazine/archive/2021/07/kodak-rochester-new-york/619009/
29 Yue-Ling Wong, *Digital Media Primer*. 3rd ed. (London: Pearson, 2016).
30 Giovanni Gavetti, Rebecca Henderson and Simona Giorgi, *Kodak and the Digital Revolution* (Cambridge, MA: Harvard Business School Press, 2005).
31 Alecia Swasy, *Changing Focus: Kodak and the Battle to Save a Great American Company* (New York: Random House, 1997).
32 DeLaMerced, "Eastman Kodak Files for Bankruptcy."
33 Gershon, "Innovation Failure: A Case Study Analysis of Eastman Kodak and Blockbuster Video," 46–68.
34 Gail DeGeorge, *The Making of a Blockbuster: How Wayne Huizenga Built a Sports and Entertainment Empire from Trash, Grit, and Videotape* (New York: John Wiley, 1996).
35 Richard Gershon, "Digital Media, Electronic Commerce and Business Model Innovation," in Yu-Li Liu and Robert Picard (Eds.), *Policy and Marketing Strategies for Digital Media* (New York: Routledge, 2014), 202–217.
36 Marc Randolph, *That Will Never Work* (New York: Little Brown and Company, 2019).
37 Gershon, "Digital Media, Electronic Commerce and Business Model Innovation," 202–217.
38 Stephen Gandel, "How Blockbuster Failed at Failing," *Time*, 2010, October 11, 38–40.
39 Jordan Crook, "What Happened to Kodak's Moment," *TechCrunch*, 2012, January 21, https://techcrunch.com/2012/01/21/what-happened-to-kodaks-moment/
40 John Antioco, "How I Did It? Blockbuster's Former CEO on Sparring with an Activist Shareholder," *Harvard Business Review*, 2011, April, 39–44.
41 Antioco, "How I Did It? Blockbuster's Former CEO on Sparring with an Activist Shareholder," 39–44.

42 Richard Gershon and Tsutomu Kanayama, "The Sony Corporation: A Case Study in Transnational Media Management," *The International Journal on Media Management* 4,2 (2002): 44–56.

43 Sony Corporation, *Genryu: Sony Challenges 1946–1968* (Tokyo, Japan: Sony Inc., 1988).

44 Gershon and Kanayama, "The Sony Corporation: A Case Study in Transnational Media Management," 44–56.

45 Richard Gershon, "The Sony Corporation: Market Leadership, Innovation Failure and the Challenges of Business Reinvention," 225–239.

46 Gershon and Kanayama, "The Sony Corporation: A Case Study in Transnational Media Management," 44–56.

47 Sea-Jin Chang, *Sony vs. Samsung: The Inside Story of the Electronics Giants' Battle for Global Supremacy* (Singapore: John Wiley & Sons, 2008), 117.

48 J. Adelstein and N. K. Stuckey, "How Sony Is Turning into a Ghost in Japan and Around the World," *Kotaku*, 2012, November 14, http://kotaku.com/5960411/how-sony-is-turning-into-a-ghost-in-japan-and-around-the-world

49 Adelstein and Stuckey, "How Sony Is Turning into a Ghost."

50 Chang, *Sony vs. Samsung: The Inside Story of the Electronics Giants' Battle for Global Supremacy.*

51 Adam Hartung, "Sayonara Sony: How Industrial, MBA-Style Leadership Killed a Once Great Company," *Forbes*, 2012, April 4, www.forbes.com/sites/adamhartung/2012/04/20/sayonara-sony-how-industrial-mba-style-leadership-killed-once-great-company/?sh=6d5f5d1765a5

52 Takashi Sugimoto, "Ex-CEO Hirai on How He Reinvented an Electronics Icon," *NikkeiAsia*, https://asia.nikkei.com/Business/Electronics/Ex-Sony-CEO-Hirai-on-how-he-reinvented-an-electronics-icon

53 *Sony 2020 Annual Corporate Report*, www.sony.com/en/SonyInfo/IR/library/corporatereport/CorporateReport2020_E.pdf

54 Andrea Murphey and Hank Tucker, "The Global 2,000," *Forbes*, 2023, June 8, www.forbes.com/lists/global2000/?sh=7b2b6f7d5ac0; See Also: "The Most Valuable Brands," *Forbes*, 2023, www.forbes.com/powerful-brands/list/

55 Collins, *How the Mighty Fall*, 1.

56 Henry Lucas and Jie Mein Goh, "Disruptive Technology: How Kodak Missed the Digital Photography Revolution," *Journal of Strategic Information Systems* 18 (2009): 46–55.

57 Rosabeth Kanter, "The Last Kodak Moment?" *The Economist*, 2012, January 14, www.economist.com/node/21542796

58 Gershon, "Innovation Failure: A Case Study Analysis of Eastman Kodak and Blockbuster Video."

59 Chang, *Sony vs. Samsung: The Inside Story of the Electronics Giants' Battle for Global Supremacy.*

60 Hartung, "Sayonara Sony: How Industrial, MBA-Style Leadership Killed a Once Great Company."

11

SMART CITIES/SMART HOMES

Smart Cities

Smart cities are communities that utilize communication and information technology for the purpose of managing people and resources in highly efficient and sustainable ways. Today, more than half of the world's population lives in urban areas. By the year 2035, the Chinese government expects that over 70% of the country's population will be living in cities.[1] Similarly, through natural growth, urban migration, and recategorization of what constitutes a city, India expects to add 416 million people to its cities by 2050; the largest projected increase in the world.[2] This shift from primarily rural areas to cities or megacities is projected to continue for decades to come, increasing the need for urban reform. As more and more people continue to cluster into larger urban centers, city planners will be faced with a number of emerging problems, including resource management, business development, education, public safety, and so forth. Additional and less obvious are the unique challenges associated with city planning and environmental sustainability.[3]

The goal of smart city technology is to leverage the collective intelligence of the city and its major constituents by coordinating community resources and skill sets. A smart city comprises various stakeholders, including, but not limited to, government, business, education, public safety, health care, energy and utilities, religious centers, transportation as well as parks and recreation.[4] The word *Smart* refers to a new generation of integrated hardware, software, and advanced analytics that provide real-time information that helps decision-makers involved with strategic and operational planning activities.

DOI: 10.4324/9781003294375-11

Electronic Government

Electronic government communication (or E-Government) can be defined as the government use of information technology and Internet based applications for the purpose of enhancing access to and delivery of government information and services to the general public as well as other government agencies and entities.[5] Smart cities put digital technology and data to work in support of better governmental decision-making and operations while helping to advance the quality of life for a community and its residents. Through the use of the Internet, governments can more easily and efficiently provide services to its citizens. A real-time based government makes life tasks simpler, such as updating tax statements, name and address changes, and settling public utility invoices. A smart government also allows for more open dialogue between the city including such public services as transportation, public safety, parks and recreation and the community for whom they serve.[6] Open communication is vital because it removes many of the administrative and legal barriers often associated with traditional government, thereby, providing increased opportunity for a community's citizenry to get involved in local initiatives while becoming better educated about issues impacting one's neighboring environment.[7]

Geographic Information Systems

Geographic information systems (GIS) involves using computer-based tools for the purpose of electronic mapping, spatial analysis, and database management. GIS analyzes and displays geographically referenced information. GIS performs four important functions. They include:

- Create and organize geographic data
- Manage and format such information into a database
- Analyze for patterns and make design plans, forecasts, working scenarios
- Create visual maps and displays[8]

The type of GIS map can vary in terms of size and scope. GIS can be used to identify underground utility lines (gas, water, electric), constructing residential and commercial survey maps, designing parks and recreation maps, analyzing city transportation patterns as well as elevation and hydrography maps to name only a few (see Figure 11.1).

Transportation is a major focus of smart city initiatives, with the goal of reducing traffic congestion, improving safety, and reducing emissions. Technologies such as intelligent traffic management systems, connected vehicles, and public transportation apps are being used to achieve these goals. Consider, for example, cities that use GIS and smart mobility applications. By 2025, cities that deploy

FIGURE 11.1   GIS—Eight-Layer Map

Source: U.S. Geological Survey.

smart mobility applications have the potential to cut commuting times by an average of 15–20% with some people enjoying even larger reductions. In practical terms, this can mean a savings of 15–30 minutes every day. A lot, of course, depends on a city's existing transit infrastructure and commuting patterns. Using digital signage or mobile apps to deliver real-time information about delays enables riders to adjust their routes on the fly.[9] Installing Internet of Things (IoT) sensors on existing physical infrastructure can help crews fix problems before they turn into breakdowns and delays. Applications that ease road conditions are more effective in cities where driving is prevalent or where buses are the primary mode of transit. Real-time navigation alerts (in combination with GPS services like Waze, Google Maps) can inform drivers regarding possible delays and help them choose the fastest route. Smart-parking apps can likewise point them directly to available spots, eliminating wasted time circling city blocks.

The ability to capture, manage, and display various kinds of geographical (and spatial data) provides obvious benefits when it comes to land use planning, conducting an environmental impact study, or contemplating disaster evacuation scenarios. The use of GIS technology reduces the amount of time necessary for planning improvements while helping to avoid costly mistakes. The demand for accurate geographical information is especially important during a crisis situation. GIS allows for database modeling in which different emergency scenarios are considered in planning for natural and man-made disasters before they occur. Database modeling, for example, can prove highly useful for those communities that are vulnerable to flooding. City planners can use that information to predict where a river is most likely to crest while recognizing the preparations needed to minimize its impact.

Another area where there is a tie-in between GIS and data modeling pertains to safety and security. A community and its residents cannot thrive or enjoy good health unless they are safe. Violence is a public health issue. While technology is not a quick fix for crime, law enforcement agencies can use data to deploy scarce resources and personnel more effectively. Real-time crime mapping, for instance, utilizes statistical analysis to highlight patterns while predictive policing goes a step further by forecasting/monitoring so-called danger zones, thereby heading off incidents before they occur. That said, data-driven policing has to be deployed in a way that protects civil liberties and avoids criminalizing specific neighborhoods or demographic groups.[10] When residents feel safe, they are more likely to have a trusting relationship with law enforcement and partner with them to proactively prevent crime. Additionally, police officers are safer when they are known and trusted by the community they serve.

Historic Preservation and Smart Cities

Creating an environment for industrial development is pivotal to a smart and sustainable city life. The potential economic benefits include enhancing the city's historic look and natural landscape, workforce development, cleaner environment, and improvements in organizational productivity. The obvious challenge is how to advance city development while decreasing the carbon footprint of that community. Further complicating the problem are the legacy costs associated with buildings that were developed decades ago and represent the city's past. While these buildings may have historic significance, they were not built to be energy-efficient by today's standards.[11] By the year 2050, 60% of the buildings currently in use will still be in operation. This begs the question. How do we make such buildings of the past smarter and more efficient going forward? Constructing new buildings and remodeling old ones that are sustainable are major environmental challenges of the 21st century. The use of broadband delivery and well-designed energy management systems are essential to making such buildings cost-effective. Developing the right approach to historic preservation has a role to play in helping to advance the smart city concept.

While opinions vary in terms of what the city of the future should include, it's important to point out that not all systems have to be high-end technical solutions. Even strategies as basic as a well-designed community website or a 211 directory that provides contact information for vital city-wide services (i.e., food, housing health care) are in keeping with the principle of smart city design. Whether its e-government (and Internet web directory) or GIS, the goal of smart city thinking is to centralize key information elements for the purpose of promoting positive economic development and social growth opportunities.[12]

Broadband Delivery and Smart Cities

The term *broadband delivery* refers to any system designed to deliver high-speed Internet access to office, education, and residential dwellings. It presupposes the use of computers, tablets, and smartphone devices. Broadband delivery is central to the principle of smart city development. It has sometimes been compared to developing the U.S. interstate highway system in the 1950s. Broadband delivery represents the great infrastructure challenge of the early 21st century. Like electricity a century ago, broadband delivery is the foundation for economic growth, job creation, global competitiveness, and a better way of life.[13] Designing a high-speed broadband delivery network is at the heart of smart city development and economic planning. It has to be understood within the larger context that it is helping to build entirely new industries, change how we educate children, deliver health care, manage energy, engage government, ensure public safety, as well as providing entertainment and value-added services.

The business community, for its part, needs broadband to compete on a global level. More and more, they seek out forward thinking "smart cities" when choosing to grow their business. Broadband delivery also makes it easier for job seekers looking for new employment opportunities. This same capability enables businesses to recruit electronically while helping to increase a larger pool of candidates. An estimated 80% of all job searches are done online.[14] And having a digitally fluent workforce brings productivity gains to firms, which can then reward employees with higher wages.

The Role of Public–Private Partnerships

Broadband delivery has become an important symbol of national development. Internationally, the best examples of broadband development and delivery rely on some kind of public–private partnership. A public–private partnership can be defined as a contractual agreement between a public agency (federal, state, or local) and a private sector entity. Through this agreement, the skills and assets of each sector (public and private) are shared in delivering an important service or facility for the general public's use. In addition to the sharing of resources, each party shares in both the risks and rewards in providing such services or facilities.[15] Examples of public–private partnerships can be seen in transportation (airport and highway construction) as well as energy (gas and electric utilities, advancing fuel efficiency, etc.).

Broadband delivery is considered a critical planning piece in helping to accelerate business development while providing new opportunities for innovation, expansion, and e-commerce. Most countries of the world place a high priority on Internet delivery speed as shown in Table 11.1. The average Internet speed by country varies significantly throughout the world. In general, wealthier countries (with strong infrastructure) have higher Internet speeds. It is worth noting also that smaller countries are often better able to deploy high-speed Internet, which is one reason why countries like Monaco, Liechtenstein, and Israel rank high on the global list of high-speed Internet delivery. These top 20 countries have been able to create a top-tier Internet infrastructure, thereby allowing their respective businesses and government agencies to take advantage of faster communication speeds and more reliable web hosting services. This, in turn, has had a major impact on a country's digital economy and financial sectors giving them a comparative advantage when compared to other nations.

TABLE 11.1 International High-Speed Internet Delivery

	Country	*Estimated Speed and Delivery Time*
1.	Monaco	319.59 Mbps
2.	Singapore	300.83 Mbps
3.	Chile	298.05 Mbps
4.	Hong Kong	292.21 Mbps
5.	China	280.01 Mbps
6.	Switzerland	279.08 Mbps
7.	France	271.33 Mbps
8.	Denmark	270.27 Mbps
9.	Romania	260.97 Mbps
10.	Thailand	260.54 Mbps
11.	United Arab Emirates	256.04 Mbps
12.	United States of America	256.03 Mbps
13.	Japan	248.34 Mbps
14.	Spain	248.25 Mbps
15.	Hungary	245.97 Mbps
16.	Canada	240.03 Mbps
17.	Liechtenstein	240.25 Mbps
18.	Israel	216.29 Mbps
19.	New Zealand	214.47 Mbps
20.	The Netherlands	209.11 Mbps

Source: Wisevoter.[16]

Smart Cities and Internet Governance

The 21st century-digital economy stands in marked contrast to the very assumptions and technology patterns of the industrial age. The industrial age gave us the concept of mass production that relied heavily on centralized manufacturing facilities, where the methods of assembly were highly routinized and standardized.[17] In contrast, the 21st century-digital economy celebrates the entrepreneur and the power of a good idea. The Internet has become the great equalizer in terms of affording increased opportunity for the person who wants to advance a creative idea or an innovative solution to a problem. The Internet can be considered an example of a common good. The term *common good* has a time-honored tradition dating back to the time of Aristotle. It is a utilitarian ideal and should be thought of as representing the best possible good for the greatest number of people. Today, the principle of common good can be seen in such things as national parks, interstate highways, and the electromagnetic spectrum. The goal is to provide the maximum value and benefit for the greatest number of people.[18]

In her book , *Governing the Commons*, Nobel laureate economist Elinor Ostrom raises the central question, how do a group of people who share a common resource organize and govern themselves while avoiding the temptation to act opportunistically.[19] At the time of her writing she was talking about fisheries, forests, and groundwater use. There are a range of choices between government ownership and purely private control. Ostrom's goal is to develop a framework for self-governing and creative institution building while serving the interests of diverse populations. As she points out, the prospect for success will vary depending on the circumstances citizens face. Some self-governance structures will succeed, whereas others will fail so that the common resource will be depleted or destabilized.

In Ostrom's work, there is a tacit recognition for what economists refer to as tragedy of the commons, which refers to a situation in which individuals with access to a public resource (also known as the commons) act in their own self-interest and, in doing so, ultimately deplete the resource. This economic theory was first conceptualized in 1833 by British writer William Forster Lloyd. Ostrom demonstrated how local property can be successfully managed by local common ownership without the need for regulation by central authorities or privatization. In the 30 plus years since Governing the Commons appeared, hundreds of studies have used Ostrom's analytic approach to evaluate and identify common property issues such as groundwater use, roads and highways (traffic flow patterns and congestion), and electromagnetic spectrum to name only a few examples.[20] Today, Ostrom's work has equal relevance if we consider the Internet as an example of a common good. The common good, in this case, means allowing the Internet to function like a vital service (not unlike water and electricity) where users can and should have equal access. The common good also means protecting the Internet from those users who would misuse or destabilize its operation. This idea becomes especially salient when one considers that no one (and no country) owns the Internet. And yet there is no question that managing it well is in everyone's best interest. To accomplish that, let's consider for a moment the importance of Internet governance.

Key Internet Governance Issues

Internet governance is the process of guiding and managing the development and use of the Internet. It's responsible for setting the rules and regulations that keep the Internet running smoothly as well as protecting the general public who use it. Government, business, education, social/religious organizations, and citizens alike have a role to play in shaping the future of the Internet. It can be a complex and challenging process, but it is ultimately essential for ensuring that the Internet remains a safe and secure space for everyone. There are some key issues in Internet governance, which are constantly changing and evolving. The following are just a few examples:

* Setting technical standards for Internet use
* The protection of intellectual property
* Monitoring and regulating against Internet fraud
* The protection of online privacy and data
* Monitoring and regulating against cyberbullying
* Monitoring and regulating against misinformation and censorship

As the Internet takes on increasing importance in our lives, the need for effective governance becomes ever more important.

Smart Homes

A smart home is a residential dwelling that uses highly advanced automatic systems for lighting, temperature control, information and entertainment services, window and door operations, security, and many other functions. A smart home relies heavily on Internet-connected devices and help to enable digital lifestyle in its many forms. A smart home appears "smart" because a variety of sensors monitor the daily activities of house use. The setup for both appliances and devices can be automatically controlled remotely by a homeowner using both mobile or other type of networked devices. One important feature of a smart home design is that it's built with a strong sense of sustainability and efficiency. Smart houses combine the best features of built-in intelligence with the ability to adapt. A smart house is typically designed around four operating principles. They include 1) the smart hub, 2) smartphone apps, 3) broadband delivery, and 4) smart home design features.

The Smart Hub

A smart house is typically designed around four operating principles. The first is the smart hub which functions as the command center. It's the organizing piece that connects various individual devices which allows them talk to one another. The design and construction of new homes will typically start with a Wi-Fi router as a standard feature as well as having voice assistant smart speakers located strategically throughout various rooms. The smart hub is often paired with digital voice assistants such as Amazon Alexa, Apple Siri, and Google Assistant.

The Internet of Things: Smart Homes

The Internet of Things (IOT) is a working concept that describes a smart, actively engaged network that monitors physical objects "things" and shares the said information between one or more devices and a system platform. Think of IoT as a type of information ecosystem which contain built-in sensors and communication hardware that are connected to a system platform.[21] Central to this idea is the importance of interoperability which means the ability of different monitoring devices and software applications to connect and communicate in a coordinated way. The job of the system platform is to integrate the various data inputs and apply analytics to address specific user needs.[22] The IoT is not one network but a series of smart networks used in variety of settings such as homes offices, factories, retail stores, vehicles as well as human use. The IoT assumes a wide range of devices and physical objects including:

- Smart refrigerators
- House and business security monitors
- Energy management
- House and business smart thermostats
- Traffic control in major cities
- Health and fitness devices
- Automobile collision avoidance systems
- Heart rate monitors
- Mail and package delivery tracking
- Self-checkout in retail stores

As one example, consider how a heart rate monitor works. A heart rate monitor is a small, wearable device (chest straps or wrist worn) that continually measures a person's heart rate. They detect each heartbeat and transmit the data to a receiver such as a watch, fitness wearable, or phone app. The data is displayed as the number of beats per minute. The chest strap heart monitor, for example, uses electrode sensors and are considered accurate as electrocardio-grams (EKG). Most heart rate monitors have indicators showing whether the person exercising is operating within their target heart rate zone and gives audi-ble or visual alerts when the person is above or below that zone.

The role of IoT in a smart home setting enables the hub center to create a highly connected and intelligent living space. IoT technology allows devices and appliances to communicate with each other and with homeowners by providing enhanced automation and control. Specifically, IoT integrates multiple services and applications, including heating/AC, lighting, security and energy manage-ment. One of the important benefits of IoT in smart home design is the ability to remotely control the switching on of lights, adjusting a thermostat for tempera-ture control, and/or checking security cameras. IoT's remote capabilities allows for greater convenience and efficiency.

Smartphone Apps

The smartphone app gives the user the ability to control or monitor their homes remotely. The user simply downloads the specific app in combination with the utility or equipment that they wish to monitor and control. A mobile app also gives the user ability to fine-tune the home's settings and schedules. This be-comes especially important when trying to control heating and air-conditioning, security systems, and energy monitoring. Also important is the ability to adjust settings and schedules remotely via one's smartphone.

Broadband Delivery

Broadband delivery in smart home design has to be understood in the larger context that it is providing an electronic gateway for a whole host of entertain-ment, utility, and value-added services. There are several different ways in which high-speed Internet access can be delivered to the home. The principle methods include cable television, telephone-based fiber optic cable, and mo-bile wireless.

Cable Television

A cable television system is a communication system that distributes broadcast and satellite-delivered programming by means of coaxial and/or fiber-optic ca-ble to people's homes. Broadband delivery in a cable television context means multichannel television, high-speed Internet access as well as enhanced infor-mation services. A cable television system is patterned after a tree-and-branch network. The signals from the headend point (i.e., master receiving site) are distributed to population centers (or neighborhoods) on heavy-duty cable called

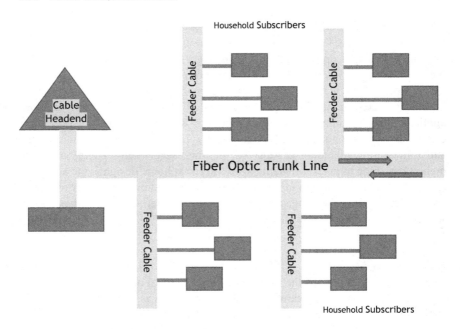

FIGURE 11.2 Cable Television: Tree and Branch Architecture

trunk lines (see Figure 11.2). In the typical cable system, the drop line coming into a subscriber's home connects to an external converter box, which in turn, delivers the signals to the user's television set. At the same time, a cable television operator is capable of delivering high-speed Internet access to a residential dwelling via a cable modem (see Figure 11.2).

Fiber Optics

Optical fiber are thin strands of extremely pure glass capable of transmitting large quantities of information over long distances with little signal loss. Fiber optics uses light as a method for encoding a transmitted signal. A standard fiber optic link consists of three parts: a light source, optical fiber as the primary transmission medium, and a transducer receiver/detector. The light source is a light-emitting diode (LED) or an injection-laser diode (ILD) laser. The LED modulates an incoming electrical signal into an optical one which is then transmitted directly to a house or an office. At the receiving end, the transducer converts the optical signal back into an electrical signal. The electronic information is then ready for input into electronic-based communication devices such as a computer or television set. Fiber optic systems offer users more potential bandwidth than any other type of transmission medium.

Smart Home Design Features

Smart home design features refer to the many devices and software applications that make a smart home, smart. No two smart homes are alike. A smart home is customized to the unique priorities, goals, and interests of the homeowner. A smart home allows homeowners to control appliances, thermostats, lights, and other devices remotely using a smartphone or tablet through a Wi-Fi Internet connection. Smart home appliances are often designed with self-learning capability so they can learn the homeowner's schedules and make adjustments as needed. A smart home design can generally be divided into six general categories. They include 1) home entertainment systems, 2) high-speed Internet access, 3) energy

1. Home Entertainment Systems

- Ultra-High-Definition Television
- Home Theatre Surround Sound
- Multiroom Speakers and Audio Zones
- OTT Video Streaming
- Multichannel Television
- Digital Video Recording

2. High-Speed Internet Access

- Electronic Commerce
- Videoconferencing
- Music File Sharing and Delivery
- Electronic Banking
- Education and Training
- Research
- Online Gaming

3. Energy Management

- Smart Thermostat—Heating and AC
- Monitor Individual Appliance Use
- Track Gas and Electric Use

4. House Management and Security

- Smart Refrigerators
- Smart Lighting and Enhancements
- Security Cameras, Motion Detectors
- Garage Door Opener

5. House Cleaning Automation Support

- Robot Vacuums
- Dishwashers
- Water Softeners
- Robotic Pool Cleaners

6. Medical and Health-Care Monitoring

- Remote Patient Monitoring
- First Alert Response for Elderly Residents

FIGURE 11.3   Smart Home Design: Enhanced Features

management, 4) house management and security, 5) house cleaning automation support, and 6) medical and health-care monitoring (see Figure 11.3).

Home Entertainment Systems

Home entertainment systems are designed to maximize the user's audio and video equipment using a combination of high-definition television, surround sound speakers, and a high-speed Internet connection. The goal is to recreate a high-end movie theater experience. Two of the distinguishing features of a home entertainment system is the high-definition monitor and the sound experience. A large 38–60-inch-high-definition television set creates a level of sharpness and clarity that makes for a theater-or sports-like experience (see Figure 11.4). The design of an ultra-high-definition television set is multifunctional providing both ports and wireless capability that allow the set to serve as the video screen for different kinds of applications, including:

- Multichannel television
- High-speed Internet access
- OTT video streaming
- Video games

FIGURE 11.4   Home Entertainment System

- Videoconferencing
- Music and DVD playback

When a person attends a movie theater, they hear music, dialogue, and sound effects not just from the screen but from throughout the movie theater. In a well-designed surround sound system, (typically 4–6 speakers), the audio signal is split into multiple channels so that different sound information comes out of the various speakers. The most direct and noticeable sounds come from the front speakers. The speakers to the rear fill in various types of background sound in the movie such as dogs barking, rushing water, or the roar of an airplane overhead. The side and rear speakers work in tandem with the front speakers to create the sensation of movement, specifically, a sound that starts from the front and then moves toward the back.[23]

In creating a home entertainment system, there are non-media elements to consider, including proper lighting, wall mounting or equipment cabinetry, as well as comfortable seating. Sun glare, for example, can undermine the clarity of a television picture. Lighting control (or automated lighting) gives homeowners the ability to adjust light levels to maximize the television viewing experience. A second important consideration is selecting equipment cabinetry that is properly sized. If the equipment cabinet is too small (or does not provide enough air circulation) the homeowner runs the risk of the equipment overheating which can directly affect the performance and life span of the television receiver, modem, and related equipment. In modern home design, it often happens that high-definition television sets are configured (and wall-mounted) to be placed over the user's fireplace. While efficient from a design standpoint, it is less than ideal from a viewing perspective since the person is forced to look up at the television screen. A third consideration is in creating the proper seating. Home entertainment seating should be visually attractive, comfortable, and built at the right height to maximize the television viewing experience.

House Management and Security

From lighting and energy management to home security, the design of such systems are tied together by one or more IoT system platforms. A smart refrigerator, for example, informs the homeowner that the family is running low on milk and that the lettuce is now four days old. The smart fridge app creates a shopping list and provides notifications regarding sales in neighboring grocery stores. Similarly, the goal of smart lighting is to create a system of lighting that is designed to be both creative and energy efficient. Such lights are controlled remotely using a wireless connection and a smartphone app. The homeowner sets timers and creates schedules for different lighted rooms based on personal preferences and/

or household routines. They can also be designed to turn on and off automatically based on motion and/or room occupancy. Motion sensors turn lights on automatically when a person enters a room or when they have left. These same lights can also be controlled using voice commands.[24]

Consider further, the functioning of a home security system. Nearly all security systems are now wireless and many also double as part of a smart home automation system. The goal of a home security system is to protect the safety and security of a home as well as the people inside it. Such threats to safety and security can come in many forms such as a burglary, home invasion, fire, flood, or other environmental disaster. Home security systems are designed to monitor for various types of intrusions. The first level of security is smart doorbells that allow homeowners to see and communicate with people who come to their doors even when they're not at home. A home security system uses a combination of sensors that communicate over radio frequencies or wires to a central hub, which then communicates with the outside world using a cellular telephone connection or landline. The hub is generally a touch screen mounted to the homeowner's wall or placed on a countertop. The sensors are strategically located throughout a person's home; specifically at doorways and first floor windows as well as hallways and high-traffic areas. These sensors detect when a door or window is opened or closed, when someone is moving inside a home, or both. When the system is triggered, it sends an alert to the hub which then sounds an alarm as well as sending a text notification to the user's smartphone. It also sends a signal to a home security monitoring center.[25]

Smart Cities/Smart Homes: Building the Right Synergy

A smart city becomes "smart" when it connects the government, business, and educational infrastructure to leverage the collective intelligence of the city. Cities that are able to fully integrate all aspects of government, business, education, and other community stakeholders are more likely to see increases in economic productivity, quality of life, as well as better living standards.[26] And just as cities are recognizing the need to be smarter, so too are the homes to which such people occupy. If one of the goals of smart city development is to become more energy efficient and sustainable, smart homes play an essential role in helping to accomplish this. There are several touch points that connect city planning with homeownerships; specifically in such areas as environmental initiatives, public safety, enhanced transportation systems, emergency evacuation procedures, and sustainable development. There can and should be a natural synergy between smart cities and smart homes; the goal of which is to optimize and promote the betterment of a city and its residents by using effective information technology and support services.

Smart People and Digital Literacy

The Digital Divide and ICT4D

As the world's population gains greater access to the Internet, digital lifestyle brings with it a certain measure of social and technological inequality. There is a noticeable gap that separates people within the same community, region, or country. Social scientists refer to this as the problem of the *digital divide*.[27] Simply put, the digital divide refers to the disparity between the technological haves and have-nots in terms of geographic locations or demographic groups.[28] The term *digital divide* came to the forefront of public discussion when it first began appearing in several United Nations (UN) reports.[29] ICT4D (Information and Communications Technologies for Development) is an international movement originating with United Nations Development Program (UNDP), whose goal is to bridge the digital divide by making access to digital technologies more equitable among poor and marginalized countries. ICT4D is viewed as a force for economic and social development around the world. It is generally recognized that people living in developed countries, especially those in urban areas, tend to have easier access to technology compared to people in underdeveloped countries. This is particularly true in rural or remote areas.[30] ICT4D presupposes the use of communication and information systems technology for the purpose of advancing worldwide digital literacy. ICT4D takes into consideration both the strategies for educating the public as well as methods for financing. The goals of ICT4D are to create enhanced learning opportunities, better economic freedom, personal and professional empowerment and community engagement.

While the focus of this chapter has been on smart cities and smart homes, we also need to consider the importance of smart people and what it means to be digitally literate. The term *digital literacy* means knowing how to use digital technologies and services. Digital literacy is an indispensable 21st-century requirement for all global citizens, whether to seek out information, communicate, find employment, engage in professional training, and/or to socialize.[31] There are a couple of key components to digital literacy. They include 1) the ability to find information, 2) computer skills proficiency, 3) recognizing the importance of online safety, and 4) the ability to communicate effectively.

Finding Information

Searching for information represents the most basic reason why someone uses the Internet, namely to gather information about topics and issues that are important to the user. The search engine in combination with hypertext linking provides a structured road map while making the Internet more accessible to navigate. The Internet provides the general user with a wealth of information. At issue is the fact that there is often too much information to choose from. It is sometimes difficult to sort between real information, misinformation, online marketing, and social media opinion. Information that is ranked high on a search engine, for example, may having nothing to do with the quality of the content itself. Being digitally literate means knowing how to navigate the Internet to find the best information.

Computer Skills Proficiency

Twenty-first century business, government, and education need to hire employees who have the right computer skills. However, not everyone entering today's workforce is fully equipped with the requisite digital skills training. It often happens that many of the said organizations struggle to find qualified talent. Digital skills are at a premium, even in advanced economies. As an example, the European Union's Digital Economy and Society Index (DESI) shows that approximately 42% of Europeans lack basic digital skills, including 37% of those in the workforce.[32] In practical terms, those who are digitally literate have the ability to perform basic tasks on the computer. This includes the ability to navigating a browser, learning keyboard commands, operating different kinds of software systems, and knowing how to download various kinds of software programs. These same set of skills should be translatable and adapted to the unique requirements of any business or organization.

Online Safety

Being safe online means that the user has the knowledge to recognize and identify potential cybersecurity issues as well as understand how to handle websites, email phishing and ransomware attacks as well as smartphone texts that engage in misinformation and fraud. Disinformation and misinformation erode trust in public institutions, exacerbate class conflict, foment fear and hatred, weaken the credibility of business and government organization while emboldening hostile actors.[33] Online safety means having the knowledge to identify such potential risks while browsing, sharing, or surfing the Internet. It enables individuals to use tools such as firewalls, antivirus software, and two-factor authentication to secure their computers and phones. Online safety also means parents teaching their children to know how to recognize and avoid strangers online.

Communication Skills

Communication skills presuppose the ability to know how to effectively communicate via the Internet. This can include sending email, texting, using social media, live streaming, engaging in chat room discussions, and so on. Message design is important in being able to send and receive information and react in ways that empower the individual and those for whom a person works and associates with. It's also important to remember that all forms of online communication are fast and immediate. Online communication is also interactive and highly reactive. Choosing one's words carefully is important as well as knowing when it's time to step back and not hit the immediate send button.

Discussion

The starting point in overcoming such digital divide barriers is to use a combination of strategies in helping to promote Internet access and digital literacy. To accomplish that, smart city planners recognize the value of public–private partnerships and the essential role that municipalities can play in helping to advance both private and publicly owned broadband networks. In working with private ISPs, local municipalities will often incentivize the ISP to invest in larger community outreach programs as well as allocating public funding to construct public networks and digital skills training.[34] These public networks can take various forms, including libraries, schools, senior citizen centers, free municipal networks, and discounted "lifeline" services financed by local government. In addition, schools and local government can provide free (or leased) laptop/tablet equipment to those students or members of a community who cannot afford them. Digital skills training is also important. Many municipalities will engage various community stakeholders to accomplish that goal including schools, community colleges, workforce and religious organizations, libraries, senior citizen centers, and the like.

Making a community digitally literate is an important step in helping to promote civic engagement. A smarter, more informed community has a better understanding of how government works as well as knowing the types of social services support that are available within a community and how to access them. Civic engagement means registering people to vote, organizing community meetings, and sponsoring community-based initiatives such as food drives and community restoration efforts. Acquiring the right set of digital skills is not only important for learning and workforce readiness; digital skills are also essential to foster a more open, inclusive, and secure society.[35] All this points to the fact that broadband delivery and digital skills training are essential requirements in helping a smart city be smarter.

Notes

1 Jonathan Chatwin, "The Shenzhen Effect: Why China's Original 'Model' City Matters More Than Ever," *CNN*, 2020, May 22, www.cnn.com/style/article/shenzhen-effect-china-model-city-intl-hnk/index.html
2 Kristina Garcia, "Understanding India's Urban Future," *Penn Today*, 2023, February 10, https://penntoday.upenn.edu/news/understanding-indias-urban-future
3 R. Lopez and G. Castro, "Sustainability and Resilience in Smart City Planning," *MDPI* 13 (2020): 1–25.

4 N. Komninos, C. Kakderi, A. Panori and P. Tsarchopoulos, "Smart City Planning from an Evolutionary Perspective," *Journal of Urban Technology* 26,2 (2018): 3–20.

5 U.S. Department of Agriculture, "E-Government," 2023, www.usda.gov/ocio/centers/irmc/e-government

6 Bernd Wirtz, Paul Langer and Florian Schmidt, "Digital Government: Business Model Development for Public Value Creation—A Dynamic Capabilities Based Framework," *Public Administration Quarterly* 45,3 (2021): 232–255.

7 "What Is a Smart City? Definition and Examples," *TWI*, 2023, www.twi-global.com/technical-knowledge/faqs/what-is-a-smart-city#SmartCityDefinition

8 Jean-Paul Rodrigue, *The Geography of Transport Systems*. 5th ed. (New York: Routledge, 2020).

9 Paul Bolstad, *GIS Fundamentals*. 6th ed. (Twin Cities, MN: University of Minnesota, 2019).

10 Spencer Chainey and Jerry Ratcliffe, *GIS and Crime Mapping* (London: Wiley, 2005).

11 H. Abu Bakar, R. Razali and D. Jambari, "A Qualitative Study of Legacy Systems Modernization for Citizen-Centric Digital Government," *MDPI* 14,17 (2022), www.mdpi.com/2071-1050/14/17/10951

12 Wirtz, Langer and Schmidt, "Digital Government: Business Model Development for Public Value Creation—A Dynamic Capabilities Based Framework," 232–255.

13 Richard Gershon, *Media, Telecommunications and Business Strategy*. 3rd ed. (New York: Routledge, 2020).

14 Chris Kolmer, "15+ Incredible Job Search Statistics, 2023," *Zippia*, 2023, February 27, www.zippia.com/advice/job-search-statistics/#:~:text=80%25%20of%20jobs

15 Frank Beckers and Uwe Stegemann, "A Smarter Way to Think about Public-Private Partnerships," *McKinsey & Company*, 2021, September 10, www.mckinsey.com/capabilities/risk-and-resilience/our-insights/a-smarter-way-to-think-about-public-private-partnerships

16 "Internet Speed by Country," *Wisevoter*, 2023, https://wisevoter.com/country-rankings/internet-speeds-by-country/

17 Klaus Schwab, *The Fourth Industrial Revolution* (New York: Crown-Business, 2016).

18 Antonio Argandoña, "The Stakeholder Theory and the Common Good," *Journal of Business Ethics* 17 (1998): 1093–1102.

19 Elinor Ostrom, *Governing the Commons: The Evolution of Institutions for Collective Action* (New York: Cambridge University Press, 1990).

20 Roberta Herzberg, "Elinor Ostrom, Governing the Commons," *The Independent Review* 24,4 (2020): 627–636.

21 "What Is the Internet of Things?" *Insider Intelligence*, 2023, www.insiderintelligence.com/insights/internet-of-things-definition/

22 McKinsey Global Institute, *The Internet of Things: Mapping the Value*, 2015, www.mckinsey.com/~/media/mckinsey/industries/technology%20media%20and%20telecommunications/high%20tech/our%20insights/the%20internet%20of%20things%20the%20value%20of%20digitizing%20the%20physical%20world/unlocking_the_potential_of_the_internet_of_things_executive_summary.pdf

23 Tracy Williams and Tom Harris, "How Home Theater Works," *How Stuff Works*, 2023, https://electronics.howstuffworks.com/home-theater3.htm

24 Jennifer Tuohy, "Smart Switches or Smart Blubs," *The Verge*, 2022, June 14, www.theverge.com/23156554/smart-bulbs-switch-lighting-guide-how-to

25 Jennifer Tuohy, "How Does a Home Security System Work," *U.S. News*, 2022, July 14, www.usnews.com/360-reviews/services/home-security/how-does-a-home-security-systemwork#:~:text=When%20the%20system%20is%20armed,if%20you%20have%20professional%20monitoring

26 Tooran Alizadeh, *Global Trends of Small Cities* (New York: Academic Press, 2021).

27 Sophie Lythreatis, Sanjay Kumar Singh and Abdul-Nasser El-Kassar, "The Digital Divide: A Review and Future Research Agenda," *Technological Forecasting & Social Change* 175 (2022): 121–359.

28 Eric Schmidt and Jared Cohen, *The New Digital Age* (New York: Alfred A. Knopf, 2013).

29 Shiv Ganesh and Kirsty Barber, "The Silent Community: Organizing Zones in the Digital Divide," *Human Relations* 62,6 (2009): 851–874; See also, Jan van Dijk and Kenneth Hacker, "The Digital Divide as a Complex and Dynamic Phenomenon," *The Information Society* 19,4 (2003): 315–326.

30 Richard Heeks, *Information and Communication Technology for Development* (ICT4D) (New York: Routledge, 2018), 5–15.

31 Rodney Jones, *Understanding Digital Literacies: A Practical Introduction* (London: Routledge, 2012).

32 European Commission, "Digital Skills and Jobs," *Shaping Europe's Digital Future*, https://digital-strategy.ec.europa.eu/en/policies/digital-skills-and-jobs See also: A. Blom, M. Nusrat and N. Goldin, "How to Define, Measure and Assess Digital Skills, World Bank: Arab Voices," 2020, August 10, https://blogs.worldbank.org/arabvoices/how-define-measure-and-assess-digital-skills-0

33 Eileen Culloty and Jane Suiter, *Disinformation and Manipulation in the Media* (London: Routledge, 2021).

34 A. Tomer, L. Fishband, A. Siefer and B. Callahan, "How Broadband Can Deliver Health and Equity to All Communities," (white paper). *Metropolitan Policy Program at Brookings Institute*, 2020, February 27, www.brookings.edu/articles/digital-prosperity-how-broadband-can-deliver-health-and-equity-to-all-communities/

35 R. Bandura and E. Mendez Leal, "The Digital Literacy Imperative," *Center for Strategic and International Studies*, 2022, July 18, www.csis.org/analysis/digital-literacy-imperative

12

DIGITAL NEWS REPORTING AND THE NEW JOURNALISM

Introduction

In his book, *Megatrends*, author John Naisbitt wrote that the problem with the 19th-century train industry was a failure to ask the question: What business are you really in? Naisbitt contends that many industrialists at the time incorrectly saw themselves in the train business rather than the future of transportation.[1] Today, the question for journalists and newspaper managers is the same. What business are you really in? If the answer to that question is newspaper, then the road ahead will be formidable. One of the great paradoxes of the newspaper industry is that while circulation and advertising levels are in decline, readership levels are up as a whole. The vast majority of the public worldwide gets some portion of their news online. And the same digital space has become home to both traditional newspapers and digital-only news outlets. Newspapers have more readers than ever especially among young people. The problem, however, is that most of these people get their news online for free rather than paying for a newspaper or magazine.[2]

Disruptive Technology and the Changing Newspaper Environment

Before the era of digital communication, the gathering and presentation of news was relatively a simple and straightforward. In getting the day's news, one had only to buy a paper, listen to the radio, or watch television. All that has changed. Today, the international newspaper industry is feeling the full effects of creative destruction. The combination of news information on the Internet coupled with the ease and access of posting information and blog commentary has

DOI: 10.4324/9781003294375-12

fundamentally challenged the economic business model for newspaper and magazine production on a worldwide basis.[3] Moreover, the effects of the Covid-19 pandemic, complete with lockdowns and other restrictions, have had a major financial impact on printed newspapers contributing to journalistic layoffs as well as causing advertisers to scale back on their level of advertising.[4] Additionally, we are seeing a structural shift toward a more mobile and platform-dominated digital media environment, which has major implications for the business model that supports the newspaper and magazine industries.[5] At issue is the potential loss of quality news reporting and news analysis.

The New Journalism

This chapter will look at the state of the newspaper industry and consider the transformation of the journalism industry. The smartphone and computer tablet are quintessential disruptive technologies that have fully changed public readership patterns forever going forward. While patterns differ across countries, the smartphone has become the dominant way in which most people access news in the morning.[6] Digital news reporting in combination with the smartphone and computer tablet reading have created both a problem and an opportunity for the newspaper industry. This juncture represents what former Intel CEO Andy Grove refers to as a strategic inflection point, a time when a triggering event in the competitive marketplace requires new solutions or face the prospect of business extinction.[7] There is no going backwards. The rise of digital media and technology has transformed the way we access both news and entertainment.

Causes and Consequences of Newspaper Circulation Decline

Starting in 2008, the world's newspaper industry entered into an unprecedented period of decline. Facing what former *Chicago Tribune* Chairman Sam Zell called a "perfect storm" of forces roiling the media industry and the broader economy, the company filed for Chapter 11 bankruptcy protection from its creditors in December 2008.[8] It was emblematic of the problems faced by newspapers around the world, many of which were forced to either shut down or cut the pay of newsroom reporters and professional staff.

What are the "perfect storm" of forces roiling the media industry? In short, what are the triggering events that are contributing to circulation decline? The causes of newspaper circulation decline are well documented. A number of media research studies and authors have identified five major causes. They include the following.

- The availability of good substitutes in obtaining news information
- The loss of advertising dollars due to free news available on the Internet

- A change in readership demographics among younger audiences
- The high cost of newspaper production and distribution
- The failure to fully appreciate the importance of digital lifestyle

The move from print media to digital has been a difficult transition for the newspaper and magazine industries. Readers have been reluctant to pay for content on the web. The field of journalism is threatened by the sheer quantity of free news in a variety of formats ranging from radio, television, and cable to multiple Internet newspaper and magazine websites that provide varying degrees of free news information. Such changes have affected the quantity and quality of news information now available to the public. The problem is made worse by the fact that there now exists multiple websites promoting fake news and disinformation masquerading as legitimate news.[9] As a consequence, many of today's newspapers have become less substantial in their news coverage. They lack the size, depth, and quality of information to satisfy those readers still willing to pay good money for a print newspaper. As circulation continues to decline, they lose value to advertisers. The solution for many newspapers is to scale back the number of print publication days while simultaneously producing a daily electronic version.[10] It's worth noting that digital advertising revenue across all digital entities (beyond just news) continues to grow, with technology companies playing a large role in the flow of both news and revenue.[11]

Few papers today offer the same level of news coverage of its cities and surrounding community that was once provided in the past. We have now reached a point where many mid-level cities no longer have a local newspaper and, those that do, employ no more than a handful of reporters. Instead, there has been a steady shift toward regional newspapers that provide general news reporting with some local coverage. Critics point to the fact that the regional newspaper is no substitute for the once highly valued local paper. The challenge, of course, is that only a select portion of the public are willing to pay for high-quality news and information.[12] Therein, lies the problem. Specifically, how does one turn an audience that appreciates news but undervalues it into paying customers? To better understand the full measure of such changes, we need to be able to reverse engineer, that is, look more specifically at the process of news selection from a user's perspective and work backwards toward the journalistic source. Stated differently, we need to better understand that today's readers are not the same as in the past; their expectations are different.

Digital News Reporting

The Internet has transformed the reading of news into a multimedia event, including text information, embedded video, and hyperlinks to related stories. Moreover, the very concept of a daily news digest (or once-a-day news presentation) is no longer a valid premise. Readers have now come to expect regular news updates to existing stories as well as the inclusion of late-breaking stories as part of the overall news website composition. Journalists in the digital age must operate in a world where the news cycle moves faster. As a result, striking a balance between timely and in-depth reporting is often more difficult.[13] Part of this same news presentation includes a running history of the stories' evolution as well as blogs and commentary that consider what different readers have to say about an ongoing story. The smartphone and computer tablet have made the reading of news a more interactive and real-time experience.

Reframing the Question

The first rule of technology diffusion is that once you go forward, there's no going backwards. We cannot disinvest what we already know how to do. Both the smartphone and the computer tablet are here to stay. We should, therefore, reframe the question. How does the news media industry combine the best practices of traditional journalism with the best tools available in the digital world in which we live? Says Arianna Huffington, co-founder of the *Huffington Post*,

> Though the distinction between new media and old has become largely meaningless, for too long the reaction of much of the old media to the fast-growing digital world was something like the proverbial old man yelling at the new media kids to get off his lawn. Many years were wasted erecting barriers that were never going to stand.
>
> The future will definitely be a hybrid one, combining the best practices of traditional journalism—fairness, accuracy, storytelling, deep investigations—with the best tools available to the digital world—speed, transparency, and, above all, engagement.[14]

Today, we have before us an opportunity to move the conversation away from the future of newspapers to the future of journalism. In this next section, we consider four perspectives on digital news reporting and the new journalism.

Perspective # 1
News Presentation, Format, and Delivery

Digital news reporting operates in real time. The challenge is no longer about meeting an 11 p.m. deadline for tomorrow's paper delivery. Instead, the goal is to provide ongoing news coverage that includes both direct reporting and regular news updates. A digital newsroom presupposes greater flexibility in terms of digital news story technique, which may include a combination of direct reporting, video inserts, blogs, and news commentary or simply providing a helpful URL link. Among the many benefits the Internet brings to an emerging news story is the ability to stay fully committed (in real time) to an investigative piece well after the traditional newspaper has gone to print. There is a running history of the news event, containing past links that keeps the story fully accessible to the reader. Internet-delivered news allows the reader to grow with the story over time.

Digital news reporting and the computer tablet have forced a fundamental change in the economics of news delivery. Computer tablets and other mobile devices force us to rethink how we receive news. Historically, newspapers and magazines are costly to produce and distribute. Both are subject to two serious disadvantages when compared to electronic media. First, newspaper and magazine production do not realize the inherent economies of scale typically associated with radio and television broadcasting. Rather, there is an incremental cost associated with each newspaper/magazine produced, distributed, and sold. There is an environmental cost as well for any and all publications not sold, thrown away, or recycled. All this points to the mechanics of news delivery.[15]

Traditional print newspapers, today, still adhere to transaction costs and news delivery methods more typically associated with mid-20th-century newspaper practices, specifically, the newspaper carrier and the newspaper stand. Digital publishing releases the publisher/owner from the fixed costs associated with the publication and delivery of news. It levels the news delivery playing field by offering the same economy of scale advantages usually associated with the broadcast and cable television industries. Add to this the importance of digital lifestyle and one gets a very different perspective on the future of news delivery. Publishers recognize that smartphones and computer tablets have become the 21st-century version of the printed page, offering new ways to package and present news information and entertainment.

Today, most newsrooms employ social media editors whose job it is to take content produced by journalists, share it, and monitor what is going on. While these changes still reflect the perceived value and core mission of a newspaper, they also speak to another dynamic, specifically, that a person's social circle can potentially be an important news source. Sharing on social media networks has become a major distribution mechanism for news stories. Like all distribution mechanisms, social media platforms can influence the content they distribute. As stories change, so too does the tone and flavor of the newsmaking process. The audience has in many cases become a primary driver of what is reported, posted, and published. As a result, there are changes happening to the type of stories being created and consumed. Audience engagement is now a key marker of journalistic authority and a core value of the new journalism. Social media tends to reward content that is shorter, more visual, and emotive.[16]

Perspective # 2
Understanding the Importance of Digital Lifestyle

We are witnessing the demassification of media and entertainment product made possible by the Internet and the power of intelligent networking. Broadcast television and large circulation newspapers are no longer seen as the primary means of delivering news information. Traditional mass circulation newspapers and television broadcasting are examples of push technology, whereas the Internet is a decidedly pull technology. Broadcast television and large circulation newspaper take a one-size-fits-all approach; hence the idea of push technology. In contrast, Internet-delivered news gives consumers the ability to compile, edit, and customize the information they receive. Social media is currently the number one place where people start their news journeys using various mobile devices. An estimated 39% of the public use social media as their gateway to news at the start of each day. While Facebook remains the most widely used social network for news, there is steady transition underway toward more video-led networks. TikTok, for example, is fast becoming one of the most widely used social media networks for news within the Generation Z (18–24) age group.[17]

Specialized News

If cable television launched the principle of narrowcasting, that is, specialized television programming (i.e., ESPN, the Food Channel, Disney, etc.), so too has digital news become highly specialized in terms of news and arts and entertainment coverage. Today's journalist is competing for the time and attention of readers who are regularly exposed to a whole host of websites and specialty blogs on most any subject. The audience has become fragmented in terms of its interests.[18] The new journalism features a wide variety of digital storytelling capability to meet the unique interests of its readers. Table 12.1 provides a select sampling of some of today's best-known specialty news websites and blogs.

TABLE 12.1 The New Journalism: Specialty News Websites

The Huffington Post

The Huffington Post is an American online news website founded by Arianna Huffington, Kenneth Lerer, Andrew Breitbart, and Jonah Peretti. It was launched on May 10, 2005. The site covers a wide variety of topics, including general news, business, politics, entertainment, popular culture, and so forth. In February 2011, the Huffington Post was acquired by AOL for $315 million. Arianna Huffington was made editor-in-chief of The Huffington Post Media Group. In 2012, the Huffington Post was the first U.S. digital media enterprise, of its kind, to win a Pulitzer Prize. In celebrating its tenth anniversary, the company now has an editorial staff of about 500 in its New York headquarters as well as a staff of 40 in its Washington office, plus 13 international editions. www.huffingtonpost.com

(Continued)

TABLE 12.1 (Continued)

TechCrunch

TechCrunch (TC) is an online publisher of technology industry news. TC was founded by Michael Arrington and Keith Teare in 2005. TC primarily covers businesses ranging from small start-ups to established companies in the field of media and telecommunications. TC features major stories concerning new information technology as well as product announcements. TC also offers its readers newsletters as well. TechCrunch is one of the highest-read technology startup news sources available on the Internet with over 37 million readers worldwide per month. http://techcrunch.com

Politico

Politico is a political news organization that is based in Arlington, Virginia that specializes in U.S. politics and policymaking. Politico's primary focus includes the U.S. Congress, the Presidency, lobbying, and governmental policymaking. Politico Magazine was created in November 2013 by Susan Glasser, a former editor at *The Washington Post*. She was later named editor-in-chief. Politico now has an online magazine version that features a daily mix of reports, analysis, and opinion. www.politico.com

Business Insider

Business Insider is an American business, celebrity, and technology news website launched in February 2009 and based in New York City. It was founded by DoubleClick founder and former CEO Kevin Ryan. The site provides and analyzes business news and acts as an aggregator of top news stories from around the web. Business Insider covers both national and international business news stories. www.businessinsider.com

Slate

Slate is an online news magazine that covers politics, business, technology, and the arts. It was founded by former New Republic editor Michael Kinsley in 1996. While initially owned by Microsoft's MSN group, it was later sold to the Washington Post Company in 2004. The news site provides commentary and analysis with a style of writing that is both crisp and entertaining. www.slate.com

FastCompany

FastCompany is an online magazine that specializes in innovation and design. The focus of the site is on artistic and creative people as well as business and technology design issues. Fast Company magazine was launched in November 1995 by Alan Webber and Bill Taylor, two former editors of the Harvard Business Review and publisher Mortimer Zuckerman. www.fastcompany.com

Quartz

Quartz is an international business news magazine and is owned by Atlantic Media. It was launched in September 2012. Quartz serves business professionals who travel the world, are focused on international markets, and value critical thinking. Atlantic Media chose the Quartz name because it embodies the new brand's essential character: global, disruptive, and digital. Quartz, the word, is bookended by two of the rarest letters in the English language, Q and Z, an easy-to-remember contraction. http://qz.com

TABLE 12.1 (Continued)

Apartment Therapy

Apartment Therapy is a leading interior design site dedicated to making people's homes and apartment's more physically attractive and useful. Launched in 2001 by interior designer Maxwell Ryan (nicknamed "the apartment therapist") as a weekly newsletter for clients, Apartment Therapy officially became an independently owned media company in 2004 and grew to become a top source for design inspiration, house tours, home projects, organizing and cleaning, and how people live. Through a combination of expert advice, shopping guides, and how-tos, Apartment Therapy shows people how to make their homes more beautiful with true-to-life tips for a range of budgets. www.apartmenttherapy.com/

News Aggregators

Visiting multiple websites to receive information can be a very time-consuming process. News aggregators using AI help to consolidate many websites into a more customized approach for the user. A well-constructed news aggregator enables the user to customize his/her reading with select news items from multiple information and entertainment sites. This, in turn, makes for creating a unique information space or personal newspaper. Examples of news aggregators, include *Feedly, Flipboard, AP News, Apple News, Inoreader* (International news), and *Google News Reader*. Aggregators also reduce the time and effort needed to regularly check websites for updates. One of the benefits of a news aggregator is the ability to receive news feeds and updates directly onto one's smartphone.

Digital News Reading

In today's digital news environment, the smartphone, computer tablet, and laptop computer (as well as hybrid versions) have become the primary means by which consumers get their news.[19]

Smartphone

As was discussed in Chapter 6, the smartphone is used for a variety of applications. It does, however, serve as an important way to access news. Research to date suggests that users consume news on their smartphones in varying degrees throughout the day in what researcher Logan Molyneux describes as "snacking." Having direct and convenient use of one's smartphone lends to sporadic news consumption, sometimes referred to as grazing or checking in.[20] Despite the small screen space and multitasking associated with smartphone, consumers do spend more time on average with long-form news articles (articles 1,000 words or longer) than with short-form stories. The types of stories are in part driven by social media use which plays an important role in news selection and delivery.[21]

The Computer Tablet

The computer tablet is a multimedia platform that can support books, newspapers, movies, music, games, and web content. The computer tablet's multimedia platform provides users with the capability of experiencing information and entertainment on multiple levels including one or more combinations of text, audio, and video. This is the very essence of convergence. Moreover, the computer tablet allows the user to customize one's reading and media experience.

The Apple iPad

The Apple iPad was introduced on January 27, 2010 by Apple's then CEO Steve Jobs. The debut of the iPad was greeted with a great deal of public anticipation. The *Economist* magazine featured Steve Jobs on its cover, hooded, robed, and holding what was dubbed "the Jesus Tablet" because of the quasi-religious fervor with which it was greeted by consumers worldwide.[22] Similarly, the *Wall Street Journal* took a similar tone by noting: "The last time there was this much excitement about a tablet, it had some commandments written on it."[23] Apple sold three million iPads in 80 days.[24] Most importantly, the iPad more than any device of its kind pointed the way to the future of journalism. The iPad created an altogether new type of reading and video experience for the user. As before, Steve Jobs wanted to have end-to-end integrated hardware and software control for this device. Said Steve Jobs at the time,

> We do these things not because we are control freaks. We do them because we want to make great products, because we care about the user and because we like to take responsibility for the entire experience rather than turn out the crap that other people make.[25]

A second important design principle is that aesthetics in design should be as important as the product's function. Apple was not the first to design the computer tablet. It can be said that Apple did not invent the computer tablet so much as reinvent it. For chief designer, Jonathan Ive the most important aspect to the iPad experience is the display screen. The iPad's ergonomic design, clean lines, and high-resolution graphics should be simple and attractive to the touch. Apple reinvented the computer tablet by focusing on ways to improve the user experience.[26] But in doing so, it helped redefine the newspaper screen.

The Computer Tablet and Digital Lifestyle

All computer tablets are controlled by a multitouch graphical user interface (GUI) display. All tablets are designed to download books, newspapers, streaming music and video, as well as other software applications (or apps) where the focus is not on the device but instead on what you can do with it. A second important aspect of digital lifestyle can be seen in the area of mobility discussed in Chapter 6. From laptop computers to smartphones, mobility has become an important requirement for people whose personal lifestyle or professional work habits require greater portability and flexibility of movement.[27] As a device, the computer tablet most closely simulates the traditional newspaper readership experience in terms of portability and ease of use. Research performed by the Pew Research Center indicates that tablet users prefer the computer tablet over other sources of news delivery, including regular computers, print publications, and/or television as a way to obtain quick headlines as well as longer articles. Tablet users are more likely than the general public to follow the news frequently. They also turn to the Internet as a main source for news more so than the general public. In sum, tablet users appreciate having access to multiple news sources from one convenient and portable location.

Perspective # 3
Business Model Innovation—News Delivery and Value Creation

The major test ahead for the modern newspaper owner and publisher is finding the right combination of news gathering, writing, and technology delivery efficiencies that are both cost-effective and sustainable over time. Resistance to change, however, has proven particularly salient for the newspaper industry where executives acknowledge the difficulty in altering the behavior of writers and editors who were trained to write for mature and well-established newspapers. Newspaper executives describe an industry still caught between the gravitational pull of the past and the need to create a faster and more efficient digital future. For many such newspapers, past success can be a liability. The challenge is that many reporters and editors view the newspaper as a final destination point, all the while neglecting the need for social engagement with its readers.

Traditional newspapers and magazines now operate in a world where they compete against multiple free and available news and social media websites. The challenge, of course, is nothing beats free. The problems facing both print newspapers and magazines are analogous to the music industry in the early 21st century when illegal music downloads threatened to tear the music industry apart. There are essentially three ways to finance the cost of production in the field of news media and communication. They include advertising, subscription, and foundational support or a combination of all these. Most of the world's best-known newspapers and magazines have adopted a subscription model of creating a premium service which includes digital access to the said publication. In a major 2022 report and survey conducted by the Reuters Institute, newspaper publishers in general feel cautious about their business prospects for the future. In this annual survey, titled "The Reuters Institute 2022 Media and Technology Report," less than half (44%) of the editors, CEOs, and digital leaders sampled say they are confident about the future, with around a fifth (19%) expressing low confidence. The biggest concerns relate to rising costs, lower interest from advertisers, and a softening in subscriptions.[28]

This report asks the kind of questions that most newspapers worldwide have to consider. How does the newspaper industry leverage quality journalism and the principles of digital lifestyle and turn it to an advantage? The challenge for today's newspaper is to change public perception about the nature of news information and delivery. Tech companies like Apple and Amazon may provide a partial answer to this question. They, better than most, understand the importance of delivering fast and efficient service to its customers using the power of engagement. Both companies have come to recognize that consumers want to customize their music listening and shopping experience. The same principle can apply to news readers as well.

Perspective 4
Misinformation, Disinformation, and Fake News

The new world of digital journalism has set into motion a number of unintended consequences, including the increased use of misinformation, disinformation, and fake news. The term *misinformation* is false or inaccurate reporting; specifically, getting the facts wrong. *Disinformation* is false information which is deliberately intended to mislead the reader by misstating facts. These are not new ideas, but the power of digital news reporting makes it easier to spread inaccurate information. At issue is the fact that misinformation, disinformation, and fake news have the potential to polarize public opinion, promote hate speech and violent extremism while undermining the public's trust in democracy and the democratic process.

In today's digital news environment, there is a potential downside with the Internet being as publicly accessible as it is. Not all self-appointed digital opinion leaders are equal to the task. As writer Andrew Keen points out, our present-day Internet culture has succumbed to the "law of digital Darwinism," the survival of the loudest, most opinionated, and perhaps most calculating.

What the Web 2.0 revolution is really delivering is superficial observations of the world around us rather than deep analysis, shrill opinion rather than considered judgment. The information business is being transformed by the Internet into the sheer noise of a hundred million bloggers all simultaneously talking about themselves.[29]

Nowhere is this more evident than in the field of journalism where blogs, commentary, and social media postings have blurred the once-clear lines of professional journalism. The problem is further exacerbated by the number of political figures, parties, bloggers, and amateur commentators who try and manipulate the conversation and call into question the meaning and purpose of journalism itself.

Fake News

The term fake news has become a familiar phrase in recent years to describe the problem of misinformation. One definition of fake news is represented by former President Donald Trump's general dissatisfaction with the mainstream news media when they write things that are critical of him. This can include *The New York Times*, *NBC Television*, *Washington Post*, and *CNN*. He is, after all, the person who repeatedly called the mainstream media "the enemy of the people." But the real definition of fake news is the many ways in which news information has become weaponized by a host of political parties, advocacy groups, foreign countries, and political operatives.[30]

Disinformation and Anonymity

The purveyors of disinformation prey on the political leanings, personal biases, and fears of the intended audience. Words like *illegal immigrant, socialist, terrorist* can elicit strong reactions by the targeted recipient. After the 2016 U.S. Presidential election, a lot was made of the threats posed to American democracy by foreign disinformation. Stories of Russian troll farms and fake news mills loomed in the national imagination. In 2016, Russian trolls worked to contaminate U.S. political discourse—posing as Black Lives Matter activists in an attempt to inflame racial divisions by fanning pro-Trump conspiracy theories.[31] But while these shadowy outside forces preoccupied politicians and journalists, today's political parties and operatives are now adopting the same tactics of information warfare.

Micro-targeting is the process of slicing up the electorate into distinct niches and then appealing to them with precisely tailored digital messages. The advantages of this approach are obvious: An ad that calls for the defunding of Planned Parenthood might get a mixed response from a large national audience but can be very persuasive to a group of Christian fundamentalist women who are predisposed to that message. The weaponization of micro-targeting was pioneered in large part by the data scientists at Cambridge Analytica. The group's focus shifted once conservative billionaire Robert Mercer became a major investor and installed Steve Bannon as his point man. Using a massive amount of data it had gathered from Facebook and other sources, without users' consent, Cambridge Analytica built and designed psychographic profiles for every voter in the United States with the goal of microtargeting specific voters with messages that would play to their innate fears and prejudices.[32] At issue, was the fact that Cambridge Analytica acquired the private Facebook data of tens of millions of users, the largest known leak in Facebook history and sold this information to then Presidential candidate Donald Trump's political campaign team.[33]

Fake News and Information Sites

The sharp increase and popularity of well-established social media sites has created a predatory secondary market for online publishers seeking to influence public opinion by spreading fake news and disinformation. They do so by regularly printing salacious and attention-grabbing headlines under the guise of plausible sounding news or information sites to suggest legitimate news when in fact it is not. At first glance, such news sites look like regular publications complete with community notices and coverage of schools. But a closer look at these sites contain no mastheads, few if any bylines, and no address for local offices. Many of them provide advocacy for conservative lobbies or extremist organizations.[34]

Deepfake

Deepfake technology can create convincing but entirely fictional photos or video of politicians, business people, and entertainers saying things or performing actions that they really haven't. Deepfakes use AI to replace the likeness of one person with another either by photo or video or audio. Deepfakes are the 21st-century version of photoshopping but with the ability to create a fictionalized video of an event that is entirely made-up.[35] Audio can be deepfaked as well with the goal of creating voice clones of public figures saying fictional things. There are several methods for creating deepfakes, but the most common relies on the use of deep neural networks that employ a face-swapping technique. What is needed is a target video that can be used as the basis for the deepfake as well as a collection of video clips of the person who is the subject of the deepfake.[36] On one level, deepfakes can be very entertaining as is the case when the film industry brings back the likeness of a well-known actor or actress and weaves them into a film or advertisement. The same can be said for humor parody where a well-known celebrity is making exaggerated statements that the public knows to be made up.

In the hands of the wrong person, deepfakes can be used to spread false information and/or designed to harass, intimidate, or embarrass someone. Deepfakes are often used in pornography, whereby AI software imposes a person's face onto another person's body performing various kinds of sexual acts. While pornographic deepfakes were first created to produce videos of celebrities, they are now made to feature private individuals (i.e., former friend or intimate, colleague, classmate, and so forth) sometimes known as revenge porn.[37] Deepfakes are also used to spread misinformation. This is especially true during a time of upcoming political elections and can negatively impact a candidate's political reputation. In July 2023, a political ad appeared featuring images of a Chinese attack on Taiwan setting into motion scenes of looted banks and armed soldiers enforcing martial law in the city of San Francisco. A narrator comments that this is happening under U.S. President Joe Biden. These visuals are not real, and the scenarios are clearly fictional; but they are nonetheless part of a Republican National Committee spot.

Filter Bubbles and Bots

Two hazards of online news information and social media are filter bubbles and bots. To maximize reader engagement, consumers are sometimes subject to filter bubbles, which are an algorithmic bias that skews or limits the type of information that they see on the Internet. Based on past Internet searches, a user can unwittingly find themselves being exposed to information and opinions that conform with their existing beliefs. Filter bubbles can affect a person's social media news feeds, online advertisements, and web searches by essentially insulating the person from outside influences, thereby, reinforcing what the individual already thinks.[38]

News and information bots are automated social media accounts that amplify and reamplify specific tweets and text messages. Bots are used to spread disinformation, whether it's political or social. Consider, for example, the political operative whose goal is to spread a rumor or fabrication on the Internet. The idea might begin on Twitter, which in turn, elicits a strong emotional reaction by the public. The viral tweet catches fire, and suddenly there are thousands of references to it. The AI aspect of bots can efficiently plant one idea in one account and then have every other account automatically retweet that same tweet thousands of times, thereby giving credence to a story that may or may not be true. Say it enough times, and it must be true.

Trolling

The term *trolling* is Internet slang for a person who intentionally tries to instigate conflict, hostility, and/or arguments in an online social community. Platforms targeted by trolls can include the comments section of a social media platform, digital news, or chat room forum. Trolls exhibit a level of mean spiritedness by using inflammatory language designed to provoke angry responses, thereby disrupting an otherwise civil discussion. As Michael Massing points out, it didn't take long before social media and newsroom forums were inundated with insults and mean-spirited attacks posted by "trolls hiding behind the anonymity of the Internet."[39] More and more news organizations have decided to either rigorously vet them or drop them altogether. Social media is fast and immediate, and within minutes an emerging story or a set of comments can become quickly blown out of proportion and taken out of context. And it's sometimes hard for the public not to get swept up in a viral tidal wave of public comment and reaction. The Internet has become the public battlefield in which users have to routinely differentiate between news reporting, blogging, and opinion in addition to well-crafted disinformation.

The Real Problem With Fake News

The Pew Research Center finds that the public has deeply divergent views about fake news and different responses to it, which suggest that the emphasis on misinformation might actually run the risk of making people less well-informed. According to their research, most adult readers blame political leaders and activists far more than journalists for the creation of made-up news intended to mislead the public. At the same time, they believe it is primarily the responsibility of journalists to fix the problem.[40] More than making people believe false things, the rise of fake news is making it harder for people to have confidence in legitimate news information.[41] Discounting all news means also discounting accurate news reporting.

Discussion

One important change that is emblematic of the new journalism and the principle of value creation was the decision by Amazon's Jeff Bezos to purchase the *Washington Post* newspaper. Amazon, for starters, is the same company that introduced readers to its Kindle E-reader and digital books. *Washington Post* columnist David Ignatius remarked that once the shock of the sale wore off, *Post* staffers began to feel the excitement.

> [A]nd when we picked ourselves off the floor and began thinking about this, it began to dawn on people that having someone with $25 billion of net worth acquire your paper, and also to have that person be a proven disrupter of technologies, somebody who made it easy to read print, to read print content (books, magazines, newspapers) on the Kindle, which I think really preceded the tablet as a new way of reading, that's pretty exciting. So by the end of the week, people were thinking, "How do we go on the offensive? How does this dynamic new owner take us into a space where we're going to be more exciting?"[42]

If newspapers are indeed in the information/entertainment delivery business, then the future of newspapers should be about uniquely customized reading experiences and smart advertising. Such newspapers are effectively providing their readers with a news service rather than a newspaper. The delivery of digital news changes the basic relationship between the news media and reader by challenging managers and news editors to shift their emphasis from mass media distribution to relationship building and customization. Bezos is convinced that the *Washington Post,* which he called a "national institution," can be brought into the digital age by leveraging Amazon's technical expertise with the journalistic strength and capability of its news organization.[43]

Newspaper Brand and Authority

Today's newspaper should be simultaneously national and international in perspective while at the same time hyper-local. It should provide a central linking point for a community and its residents. The community newspaper has to be everything local and foster a sense of common ownership in the paper itself. It should be viewed as a community resource where everyone has a stake in its success. While the paper may be owned and published by a group publisher or an individual, the newspaper franchise belongs to the community and its citizens. Names like *the New York Times* (USA), *Yomiuri Shimbun* (Japan), and *El Pais* (Spain), to name only a few, are part of the cultural fabric of their respective communities.[44] The one obvious challenge is that a large percentage of digital subscriptions tend to favor a few select national brands, thereby undercutting some of the lesser-known brands.[45] In contrast, amateur journalism, blogs, and commentary do not carry the same weight and authority as a well-established newspaper with a history and a past.

There is no substitute for the newspaper brand and authority. Quality journalism is best exemplified by those news organizations that have both the resources and the courage to defend their work when it challenges powerful institutions and individuals. The public may perceive journalism as an enterprise comprising individual reporters, but this is rarely the case. The best work is usually done by a team that has the backing of an organization committed to the highest standards of news reporting. As researchers Downie and Schudson point out, "there is a need not just for news but for newsrooms. Something is gained when reporting, analysis, and investigation are pursued collaboratively by stable organizations that can facilitate regular reporting by experienced journalists."[46] News credibility is everything. The 21st-century newspaper should fully understand the importance of its established brand and leverage both its name and position as a starting point for delivering multiple forms of information and entertainment content and to charge a set fee for a combined news service. The truth is, today's reader wants breaking news from well-sourced reporters or smart analysis from experts who know what they're talking about.[47]

Digital news reporting creates both a challenge and an opportunity for the modern newspaper. If newspapers are going to survive the current business and technological climate, the industry will have let go of some traditional assumptions about news format, presentation, and methods of delivery. What business are you really in?—has never become a more pressing question. Today, the Internet has become steadily woven into all aspects of work and leisure. It has become the all-important network engine that drives globalization forward making instantaneous communication possible for business and individual users alike. The smartphone and computer tablet are examples of John Naisbitt's principle of "high tech—high touch."[48] Both devices do indeed change the newspaper reading experience. But it does not have to mean the end of quality journalism. The challenge before us is to transform the current moment into a redesign of modern journalism by combining the best practices from the past with new possibilities for the future. One can envision a scenario, whereby the busy working professional gets his/her daily news by subscribing to a newspaper's online edition during the week. At the same time, the same reader may desire a hard print copy of the same paper for Sunday morning over a cup of coffee. This is digital lifestyle in practical terms and speaks to the future of the 21st-century newspaper. While the technology of delivery may indeed change, the need for talented reporters and writers remains the same. The newspaper's brand and authority must remain constant over time.[49]

Notes

1 John Naisbitt, *Megatrends* (New York: Grand Central Publishing, 1988).
2 *Reuters Institute Digital News Report, 2022* (Oxford: Reuters Institute, University of Oxford, 2022), https://reutersinstitute.politics.ox.ac.uk/digital-news-report/2022
3 Robert McChesney and Victor Pickard (Eds.), *Will the Last Reporter Please Turn Out the Lights: The Collapse of Journalism and What Can Be Done to Fix It* (New York: The New Press, 2011).
4 *Reuters Institute Digital News Report, 2021* (Oxford: Reuters Institute, University of Oxford, 2021), 9–12, https://reutersinstitute.politics.ox.ac.uk/digital-news-report/2021
5 *Reuters Institute Digital News Report, 2022*. See also, Nic Newman, "Overview and Key Findings," 2022, June 15, https://reutersinstitute.politics.ox.ac.uk/digital-news-report/2022/dnr-executive-summary
6 *Reuters Institute Digital News Report, 2023* (Oxford: Reuters Institute, University of Oxford, 2023), https://reutersinstitute.politics.ox.ac.uk/digital-news-report/2023 See also, Nic Newman, "Overview and Key Findings," 2023, June 14, https://reutersinstitute.politics.ox.ac.uk/digital-news-report/2023/dnr-executive-summary
7 A. Webber, "The Apple Effect," *The Christian Science Monitor*, 2011, September 19, 26–31.
8 "Tribune Co. files for Chapter 11 Protection," *Chicago Tribune*, 2008, December 9, www.wsj.com/articles/SB122876270495988567
9 Darrell West, "How to Combat Fake News and Disinformation," *Brookings Institute*, 2017, December 18, www.brookings.edu/research/how-to-combat-fake-news-and-disinformation/
10 McChesney and Pickard, *Will the Last Reporter Please Turn Out the Lights*.
11 "Newspaper Fact Sheet," *Pew Research Center*, 2021, June 29, www.pewresearch.org/journalism/fact-sheet/newspapers/
12 Robert Picard, "A Business Perspective on the Challenges Facing Journalism," in R. Nielsen and D. Levy (Eds.), *The Changing Business of Journalism and Its Implications for Democracy* (Oxford: The Reuters Institute for the Study of Journalism, 2010), 17–24.

13 "The Rise of Digital Journalism," *Maryville University*, 2023, https://online. maryville.edu/blog/digital-journalism/#evolution

14 Arianna Huffington, "Bezos, Heraclitus and the Hybrid Future of Journalism," *Huffington Post*, 2013, August 14, www.huffingtonpost.com/arianna-huffington/future-of-journalism_b_3756207.html

15 Richard Gershon, "Digital Media Innovation and the Apple iPad: Three Perspectives on the Future of Computer Tablets and News Delivery," *Journal of Media Business Studies* 10,1 (2013): 41–61.

16 Emily Vogel and Risa Gelles-Watnik, "Teens and Social Media: Key Findings from Pew Research Center Surveys," *Pew Research Center*, 2023, April 24, www. pewresearch.org/short-reads/2023/04/24/teens-and-social-media-key-findings-from-pew-research-center-surveys/

17 Nic Newman, "Overview and Key Findings," *Reuters Institute Digital News Report, 2023* (Oxford: University of Oxford, 2023). https://reutersinstitute.politics.ox.ac.uk/digital-news-report/2023/dnr-executive-summary

18 Michael Massing, "Digital Journalism: The Next Generation," *The New York Review*, 2015, June 25, www.nybooks.com/articles/archives/2015/jun/25/digital-journalism-next-generation/

19 Matthew Lynes, "The Importance of Mobile and How It's Shaping the News Publishing Industry," *Twipe Digital Publishing*, 2022, June 30, www.twipemobile.com/the-importance-of-mobile-and-how-it-is-shaping-the-news-publishing-industry/

20 Logan Molyneux, "Mobile News Consumption: A Habit of Snacking," *Digital Journalism* 6,2 (2017): 1–17.

21 A. Mitchell, G. Stocking and K. Eva Matsa, "Long Form Reading Shows Signs of Life in Our Mobile News World," *Pew Research Center*, 2016, May 5, www. pewresearch.org/journalism/2016/05/05/long-form-reading-shows-signs-of-life-in-our-mobile-news-world/

22 "The iPad and Steve Job's Second Coming," *The Economist*, 2011, May 2, www. economist.com/blogs/babbage/2011/03/tablet_computers?page=2

23 Walter Isaacson, *Steve Jobs* (New York: Simon & Schuster, 2011), 493.

24 "Apple Sells Three Million iPads in First 80 Days," *Los Angeles Times*, 2010, June 22, http://articles.latimes.com/2010/jun/22/business/la-fi-ipad-20100623

25 Isaacson, *Steve Jobs*, 35.

26 Adam Lashinsky, *Inside Apple* (New York: Business Plus, 2012).

27 Gershon, "Digital Media Innovation and the Apple iPad: Three Perspectives on the Future of Computer Tablets and News Delivery," 41–61.

28 Nic Newman, "Journalism Media and Technology Trends and Predictions, 2023," *Reuters Institute*, 2023, January 10, https://reutersinstitute.politics.ox.ac.uk/journalism-media-and-technology-trends-and-predictions-2023

29 Andrew Keen, *The Cult of the Amateur* (New York: Random House, 2007), 15–16.

30 Eileen Culloty and Jane Suiter, *Disinformation and Manipulation in Digital Media* (London: Routledge, 2021), 11–29.

31 McKay Coppins, "The Billion-Dollar Disinformation Campaign to Reelect the President," *The Atlantic*, 2020, February 10, www.theatlantic.com/magazine/archive/2020/03/the-2020-disinformation-war/605530/

32 M. Rosenberg, N. Confessore and C. Cadwalladr, "How Trump Consultants Exploited the Facebook Data of Millions," *New York Times*, 2018, March 17, www.nytimes.com/2018/03/17/us/politics/cambridge-analytica-trump-campaign.html

33 Nicholas Confessore, "Cambridge Analytica and Facebook: The Scandal and the Fallout So Far," *New York Times*, 2018, April 4, www.nytimes.com/2018/04/04/us/politics/cambridge-analytica-scandal-fallout.html

34 Priyanjana Bengani, "Hundreds of 'Pink Slime' Local News Outlets Are Distributing Algorithmic Stories and Conservative Talking Points," *Columbia Journalism Review*, 2019, December 18, www.cjr.org/tow_center_reports/hundreds-of-pink-slime-local-news-outlets-are-distributing-algorithmic-stories-conservative-talking-points.php

35 Ian Sample, "What Are Deepfakes and How You Can Spot Them?" *The Guardian*, 2020, January 13, www.theguardian.com/technology/2020/jan/13/what-are-deepfakes-and-how-can-you-spot-them

36 Dave Johnson and Alexander Johnson, "What Are Deepfakes and How Fake AI-powered Audio and Video Warps Our Perception of Reality," *Business Insider*, 2023, June 15, www.businessinsider.com/guides/tech/what-is-deepfake

37 Douglas Harris, "Deepfakes: False Pornography Is Here and the Law Cannot Protect You," *Duke Law & Technology Review* 17 (2018): 99–128.

38 D. Wilding, P. Fray, S. Molitorisz and E. McKewon, *The Impact of Digital Platforms on News and Journalistic Content* (Sydney, Australia: University of Technology, 2018), 57–62.

39 Massing, "Digital Journalism: The Next Generation."

40 Amy Mitchell, Jeffrey Gottfried, Galen Stocking, Mason Walker and Sophia Fedeli, "Many Americans Say Made-Up News Is a Critical Problem that Needs to Be Fixed," *Pew Research Center*, 2019, June 5, www.pewresearch.org/journalism/2019/06/05/many-americans-say-made-up-news-is-a-critical-problem-that-needs-to-be-fixed/

41 Sue Ellen Christian, *Everyday Media Literacy: An Analog Guide to Your Digital Life* (New York: Routledge, 2020).

42 Huffington, "Bezos, Heraclitus and the Hybrid Future of Journalism."

43 Mike Isaac, "Amazon's Jeff Bezos Explains Why He Bought the Washington Post," *New York Times*, 2014, December 2, http://bits.blogs.nytimes.com/2014/12/02/amazons-bezos-explains-why-he-bought-the-washington-post/

44 Gershon, "Digital Media Innovation and the Apple iPad: Three Perspectives on the Future of Computer Tablets and News Delivery," 41–61.

45 Nic Newman, "Overview and Key Findings," *Reuters Institute Digital News Report*, 2023. https://reutersinstitute.politics.ox.ac.uk/digital-news-report/2023/dnr-executive-summary

46 Leonard Downie and Michael Schudson, "The Reconstruction of American Journalism," *Columbia Journalism Review*, 2009, November/December, www.cjr.org/reconstruction/the_reconstruction_of_american.php

47 Massing, "Digital Journalism: The Next Generation."

48 In his book, *Megatrends*, author John Naisbitt (1982) coined the phrase "high tech—high touch" as a way to describe the importance of finding the right balance between technology and the softer/aesthetic aspects in the way we live.

49 Gershon, "Digital Media Innovation and the Apple iPad: Three Perspectives on the Future of Computer Tablets and News Delivery," 41–61.

13

CREATING A CULTURE OF INNOVATION

Introduction

From the original AT&T Bell Labs to the modern-day Googleplex, the history of innovative discovery is really the study of how organizations set out to problem-solve. The best moments in innovation seldom follow a predictable path. What is sometimes underappreciated is that great innovators like Akio Morita (Sony), Steve Jobs (Apple), and Jeff Bezos (Amazon), to name only a few, are the faces of a team of engineers, marketers, and designers who spend thousands of hours creating the breakthrough products and services that have become real game changers. They, better than anyone, understand that great discoveries are seldom achieved quickly. Rather, greatness is achieved over time through patience and perseverance. It requires hard work and a willingness to take the long-term view toward project success. In 1997, the year Amazon.com went public, company CEO Jeff Bezos wrote in the company's report to stockholders:

> We believe that a fundamental measure of our success will be the shareholder value we create over the long term. This value will be a direct result of our ability to extend and solidify our current market leadership position. The stronger our market leadership, the more powerful our economic model . . . We can't realize our potential as people or as companies unless we plan for the long term.[1]

What has become known as his "day one" essay is still as relevant today as it was then. The purpose of this essay was to remind the reader of the importance of taking the long view toward project success.

DOI: 10.4324/9781003294375-13

Great innovation is also the story of the lone maverick who imagines an idea that heretofore did not exist. What people like Alexander Graham Bell, Nikola Tesla, Tim Berners-Lee, Susan Wojcicki, and Steve Jobs share in common is an insatiable curiosity. It starts with a compelling idea. What if we did . . . Business author Jim Collins makes the argument "that when you combine a culture of discipline with an ethic of entrepreneurship, you get the magical alchemy of great performance."[2] The best companies have both a culture of disciplined behavior and a latitude for individual action. Such companies create a space where risk and experimentation are encouraged. In this chapter, we consider what it means to create an organizational culture of innovation.

A Culture of Discipline

A culture of self-discipline is critical because it creates an environment where creative people work within a defined system. Knowing the organizational boundaries gives the individual more freedom to act within that system. Highly motivated people are self-motivated. Their sense of mission and purpose is personally driven. The need for enforced rules and structure is secondary. Success is rarely achieved in a sudden flash of insight. There is no magic formula or defining moment that brings about great product transformation. Rather, greatness is achieved over time through a constant, deliberative effort. It's not dramatic, revolutionary change but rather a passion and dedication to hard work. Momentum is built a little bit at a time. As Angela Duckworth writes,

> [T]here are no shortcuts to excellence. Developing real expertise, figuring out really hard problems, it all takes time—longer than most people imagine. . . . you've got to apply those skills and produce goods or services that are valuable to people. . . . Grit is about working on something you care about so much that you're willing to stay loyal to it.[3]

Having the Right People

Great innovation also means having the right people. Putting the right structures, people, and processes in place should occur as a matter of course—not as an exception. Jim Collins makes the point that one of the most important decisions for a senior leader is to clearly assess the performance capability of key professional staff during the start-up of that company or organization. He refers to it as "getting the right people in the right seats on the bus and the wrong ones off it."[4] When thinking about the important positions within an organization, formal titles become less important than the tasks and responsibilities that need to be performed. This is very much in keeping with the principle of hacker culture.

People don't have jobs; they have responsibilities. For Collins, there are two important essentials:

> First, if you begin with *who*, rather than *what*, you can more easily adapt to a changing world. Second, if you have the right people on the bus, the problem of how to motivate and manage people largely goes away. The right people don't need to be tightly managed or fired up. They will be self-motivated by the inner drive to produce the best results and to be part of creating something great.[5]

Having the right people means making the hiring and recruitment of professional staff one of the most important responsibilities for a CEO or senior manager. Having the right people also means not settling for those individuals who may be wrong for the organization. In practical terms, that may mean parting ways with a longtime traveling companion who needs to step off the bus in order for the vehicle to move forward. Apple's Steve Jobs makes a similar point about the importance of finding the right people. For Steve Jobs, putting together the right project team was every bit as important as the project design itself.

> I noticed that the dynamic range between what an average person could accomplish and what the best person could accomplish was 50 or 100 to 1. Given that, you're well advised to go after the cream of the cream. . . . A small team of A+ players can run circles around a giant team of B and C players.[6]

Recognizing and Valuing Talent

Is there a certain litmus test in determining who are the A people for an organization? No. It would be more accurate to say that there are certain truisms that apply in helping to advance highly successful project teams. Among the questions to consider:

1. Does the person share the organization's core values? Part of the success of any business start-up (or project group) is a sense that the person knows that he/she is engaged in some unique work.
2. Does this person possess some exceptional ability? Does this person have the potential to be one of the best in his/her field?
3. Does this person possess a sense of ownership in the work that has to be performed? Is this person willing to take responsibility (i.e., going the extra mile) for ensuring that a job gets finished correctly. This stands in marked contrast to the person who is simply holding down a job.

There is very little sentimentality in Steve Job's thinking.

> I've learned over the years that, when you have really good people, you don't have to baby them. By expecting them to do great things, you can get them to do great things. The original Mac team taught me that A-plus players like to work together, and they don't like it if you tolerate B-grade work.[7]

Mavericks Often Lead the Way

It takes a unique person in a leadership role to appreciate the talent factor when it comes to understanding the role of the maverick within an organization. Mavericks are often some of your best examples of A+ people. They stand apart from the rest of the group. It is almost an article of faith that such individuals are often eccentric, rude, and annoying. They are all too willing to challenge the system by asking tough questions. Mavericks often lead the way when it comes to experimentation. They are fully focused on developing their idea at the expense of everything else. As sometimes happens, the maverick will leave the familiarity of one's home in search of independence and a better place to apply their ideas. Smart, creative companies recognize talent when they see it. They give such individuals the freedom and artistic space to test out new ideas and working concepts.

Hacker Culture

One of the most interesting trends of the 21st century has been the emergence of hacker culture located throughout the workplace of today's best-known media and IT companies. By hackers, we don't mean people who pose security threats to computer networks. Rather, the term *hacker culture* is used to describe smart, talented people who find creative ways to overcome challenging problems and limitations to a project design. Hacker culture is very hands-on and applied. Hacker, in the Facebook sense, means building something quickly or testing the boundaries of what is possible. It's an approach that involves constant refinement. Says Meta CEO, parent company to Facebook, Mark Zuckerberg,

> Hackers believe that something can always be better, and that nothing is ever complete. They just have to go fix it—often in the face of people who say it's impossible or are content with the status quo. Hackers try to build the best services over the long term by quickly releasing and learning from smaller iterations rather than trying to get everything right all at once. To support this, we have built a testing framework that at any given time can try out thousands of versions of Facebook. We have the words, *Done is better than perfect*, painted on our walls to remind ourselves to always keep shipping.[8]

Rather than debating the merits of new ideas, the company encourages its developers to build and test prototypes. "There's a hacker mantra that you'll hear a lot around Facebook offices: Code wins arguments."[9]

One of the core values of hacker culture is a belief that talent and dedication reign supreme. The best ideas should prevail. Implicit in hacker culture is a belief that work should be fun and challenging. If work is fun, then you don't mind working long hours to see a project through to its completion. But working long hours comes at a cost to the individual and his/her family. In contrast to previous generations, hackers tend to be more casual in dress; T-shirts, jeans, and running shoes. They are less concerned about the traditional representations of professional success (business attire, professional titles, corner offices). Instead, the focus is on being smart, creative, and making really great products. The best companies also attract smart, like-minded people.

At one end of the spectrum are the large research and development tech companies such as Google, Apple, Microsoft, and Facebook whose employees are located in multiple buildings on wide-area campuses. Such campus environments feature different kinds of work zones as well as cafes, gyms, and other amenities. At the other end of the spectrum is the small five-person start-up company. Instead of high-end open space architecture, it may be a one-room office over a dry cleaning store. Whereas, the middle ground may be a 130-person start-up that occupies a set of offices that are part of an incubator program at a university. Instead of cafés and gourmet food at the Googleplex, it's pizza all the way, or at least a sandwich from home. What levels the playing field is the power of a good idea and a core group of people who are fully committed to the project at hand. The people who work for such companies and business start-ups have a strong sense of purpose. They are willing to work the long hours to make things happen. Hacker culture means giving team members a real sense of ownership in the process and outcomes for which they are committed.

Risk and Experimentation

Risk and experimentation lie at the heart of every company's ability to innovate. The most successful companies are those that are willing to experiment and not rest on their past achievements. The challenge, of course, is that well-established businesses with a proven track record find it hard to change. While many such companies like to talk a good game about being innovative, they are not inclined to take risks (and stand outside themselves) when things are going well. There is a clear pattern of success that translates into established customer clients, sales volume, and public awareness for the work that has been accomplished to date. A variety of commitments have been made in terms of people, manufacturing, production schedules, and contracts going forward. Such commitments to ongoing business activities have an established trajectory. As researcher Rosabeth

Moss Kanter points out, "mainstreams have momentum. Their path is established, the business flow is already developed."[10] At issue is the fact that most managers are unable or unwilling to sacrifice a successful product in favor of a new untested one (i.e., the innovator's dilemma). Instead of blue ocean thinking, managers become preoccupied with fine-tuning and making slight adjustments to an existing product line rather than preparing for the future. There is a tendency toward playing it safe by focusing on present-day customers and what works. New product development and innovation carry with them uncertainty and risk. The commitment to advance a new technology or service requires large start-up costs, with no guarantees of success. As Rosabeth Kanter writes,

> [A]nd the newer it is, the more likely that there will be little or no precedent, little or no experience base to use to make forecasts. Timetables may prove unrealistic Anticipated costs may be overrun. Furthermore, the final form of the product may look different from what was originally envisioned.[11]

A related problem is the self-imposed limitations of sunk costs, that is, investments in research and technology, construction of production facilities, education and training, contract obligations, and so forth. Such companies feel that they can't afford to change given the amount of time, money, and investment spent in the current research or project design effort. The difficulty, however, is that mainstream technology can become steadily obsolete. It is only when faced with a rival product or a disruptive technology that the same set of managers feel the urgency to adapt and innovate. By then, it may be too little or too late. Response time is critical. Those companies whose response time is slow pay a heavy price in terms of revenue decline, lost market share, and missed opportunity. As was discussed earlier, companies like Kodak, BlackBerry, and Blockbuster were slow to react. Such companies did not anticipate a time when a substitute product (or changing market conditions) might come along and dramatically alter the playing field.

To offset the playing-it-safe mindset, highly innovative companies foster a culture of risk and experimentation. It goes with the territory of making new discoveries. Accordingly, the CEO and senior leadership team help set the tone by putting their full weight behind such experimentation. Leadership plays an essential role in helping to drive digital transformation, and changing the culture is the most significant task facing those leaders.[12] Such companies create a culture of innovation, where experimentation and mistakes are all part of the process for testing new boundaries. They fully accept the possibility of failure. As Microsoft founder Bill Gates writes, "it's fine to celebrate success but it is more important to heed the lessons of failure."[13] David Kelley, founder of IDEO, believes that it is important to rethink the role of failure in the design process. When a novel idea fails in an experiment, the failure can expose important knowledge gaps.[14]

But such efforts can also reveal unique ways of looking at the problem. It can refocus the group's efforts in more promising areas. A culture of innovation means taking risks and with it the very real possibility of product failure. It's part of the DNA of what it means to be innovative.

Creating the Proper Work Space

Creating a culture of innovation presupposes having the right work environment with which to develop and implement great ideas. From the corner office to the nondescript cubicle, there is considerable difference of opinion as to what makes for a highly productive work environment. There are, however, certain truisms in terms of what makes for a creative work space. Innovation needs a place to flourish and grow. The creative office should function like a well-designed stage or movie set, thereby contributing to great performance. Good design space creates opportunities for prototyping new ideas.

Many of today's more innovative companies have abandoned the very notion of the corner office. Certainly, within media and IT circles, the private office is considered a relic of the 20th century.[15] Gone are the immense executive desks from the past symbolizing power and authority as well as trophy-laden walls. Large drawers and closet space for storage are now deemphasized, reflecting the shift away from paper and more toward cloud computing and the electronic storage of information.[16] More and more of today's media and IT executives have given up the private office to be in close proximity with employees, thereby improving overall communication and collaboration.

At the same time, there is still a very obvious need for privacy. Working professionals still need to be able to have quiet, deliberative time to think and work without interruption. The more demanding the task, the more individuals need brief moments of private time to think or recharge. The challenge is that critical thinking time is hard to come by when one is faced with constant interruptions. As Congdon, Flynn, and Redman write,

> The increased focus on collaborative work means we're rarely alone, and the ubiquity of mobile devices means we're always accessible. In light of these pressures, it's not surprising that the number of people who say they can't concentrate at their desk has increased.[17]

Privacy versus open work space is not a zero sum game. Rather, it's about finding a balance between the work that needs to get accomplished and creating the proper work space that will enable that to occur. The professional workspace should reflect the way people actually work. *New York Times* writer Allison Arieff makes the argument that furniture is not the problem. Rather, it has more to do with understanding how people really work in a fast-paced business environment. The key design principle is sustainability where the emphasis is on energy efficiency and economy of space. The designers of the 21st-century office recognize the importance of creating work zones, that is, areas where specific types of tasks get accomplished.[18]

Another consideration is the importance of building intelligence into the design of the modern office work space. The combination of computer and telecommunications technology has had a major effect on the spatial design of the modern-day office. The buildings and office space that workers occupy are not nearly as important as the tools they use to get work done. The blending of powerful communication tools with flexible work space can greatly enhance productivity and innovation.[19] Related to this idea is the importance of mobility which recognizes that business professionals and creative teams need flexibility of movement. Today's working professional should be able to access the Internet anytime, anywhere. Location should never be an obstacle.

Serendipitous Connections

One of the important lessons in innovation is that some of the best moments in creativity and discovery are the result of a chance encounter. The history of business and technological discovery often starts with the chance encounter: "I was sitting next to this guy on an airplane and he said . . . I met this woman at a conference and she told me." The pacemaker was invented by an electronics technician who happened to have lunch with two heart surgeons; Starbucks became a national chain after salesman Howard Schultz stopped by the original single store in Seattle's historic Pike Place Market and realized that his future lay in cafés and fresh-roasted whole bean coffee.

As writer Steven Johnson points out, some of the best discoveries occur when different people with diverse backgrounds and skill sets find themselves in a common space sharing their ideas.[20] The unfiltered exchange of a chance idea can sometimes spawn a radically new working concept. And so it is that some of today's most innovative companies create spaces for chance encounters— enabling good ideas to move freely, making connections in unexpected ways. Steve Jobs makes a similar point when he writes:

> Innovation comes from people meeting up in the hallways or calling each other at 10:30 pm at night with a new idea, or because they realized something that shoots holes in how we've been thinking about a problem. It's ad hoc meetings of six people called by someone who thinks he has figured out the coolest new thing ever and who wants to know what other people think of his idea.[21]

Innovation and Adaptation

The New York Times columnist Thomas Friedman writes that the world at large is being subjected to three simultaneous and interlocking changes: technology, the environment, and the global economy.[22] In the midst of the greatest-ever velocity of change, we must become better skilled at the power of adaptation. The future world of work, for both individuals and organizations, will rely on rapid learning, unlearning, and adaptation. As researchers McGowan and Shipley write, "to successfully learn and adapt, we have to let go of the way we have always done things and perhaps equally more challenging—who we think we are."[23] To accomplish this, we must become comfortable with ambiguity and not knowing. Microsoft's Bill Gates makes the same point when he says, "you are never too smart to be confused. Everything I have accomplished happened because I sought out others who knew more than me."[24] Technology is accelerating the pace of business at unthinkable speeds, so much so that today's working professional may undergo several job changes in a single career. In practical terms, this means learning to adapt, specifically, being able to let go of old ways of doing things including fixed occupational identities and regular/routine work patterns.

The Lessons of the Covid-19 Pandemic

Starting in the spring of 2020, the Covid-19 pandemic disrupted the world's economy by forcing the closing of schools, business, and government agencies throughout the world. But like a natural disaster or war, necessity proved to be the mother of invention. During the initial stages of the pandemic, countless organizations worldwide were forced to pivot and develop remote working from home options. One of the direct consequences of the Covid-19 pandemic is that it led to an exponential increase in the use of Zoom and equivalent conferencing software, thereby creating a new comfort level in terms of its use for business, education, health care as well as the general public.

The Covid-19 pandemic disrupted both large and small businesses alike. It forced the relocation of working professionals from a dedicated place of work to a person's home, apartment, or remote setting. Prior to Covid-19, the term "telecommuting" was an idea in principle that applied to some working professionals but never got the full support of mainstream business. At issue, in the telecommuting debate, was whether employees working at home could be trusted to work efficiently, be productive, and not game the system. Now suddenly, the question of whether people could be trusted to work at home was a moot point. The home office would undergo a major redefinition in terms of setup and design. The new office environment would require a desktop or laptop computer, a high-speed Internet connection, videoconferencing capability, and a cell phone. It should be noted that dedicated videoconferencing facilities for business have been in place since the late 1990s. The Covid-19 pandemic, however, proved to be a major tipping point in terms of promoting remote working at home and the regular use of videoconferencing software. It became an object lesson in the power of adaptation.

Similarly, the field of education—ranging from grade schools to universities—was forced to adapt and modify their approach to classroom instruction. During the initial weeks of the Covid-19 outbreak, educators around the world were forced to learn the basics of online instruction in a short period of time. But steadily, these same educators would adapt and make the transition by creating a virtual classroom space for their students. One of the very real turning points for educators was a letting go of traditional views that classroom instruction could only be taught in person. As we look to the future, online instruction and degree programs now represent a viable training platform for tomorrow's students and working professionals.[25] In fact, many of today's university students prefer a combination of in-class meeting sessions and virtual courses as part of their regular semester work schedule.

One of the other lessons from the Covid-19 pandemic was the level of success and productivity accomplished by many working professionals then operating from home or remote setting. Today, many worldwide organizations are giving their employees the option to work from home full time or in a hybrid capacity, that is, a combination of some days at home and some days in the office or work setting. In fact, many such employees have indicated that they would quit if forced to return to the workplace full time.[26] The aftermath of Covid-19 has also forced many business enterprises to reconsider the need for massive building infrastructure and office space going forward. Another consequence of the Covid-19 pandemic has been a reduced need for physical travel and the standard weekday flight for a two-day meeting. Remote working from home has forced a reimagining of how work gets performed. It is now part of any discussion on workplace productivity and employee satisfaction.[27]

Disney's Pixar and the Serendipitous Encounter

Pixar Animation Studios is an internationally respected film studio known for its critically and commercially successful computer-animated feature films. Creating a work environment that people enjoy working in can be one of the most challenging aspects of modern office design. At Pixar, employees are encouraged to be creative. There is a lot of wide open space that greets a visitor when arriving at Pixar's football-sized atrium. The story behind Pixar's headquarters starts in 1999 with Steve Jobs. As Pixar's co-founder, Steve Jobs brought in the architectural firm of Bohlin Cywinski Jackson, then highly recognized for designing Bill Gates' 66,000-square-foot estate. Steve Jobs wanted to design a building that fostered creativity and where people would interact naturally. The plan called for a central atrium where mailboxes, meeting rooms, cafeteria, and most importantly, the bathrooms were to be located. His intention was to make it so that Pixar's professional staff would casually interact as opposed to going off into separate silos of software coding, animation, and production.[28] The Pixar architectural design makes the serendipitous encounter with different employees from other departments a mainstay of the Pixar organizational culture. Steve Jobs believed that when people casually interact and have fun, good things can sometimes happen.

Décor also contributes to a playful, fun atmosphere. Steve Jobs was well-known for his meticulous eye for design when it comes to Apple's products. But another area where this fanaticism for detail came out was with regard to the steel beams used in the construction of the atrium. The atrium at Pixar is decorated with larger-than-life statues of Pixar characters, concept paintings on the walls, and storyboards and color scripts in clear view. Pixar's rolling, 16-acre campus also includes offices, studio and sound rooms, screening rooms, a lap pool, volleyball courts, and a 600-seat outdoor amphitheater—all of which makes for a welcome escape from the daily routine of work.

According to Pixar Technical Director Danielle Feinberg, collaboration and working together are the central tenets of producing films at Pixar.

Pixar is this wonderful place where we get to make these great movies. It's full of smart, talented, creative and technical people, storytellers, all these great people. One of the cool things here is that the culture of Pixar really is to be nice . . . When you walk in, you're around nice people. There aren't people trying to jam their superiority down your throat. You're making movies. It's this very collaborative endeavor. It works out well that people have varied talents that can plug in. I don't think you work here unless you understand what a team project it is to pull together a movie. All of that works well in tandem. Having people of all talents leads to people appreciating all those talents.[29]

The Googleplex

Over the years, Google has evolved a unique business culture. The company's headquarters referred to as the Googleplex is an informal, highly charged atmosphere that encourages collegiality and innovation. Writer Adam Lashinsky refers to it as *chaos by design*.[30] One of the most important features of the Googleplex is that its overall design and aesthetic can be likened to a university campus. The entry point for the Googleplex was designed and built in less than a year from one of Google's existing buildings. Architect Clive Wilkinson and project team imagined the space as a type of urban campus, a gathering point for visitors as they make their way from the lobby. It is flanked by cafés and dominated by a grand central staircase that encourages people to sit on its steps with their laptops. The welcoming atmosphere was something that co-founders Page and Brin wanted to foster. At lunchtime, the high-ceilinged space is crowded by groups of coworkers eating together in front of a whiteboard that is 20 feet long.[31]

In the beginning, the designers and the engineers had a difficult time adjusting to one another. Wilkinson's team had to fully understand the workstyle of an engineer which involves high levels of engagement and time spent with one's computer. Says Wilkinson, "engineers are very left brain. They might work in teams, but they require a high level of concentration; they sit in front of the computer and crunch formulas in the most extraordinary way." After examining the ways in which employees actually use their space, the architects came up with a list of 13 different types of work zones that include glassed-in offices, library, conference rooms, lecture halls as well as shared workspaces. Page and Brin placed a high priority on air quality and preservation of natural daylight. They instructed Wilkinson's group to have all side offices be fully glassed which allows natural light to stream into the center of the floor.[32]

One of the other important changes that affected Google's building infrastructure and work space was the direct result of the Covid-19 pandemic. Since the end of the pandemic, Google has adopted a hybrid work model in which most staff have the option to work remotely two days a week. They are also given the option to work remotely up to four weeks per year. This provides a great deal of flexibility for its employees who have likely gotten used to working remotely. This approach is intended to strike a balance between in-office and at-home work while helping to avoid the potential initial shock of returning to the office five days per week.[33] Google has subsequently updated its hybrid work policy and notified employees of the need to return to the office and that in-person attendance will be part of an employee's future performance review.[34]

Facebook and Hacker-Style Décor

Today, Meta (parent company to Facebook) claims an international workforce of more than 87,000 employees. Facebook's 30 building campuses are located in Menlo Park, CA on more than 250 acres on the edge of the San Francisco Bay. The campus is split into four sections and is home to more than 10,000 employees. Its two main buildings, MPK20 and MPK21, were designed by Canadian architect Frank Gehry. The company's new corporate headquarters was completed in 2015 and was designed to embody its hacker culture. It is perhaps fitting that the company's main address is 1 Hacker Way, Menlo Park, California. As architectural critic Christopher Hawthorne writes,

> For a field that has long taken pride in generic work spaces—garages, dorm rooms, and suburban office parks—this emerging architectural arms race is a major shift. Unlike Apple and Google, Facebook has managed to have it both ways. It has maintained Silicon Valley's quick-and-dirty aesthetic, its sneaker-wearing and ramen-eating ethos, while also signing up one of the most famous architects in the world.[35]

The new Facebook headquarters features a nine-acre green roof with a half-mile loop that is spaced among trees, cafés, plants, and various types of gathering spaces. The new building is connected to the company's old headquarters, located on the other side of the highway via an underground tunnel. Employees can walk, bicycle, or take a tram from one side to the other. Inside, the building has an open floor plan and features large murals and art installations from local artists.[36] It is a vast warehouse with 24-foot ceilings. There are no private offices or cubicles to divide coworkers. Instead, software designers and engineers occupy rows of shared desk space.[37] Workers roam with laptops, meet on sofas, and scribble on walls, where rusted steel beams, exposed heating ducts, and plywood-covered corridors are part of the decor. The design was intended to express the culture of the world's largest social networking company. Hawthorne describes the workspace as "a dense view of unpainted steel beams alongside cords and wires running from the ceiling, with the heads of employees half-hidden behind giant monitors."[38] The goal is to create distinct neighborhoods of interior space. Zuckerberg elaborated on the design concept:

> It's pretty simple and it isn't fancy, but that's on purpose. We want our space to feel like a work in progress. When you enter our buildings, we want you to feel how much there is left to be done in our mission to connect the world.[39]

Creating Innovation Centers Within a Larger Organization

It's one thing to be a large research and development company such as Apple. It's quite another when one is operating as a small project team that is part of a larger mainstream company. More and more companies have created so-called innovation centers or incubator programs whose goals are to develop next-generation products and services. It sometimes happens that building a new innovation center is met with a certain measure of skepticism from other divisions and groups within the company. It's not uncommon that division heads from other areas become resentful when needed resources are being diverted away from businesses with an established track record to support what appears to be a speculative project venture. This can include privileges and rewards that may exceed what other established businesses are getting. Over time, there evolves an unspoken culture clash between those who are free to experiment (and by extension have all the fun) and the serious business enterprise that generates revenue by providing reliability and growth.

Open Communication and Keeping Everyone Involved

Innovators and project leaders should not work in isolation if they want buy-in and support from the rest of the organization. If they want their ideas to catch on, the project manager would do well to engage in open communication by keeping the larger organization informed and involved. Open communication will go a long way in building a coalition of supporters who will provide project support during both formal meetings and behind the scenes. There should never be a perception that the new start-up group is off doing its own thing. Rather, the goal is to make everyone feel that they are a legitimate stakeholder in the project outcome.[40]

Product Demonstrations and Updates

It's important that everyone understands the proposed plan and long-term goal of the project undertaking. If the idea is compelling enough, even people who are not directly involved will feel some measure of ownership and that careful thought and applied strategy are being directed toward the project start-up. One way to help define the movement is to pilot (or showcase) the project. By giving periodic demonstrations or updates, this will go a long way in helping to build support among the various departments and divisions that are part of the organization's larger mission.

Keep the Project Review Process Flexible

Another important lesson is that overly tight performance review measures can strangle innovation. There is a tendency among well-established companies to apply the same performance review metrics to new project start-ups, thus weakening the venture before it has the opportunity to get some traction. As Google's Sergei Brin comments, "too many rules will stifle innovation."[41] Too much emphasis on demographic research or performance metrics like return on investment (ROI) at an early stage of development can kill a good project before it gets off the ground. Traditional demographic research reflects information that is currently available, but it cannot accurately forecast what customers want and would be willing to pay for in the future.[42] It cannot fully consider blue ocean opportunities because there is no basis for analysis and comparison. Demographic research and strict control measures have their place, but flexibility goes a long way in ensuring that promising ideas and project start-ups will see the light of day.

The Value of Partnerships and Collaboration

One of the most important lessons executives have learned about innovation is that companies can no longer afford to go it alone. The traditional model of research and development is to create and manufacture products exclusively within the confines of one's own company. The basic logic is if you want something done right, you've got to do it yourself. Researcher Henry Chesbrough challenges that basic assumption and makes the argument that the not-invented-here approach is no longer sustainable. Accordingly, companies should be drawing business partners and suppliers into the so-called innovation networks.[43] The idea behind open innovation is that there are simply too many good ideas available externally and held by people who don't work for your company. They simply cannot be ignored. Even the best companies with the most extensive internal capabilities have to take into consideration external knowledge and information capabilities when they think about innovation. One such example can be seen with the partnership that was formed when Microsoft purchased LinkedIn for $26.2 billion in 2016. It was an example of boundary spanning in its most essential sense. The LinkedIn business professional networking provided an important value-added factor and soon became a part of Microsoft's enterprise business software package.[44] Since that acquisition, LinkedIn's user base has grown by over 50% from 433 million users to an estimated 930 million worldwide members in more than 200 countries and territories.[45]

Value of Customer Insights

What is the value of one good idea or suggestion? No one knows better than one's customers what they want in terms of improved product design or service performance. Many new product development opportunities originate from customers who have difficulties with existing products or have needs that are not being fully addressed. Customers want solutions to their problems. They seek better value from the products and services they buy. Taking time to understand the behavior activities of one's customers in their daily work routine can go a long way in helping to understand the kinds of special features and benefits that may be of interest to them in the long term. The principle of engaging one's customers goes well beyond the focus group model. Instead, the emphasis should be on trying to understand the essential habits (and support technology) that drive the customers' everyday work process. It must solve a practical problem.[46]

Discussion

Companies, like people, can become easily satisfied with organizational routines that stand in the way of being innovative. Respect for past success is important. However, too much reliance on the past can make an organization risk-averse. Such companies become preoccupied with fine-tuning and making slight adjustments to an existing product line rather than preparing for the future. The lessons of business history have taught us that there is no such thing as a static market. There are no guarantees of continued success for any business enterprise, no matter how good its reputation or past performance. Over time, tastes, preference, and technology change. Innovative companies keep abreast of such changes, anticipate them, and make the necessary adjustments in terms of strategy and new product development.

The irony, of course, is that even the best-managed companies are susceptible to innovation failure. Specifically, a company's very strengths and ongoing success can lay the groundwork for its eventual decline. This can occur at a time when the company is realizing some of its highest profits. Failure sometimes goes with the territory of introducing game-changing technologies and services. The challenge, therefore, is to develop a culture of innovation where risk and experimentation are fully supported. Forward-thinking companies create a culture of innovation where risk and experimentation are an accepted part of the process of testing new boundaries. If innovation can be likened to the game of baseball, and more specifically being a professional pitcher, there is no such thing as a perfect 30–0 season. Rather, innovation is about putting together a winning record (perhaps 26–4) and making innovation (like games) a sustainable, repeatable process.

Notes

1 Amazon Inc., *Annual Report to Stockholders*, 1997. www.scribd.com/doc/43386750/Amazon-Letter-to-Shareholders-in-1997
2 Jim Collins, *Good to Great* (New York: Harper Collins, 2001), 13.
3 Angela Duckworth, *Grit: The Power of Passion and Perseverance* (New York: Scribner, 2016), 54.
4 Collins, *Good to Great*, 41.
5 "Get the Right People on the Bus," *The Wunderlin Company*, 2013, August 14, http://wunderlin.com/get-the-right-people-on-the-bus-2/#.VUEaG3rqK-8
6 Bernadette Eichner, "Steve Jobs' Top Hiring Tip: Hire the Best," *Zippia*, 2022, December 20, www.zippia.com/employer/steve-jobs-top-hiring-tip-hire-the-best/
7 Walter Isaacson, *Steve Jobs* (New York: Simon & Schuster, 2011), 124.
8 David Cohen, "Annual Meeting: Mark Zuckerberg Addresses Facebook's Hacker Culture," *Adweek*, 2013, May 23, www.adweek.com/socialtimes/annual-meeting-mark-zuckerberg-hacker/435177
9 "Mark Zuckerberg's Letter to Investors," *Wired*, 2012, February 1, www.wired.com/2012/02/zuck-letter/
10 Rosabeth Moss Kanter, *When Giants Learn to Dance* (New York: Simon & Schuster, 1989), 175.
11 Kanter, *When Giants Learn to Dance*, 217.
12 Lucy Kueng, *Hearts and Minds: Harnessing Leadership Culture and Talent to Really Go Digital* (Oxford: University of Oxford, The Reuters Institute, 2020).
13 "Failure and Success Go Together," *Excelerate*, 2020, August 16, www.exceleratellc.com/blog/failure
14 Tom Kelley, *The Ten Faces of Innovation* (New York: Doubleday, 2005).
15 Allison Arieff, "Beyond the Cubicle," *New York Times*, 2011, July 18, http://opinionator.blogs.nytimes.com/2011/07/18/beyond-the-cubicle/?_r=0
16 Sue Shellenbarger, "Designs to Make You Work Harder," *Wall Street Journal*, 2011, June 22, www.wsj.com/articles/SB10001424052702304070104576399572462315158
17 Christine Congdon, Donna Flynn and Melanie Redman, "The Best Collaborative Spaces also Support Solitude," *Harvard Business Review*, 2014, October, https://

hbr.org/2014/10/balancing-we-and-me-the-best-collaborative-spaces-also-support-solitude

18 Arieff, "Beyond the Cubicle."

19 Ben Waber, Jennifer Magnolfi and Greg Lindsay, "Workspaces that Move People," *Harvard Business Review*, 2014, October, 69–77.

20 Steven Johnson, *Where Good Ideas Come From: The Natural History of Innovation* (New York: Riverhead Books, 2010).

21 "Steve Jobs in His Own Words," *The Guardian*, 2011, October 6, www.theguardian.com/technology/2011/oct/06/steve-jobs-quotes

22 Thomas Friedman, *Thank You for Being Late* (New York: Farrar, Straus and Giroux, 2016).

23 Heather McGowan and Chris Shipley, *The Adaptation Advantage* (Hoboken, NJ: John Wiley & Sons, 2020), xxxvii, 3–15.

24 Jana Turner, "Bill Gates: '5 Things I Wish I Was Told at the Graduation I Never Had," *Rets Associates*, 2023, May 18, https://retsusa.com/bill-gates-5-things-i-wish-i-was-told-at-the-graduation-i-never-had/

25 J. Singh, K. Steele and L. Singh, "Combining the Best of Online and Face-to-Face Learning: Hybrid and Blended Learning Approach for COVID-19, Post Vaccine, & Post-Pandemic World," *Journal of Educational Technology Systems* 50,2 (2021): 140–171.

26 Liam Tung, "A Ban on Hybrid Working? Workers Say They Would Rather Quite Instead," *Zdnet*, 2021, December 13, www.zdnet.com/home-and-office/work-life/a-ban-on-hybrid-working-half-of-workers-say-they-would-quit-instead/

27 Charlie Warzel and Ann Peterson, *Out of Office* (New York: Alfred A. Knopf, 2021).

28 Walter Isaacson, *Steve Jobs* (New York: Simon & Schuster, 2011), 430–432; See also: "Pixar Headquarters and the Legacy of Steve Jobs," *Office Snapshots*, 2012, July 16, https://officesnapshots.com/2012/07/16/pixar-headquarters-and-the-legacy-of-steve-jobs/

29 Dean Takahashi, "How Pixar Finds Ways to Inspire Creativity and Diverse Thinking," *VentureBeat*, 2019, June 23, https://venturebeat.com/business/how-pixar-finds-ways-to-inspire-creativity-and-diverse-thinking/

30 Adam Lashinsky, "Chaos by Design," *Fortune*, 2006, October 2, 86–96.

31 "The Googleplex and the Rise of the Corporate University Campus," *Office Snapshots*, 2023, https://officesnapshots.com/articles/the-googleplex-and-the-rise-of-the-corporate-university-campus/

32 Jade Chang, "Designing the First Googleplex Office," *Metropolis*, 2006, July, https://metropolismag.com/projects/googleplex-google-hq-clive-wilkinson/

33 Kelly Main, "How Google's Reimagined Work from Anywhere Policy Gets Staff Back in the Office," *Inc.*, 2023, www.inc.com/kelly-main/how-googles-reimagined-work-from-anywhere-policy-gets-staff-back-in-office.html

34 Jennifer Elias, "Google to Crack Down on Office Attendance," *CNBC*, 2023, June 7, www.cnbc.com/2023/06/08/google-to-crack-down-on-hybrid-work-asks-remote-workers-to-reconsider.html

35 Christopher Hawthorne, "Facebook's Campus in Menlo Park," *AV*, 2023, June 11, https://arquitecturaviva.com/works/facebook-campus-in-menlo-park

36 Ellen Sheng, "Why the Headquarters of Iconic Tech Companies Are Now Among America's Top Tourist Attractions," *CNBC*, 2018, December 3, www.cnbc.com/2018/11/03/why-the-headquarters-of-iconic-tech-companies-are-tourist-attractions.html

37 Kindra Cooper, "An Inside Look at Facebook's Headquarters," *Candor*, 2021, October 22, https://candor.co/articles/tech-careers/an-inside-look-at-facebook-s-headquarters

38 Hawthorne, "Facebook's Campus in Menlo Park."

39 Hawthorne, "Facebook's Campus in Menlo Park."

40 Lorraine Marchand, *The Innovation Mindset* (New York: Columbia University Press, 2022), 164–189.

41 Dan Farber, "Google's Sergey Brin: Facebook and Apple a Threat to Internet Freedom," *CNET*, 2012, April 15, www.cnet.com/tech/services-and-software/googles-sergey-brin-facebook-and-apple-a-threat-to-internet-freedom/

42 Clayton Christensen, *The Innovator's Solution* (Boston, MA: Harvard Business School Press, 2003).

43 Henry Chesbrough, *Open Innovation: The New Imperative for Creating and Profiting from Technology* (Boston, MA: Harvard Business School Press, 2003).

44 "What Makes a LinkedIn Profile Most Successful," *RETS Associates*, 2022, January 26, https://retsusa.com/what-makes-a-linkedin-profile-most-successful/

45 Jon Erlichman, "Three Years after Microsoft Acquisition, Linked-In Keeps Quietly Climbing," *BNN Bloomberg*, 2019, October 23, www.bnnbloomberg.ca/three-years-after-microsoft-acquisition-linkedin-keeps-quietly-climbing-1.1335990 See also: Maddy Osman, "Mind Blowing Linked-In statistics and Facts," *Kinsta*, 2023, March 21, https://kinsta.com/blog/linkedin-statistics/

46 Marchand, *The Innovation Mindset*, 20–36.

INDEX

Printed in the United States
by Baker & Taylor Publisher Services